Representation and Its Discontents

Representation
and Its Discontents

The Critical Legacy of German Romanticism

Azade Seyhan

University of California Press

Berkeley / Los Angeles / Oxford

University of California Press
Berkeley and Los Angeles, California

University of California Press
Oxford, England

Library of Congress Cataloging-in-Publication Data

Seyhan, Azade.
    Representation and its discontents: the critical
legacy of German romanticism / Azade Seyhan.
        p.   cm.
    Includes bibliographical references and index.
    ISBN 0-520-07675-3 (alk. paper).
    ISBN 0-520-07676-1 (pbk.: alk. paper)
    1. German literature—18th century—History and
criticism.   2. German literature—19th century—
History and criticism.   3. Romanticism—Germany.
4. Criticism—Germany—History.
I. Title.
PT361.S48   1992
830.9'145—dc20   91-31938
                                                        CIP

Printed in the United States of America

1   2   3   4   5   6   7   8   9

To the Memory of my Father
Muvaffak Seyhan
Scientist, Writer, Wit

Contents

Acknowledgments

At various stages, this work was supported by an American Council of Learned Societies Research Fellowship, a National Endowment for the Humanities Summer Stipend, and a generous junior faculty research leave from Bryn Mawr College. I am deeply indebted to my dissertation director, Ernst Behler, for his ongoing support of my work and for his invaluable editorship of the multivolume Friedrich Schlegel critical edition which has been instrumental in bringing the theoretical sophistication of Jena Romanticism and the *Athenäum* to the attention of contemporary critics. Hazard Adams, Diana Behler, Carol Bernstein, Sander Gilman, Ingeborg Hoesterey, Peter Uwe Hohendahl, Alice Kuzniar, Jeffrey Peck, Hinrich Seeba, and Kathleen Wright provided the intellectual inspiration and exchange of ideas that have left their mark on the following pages. I would also like to extend my sincere gratitude to my editor, Edward Dimendberg of the University of California Press, for his genuine interest in and steady support of this study.

For the information of the reader, standard and available English translations of the texts cited are given in the bibliography. Although I have occasionally consulted these translations, which by and large skillfully preserve and convey the letter as well as the spirit of the original works, I translated all cited passages in order to maintain a certain consistency in the style and tone of my own text. Some passages from this book were previously published in a modified form in "Labours of Theory: The Quest for Representation in Early German Romanticism," *Seminar* 25 (1989): 187–204. Passages from Jorge Luis Borges's *Labyrinths* are reprinted by permission of New Directions. Copyright © 1962, 1964 by New Directions Publishing Corporation.

1. Introduction
Representation and Its Discontents

> It is characteristic of philosophical writing that at every turn it must confront the question of representation anew.
>
> Walter Benjamin,
> *The Origin of German Tragic Drama*

Walter Benjamin's opening lines in the *Ursprung des deutschen Trauerspiels* (The origin of German tragic drama) is a clear echo of the critical problem that informed the intellectual life of the early years of German Romanticism, known as the *Frühromantik*, a brief yet revolutionary period of literary activity that revolved around the journal *Athenäum* published during the years 1798–1800 in Jena. The founders of the journal were two brothers, August Wilhelm and Friedrich Schlegel. In the course of their literary careers, the Schlegels published three more journals: *Europa* (1803–1805), *Deutsches Museum* (1812–1813), and *Concordia* (1820–1823).[1] Both brothers were accomplished classical philologists and translators. They and August Wilhelm's wife, Caroline, were later joined by Friedrich's wife, Dorothea, poet-philosopher Novalis (Friedrich von Hardenberg), writer Ludwig Tieck, theologian-philosopher Friedrich Schleiermacher, and philosopher Friedrich Wilhelm Joseph Schelling. Schelling actually never published in the journal but was interested in Caroline, whom he married shortly after the group disbanded.[2] Such dangerous liaisons or extracurricular activities of the *Athenäum* circle become the butt of Heinrich Heine's relentless jokes in his long essay *Die romantische Schule* (The Romantic School), an amusing and thought-provoking critique of German Romanticism. But that is the subject of another story.

Though not strictly a movement or a school, Jena Romanticism represents a prescient critical consciousness that has found forceful expression in contemporary literary theory. The work of Friedrich Schlegel and Novalis is informed by a strong interest in the philosophical, moral, aesthetic, and social implications of the problem of representation. The theoretical imagination of Jena Romanticism was not laid to rest with the *Athenäum*. Schlegel and Novalis carried out their mission of establishing literature's critical foundation with unabated passion until the end of their lives. Schlegel's following tribute to Novalis bears testimony to the intellectual affinity and compatibility of the two writers and to their close cooperation in the critical ventures of German Romanticism:

> You don't dwell on the boundaries; rather your soul is deeply steeped in poetry and philosophy. It was closest to me in these images of uncomprehended truth. What you've thought I think; what I've thought you will think or have already thought. There are misunderstandings that confirm anew the greatest shared understanding. Every doctrine of the eternal Orient belongs to all artists. I name you instead of the others. (1958, 2: 272, no. 156)

The ramifications of the *Athenäum* project extend well into Friedrich Nietzsche's work and beyond. The journal envisioned its intellectual task to be re-presenting representation, in other words, recasting narrative accounts of philosophy, history, literature, and art in terms of their present or modern configuration. The critical attention of the *Athenäum* encompassed a set of interrelated questions on the nature of literary and philosophical representation which had challenged major thinkers since the days of the pre-Socratic philosophers. As Philippe Lacoue-Labarthe and Jean-Luc Nancy state in the preface to *L'absolu littéraire* (The literary absolute), the *Athenäum* does not claim to represent a rupture: "It makes no pretense of starting out with a *tabula rasa* or of ringing in the new. It sees itself, much to the contrary, as a commitment to the critical 'recasting' of what is" (1988, 10).

Indeed, the early Romantics lay no claim to the originality of their critical formulations. In fragment 110 of the *Athenäum*, Friedrich Schlegel states: "It is a sublime taste always to prefer things that have been raised to the second power. For example, reproductions of imitations, critiques of reviews, postscripts to addenda, commentaries on notes" (1958, 2: 181). The accreditation of copy, repetition, imitation, or intertextuality poses a radical challenge to the humanist notions of originality and authenticity. It is interesting that many contemporary works of art and literature defy these concepts in their deliberate use of copies, collages, parodies, and intertexts. Although the Romantics, with their usual ironic disposition, declined to accept credit for critical innovation, the conceptual paradigms they deployed as a result of the fragmentation, revision, and configuration of previous texts have radically changed the ways of reading and writing literary history. In the words of Lacoue-Labarthe and Nancy, "our 'modernity,'" does not cease to "use romanticism as a foil," tirelessly reinventing its central concepts. "What interests us in romanticism," they state, "is that we still belong to the era it opened up" (ibid., 15). The unfinished critical agenda of Jena Romanticism is, indeed, frequently discussed, alluded to, or paraphrased in the work of contemporary literary theorists. Lacoue-Labarthe and Nancy describe the Jena "project" as "that brief, intense, and brilliant *moment of writing* (not quite two years and hundreds of pages) that by itself opens an entire era, but exhausts itself in its inability to grasp its own essence and aim— and that will ultimately find no other definition than a place (Jena) and a journal (the *Athenäum*)" (ibid., 7).

Even a brief glance at the pages of the *Athenäum* readily reveals that its contributors addressed, in one way or another, every critical question literature could imagine. They never attempted, however, to fully answer these questions. On the contrary, their writings sustain our interest today probably because they maintain an unresolved critical tension. This tension results, as Schlegel implies, from the awareness of the impossibility of representing the absolute:

> Once one becomes infatuated with the absolute and simply can't escape it, then the only way out is to constantly contradict oneself and unite opposite extremes. The principle of contradiction is inevitably doomed, and one only has the choice of either suffering from it or else ennobling necessity by acknowledging its status as free action. (1958, 2: 164, no. 26)[3]

The possibility of "free action" implies freely motivated representation that is only possible in the realm of art and which a belief in the availability of truth or being would exclude. Clearly positioning themselves against the representational conceit of philosophy and the noncontradiction rules of logic, the Romantics demonstrate that the critical adventure of art and literature thrives on moments of discontinuity, rupture, and reversal.

True to the spirit of Romanticism's interest in copies, commentaries, and intertexts, I would like to start my investigation with a quote that is several times removed from its original source. In *Les mots et les choses* (The order of things), Michel Foucault writes that this book was conceived in a burst of laughter triggered off by a passage in a work by Jorge Luis Borges which, in turn, was a reference to a Chinese encyclopedia that classifies animals as " '(a) belonging to the Emperor, (b) embalmed, (c) tame, (d) sucking pigs, (e) sirens, (f) fabulous, (g) stray dogs, (h) included in the present classification, (i) frenzied, (j) innumerable, (k) drawn with a very fine camelhair brush, (l) *et cetera,* (m) having just broken the water pitcher, (n) that from a long way off look like flies.' " This amusing taxonomy, which so markedly differs from all our known conventions of classification, this "exotic charm of another system of thought" makes us immediately realize "the limitation of our own [thought], the stark impossibility of thinking *that*" (1970, xv). The realization of "the stark impossibility of thinking that," in other words, the awareness of difference and the recognition of otherness, often coincide in intellectual and literary history with a heightened perception of a crisis in representation.

The problem of representation is inherent to the never fully answered question of how philosophical or literary language can mediate and account for the world of experience and for concepts. That question pursues the ideal correspondence of object to subject, word to meaning, image to concept. Representation always aims to make the subject or presence present to itself. It strives to present concepts of presence, identity, and being in their totality. However, if it were to achieve its objective completely it would negate itself, for then it would become the object represented. If representation is to re-present presence, it can only do so in a formal or material way, that is, through the mediation of synthetic or constructed entities, such as words, symbols, and images. These constructs are not what they represent. Thus, representation always involves the duplication or presentation of an object or a concept by means of something that it is not, which also means that representation begins with a duplication or repetition of identity. The form of this repetition, however, is difference, that is, a split in subjectivity and identity. Since representation can never fully recover presence or coincide ideally with it, it will always pursue strategies to cover absence. "Instead of presenting presence," any attempt at mimetic representation "testifies to absence by tracing and retracing ever elusive presence" (Taylor 1984, 82). The recognition that some primary presence or truth remains inaccessible to consciousness lies at the heart of the problem of representation.

The uneasy confrontation with the impossibility of knowing the truth, hidden in some other—be it the noumenal world, a forgotten time, or an occulted code—creates an intellectual anxiety during periods poised on the thresholds of revolutionary change. As Foucault has observed, the definite transition to modernity was marked "when words ceased to intersect with representations and to provide a spontaneous grid for the knowledge of things" (1970, 304). The social and political upheaval generated by the French Revolution was paralleled by a relentless search for the understanding of the conditions and limits of human reason, by the praxis of critique introduced by Immanuel Kant. Kant's critical philosophy represents, in his own words, "a new Copernican revolution" by placing the human mind at the center of all operations of knowledge. It is impossible to ascertain, however, whether the cognitive powers with which the human subject is equipped can represent things as they "really" are. Therefore, it is necessary to distinguish between the thing as it is synthesized by a priori forms of intuition and the thing-in-itself (*das Ding an sich*). The thing-in-itself is not accessible by the faculties and forms a limit to human knowledge. The implications of the Kantian problem of representation that gave rise to Romanticism's speculative idealism will be discussed in more detail in the next chapter.

Here I would like to explore the extent to which the critical discourse of the *Frühromantik*—as articulated in the works of its major theorists, Friedrich Schlegel and Novalis—constitutes a response to the problem of representation that acquired renewed currency in the aftermath of the revolution in German Idealism. The crisis of representation, witnessed in the radical shift from poetic mimesis to critical poiesis during the late eighteenth century, corresponds to the profound socio-political, economic, cultural, and moral crises that accompanied the French Revolution. These crises are not the direct object of my study; however, their traces are unmistakable in the work of the early Romantics. History and the history of philosophy constitute the condition and context of literature. "The French Revolution, Fichte's philosophy, and Goethe's *Meister* are the greatest tendencies of the age," writes Schlegel in the *Athenäum,* adding:

Whoever is offended by this juxtaposition, whoever cannot take any revolution seriously that isn't noisy and materialistic, has not yet achieved

a lofty, broad perspective on the history of humanity. Even in our inadequate cultural histories—which usually resemble a collection of vari-
ants accompanied by a continuous commentary for which the classical
text was lost—many a little book, scarcely noticed by the noisy masses
at the time, plays a greater role than anything they did. (1958, 2: 198–
199, no. 216)

Romanticism's critical anxiety is largely triggered by the hitherto
inexperienced violent births in political and intellectual history. The
observers cannot name the newborns. Furthermore, they are ill at
ease at the sight of the Janus-faced progeny of the time. The French
Revolution that represented the golden age of freedom and social
justice for German intellectuals turned into a nightmare of dashed
hopes with the French occupation. Kant's critical paradigm was
both daunting and liberating and had to be revised to allow for a
self-reflexive praxis. In the *Athenäum* Schlegel calls the French Revolution the "prototype [*Urbild*] of revolutions," yet goes on to state
that one could also regard it as "the most frightful grotesque of the
age where the most deep-seated prejudices and their most brutal
punishments are joined in a gruesome chaos and interwoven as
bizarrely as possible with a colossal human tragicomedy" (ibid.,
2: 248, no. 424). Faced with an unrepresentable chaos on the political and intellectual landscape, the Romantic mind initiates a discursive plan intent on inventing new paradigms of understanding and
redefining the objectives of criticism and representation. This project, if one can call it such, is nevertheless neither self-avowedly innovative nor theoretical in a strict sense. The Jena Romantics see
it as the creation of a "new mythology." The very term denotes the
impulse to look for appropriate conceptual models in the past. The
archaeology of these models in itself is not the major task; once
found they need to be fragmented, realigned, and resynthesized in
order to be conceptually useful in a new age. Novalis states that
the problem of representation "needs, by all means, to be cast in
another language" (1960, 2: 255, no. 477). The search for this language leads Romanticism to an investigation of the connections
between literature and history as well as those between literary criticism and historiography.

In his dissertation, *Der Begriff der Kunstkritik in der deutschen
Romantik* (The concept of art criticism in German Romanticism),
Benjamin (1972–, 1.1: 51) observes that the words *Kritik* (critique,

criticism) and *kritisch* (critical) are the most frequently used philosophical and aesthetic expressions in the writings of early German Romantics. The word *Darstellung* (sensible or sensory representation) is probably a close second. In Romantic idealism, representation is often designated by three words, *Darstellung, Vorstellung,* and *Repräsentation.* Without attempting an etymological detour, I shall briefly examine the contextual use of these words in Romantic criticism. All point to the initial absence of what is being represented. However, in Romantic usage, only *Darstellung* attains to a materiality of figural representation. The concept of *Darstellung,* which rejects the imitative claims of mimesis and mimetic representation, appears with growing frequency in modern literary criticism beginning in the eighteenth century. In a well-documented study on the emergence of this term in the aesthetic discourse of eighteenth-century Germany and its definitive formulation in Schiller, Fritz Heuer (1970, 12–13) maintains that *Darstellung* distinguishes itself from existing notions of representation in its emphatic focus on poetic presence. Poetic representation is inextricably bound to the figural. Schlegel clearly invests the concept with a material form by stating that knowledge becomes knowledge only through *Darstellung* and that "poetry as *Darstellung* is knowledge and more than that" (1958, 18: 569, no. 84). *Vorstellung,* on the other hand, designates a latent metaphor or an image in the subject's mind. In "Gespräch über die Poesie" (Dialogue on poetry), Schlegel emphasizes the semantic distinction between the two words in an analogy to the distinction between inside and outside: "The inner vision [*Vorstellung*] can become clearer to itself and quite alive only through external representation [*Darstellung*]" (ibid., 2: 306). Finally, Novalis reserves the term *Repräsentation* for the act of making present in a material and visual but not necessarily poetic sense: "A thing becomes clear only through *Repraesentation.* One understands something most easily, when one sees it represented" (1960, 3: 246, no. 40). On the other hand, poetry "represents the unrepresentable" (*stellt das Undarstellbare dar;* ibid., 3: 685, no. 671).

Several important studies have investigated the function of the artistic or literary work as the representation of the idea(1) in early German Romanticism. Benjamin's *Der Begriff der Kunstkritik in der deutschen Romantik,* a prescient text that anticipates the contemporary theoretical interest in the problem of representation, ar-

gues that in early Romanticism the idea of form replaces the idea
of the absolute. "The representational form" (*Darstellungsform*) is
the medium of the reflective function. It "reveals itself in criticism"
and, in the final analysis, transforms itself "into an orderly continuum of forms" (1972–, 1.1: 88). The novel, which the Romantics
called a *Mischgedicht* (mixed poem), represents a repertory of various genres and therefore embodies almost ideally the concept of this
"continuum" (ibid., 1.1: 100). "The Romantic theory of the work
of art," concludes Benjamin, "is the theory of its form" (ibid., 1.1:
72). The figural or representational form is simultaneously the
medium of reflection and of knowledge—which is constituted in
reflection. Representation is clearly no longer an inadequate repetition of the concept but a way of empowering reflection. In this
sense, representation institutes critical praxis.

In *The Literary Absolute* Lacoue-Labarthe and Nancy also investigate early Romanticism's indebtedness to idealistic philosophy. They maintain that Jena Romantics, most notably Friedrich
Schlegel, define the status of literature as the representation of
philosophy, as the aesthetic reflection on the concept. Like Benjamin, Lacoue-Labarthe and Nancy maintain that the Romantics
considered the work of literature to be inscribing onto itself the conditions of its own production and producing its own truth. What
this means is that literature is neither purely literature nor simply
literary theory. Rather it is literature that creates its own theory
as it is being written. Schlegel and Novalis insist on this definition
of the work of literature as a mode of critical self-reflection. Since
literature produces its own truth, the literary form is ultimately
the representation of the absolute. As Lacoue-Labarthe and Nancy
put it, "Romanticism is the inauguration of the literary absolute"
(1988, 12). They argue that the Romantics reinvent literary form
as the definitive equation between presence and representation,
an operation that Kant left incomplete even in the *Kritik der
Urteilskraft* (Critique of judgment).

Although the present study acknowledges a great debt to the insights of Benjamin and Lacoue-Labarthe and Nancy, it seeks to
demonstrate that the "literary absolute" constitutes the very space
where the problem of representation as mediation of presence becomes most visible in its irremediable ambiguity rather than to reaf-
firm that the Romantics elevated the literary to the absolute. After

all, the dominant figural forms (the arabesque and the fragment) and tropes (allegory and irony) of Romanticism are characterized by discontinuity, rupture, and indirect reference. Furthermore, the interest of this investigation lies ultimately not so much in the question of representation alone as in the relation of representation to the concepts of time and otherness.

Philosophy is based on the premise of absolute identity as in A = A, a proposition with which Johann Gottlieb Fichte's *Wissenschaftslehre* (The science of knowledge) starts.[4] Absolute identity is fulfilled in self-consciousness where the subject and the object are one. In Fichte's philosophy, which, as Benjamin argues, provides the direct model for early Romanticism's work on representation, the self (*Ich*) represents itself to itself by positing a not-self (*Nicht-Ich*). Only the presence of the not-self validates the self. In reflection upon the not-self, the self sees its own presence as representation. Thus, identity always involves both a temporal (or diachronic) element, that is, the process of dividing and positing, and a synchronic one, which involves coexisting with difference. "The notion of the *same* captures the play of time and space by pointing to the representative character of all presence and every present and by underscoring the repetitiousness of all identity," writes philosopher Mark Taylor, "the same is not a simple identity; it is, rather, a 'structure of iterability' that includes *both* identity and difference" (1984, 48). It is only by embodying difference that identity fulfills its destiny. In fact, Jacques Derrida has argued that "just as . . . simple internal consciousness could not provide itself with time and with the absolute alterity of every instant without the irruption of the totally-other, so the ego cannot engender alterity within itself without encountering the Other" (1978, 94). This duplication of identity as difference and the concept of the doubling self are recurring motifs in Romantic writing. Since the self can represent itself only through the other, it is not surprising to see that Romantic discourse is populated by many others. Both Weimar Classicism and Jena Romanticism, for example, return to ancient Greece to uncover there an "archaeology" of themselves. Schlegel and Novalis add India and the Near East respectively to their historical-textual itinerary. Thus, representations of antiquity and the Orient are thinly veiled allegories of contemporary Germany. In other words, representations of otherness are self-representations. In a broader analogous context, then, criticism is the self-representation of art or literature, fiction (*Geschichten*) that of history (*Geschichte*), and the past and the future that of the present.

In the history of Western philosophy being and time have always been intimately linked. Numerous treatises in the history of science and philosophy, among them Martin Heidegger's *Sein und Zeit* (Being and time), attest to the monumental human endeavor to grasp and analyze the relation of temporality to existence (1975, vol. 2). "Being has been consistently interpreted as presence and hence constantly regarded in terms of the present," observes Taylor, "to be is to be present, and to exist fully is to be present totally" (1984, 49). An understanding of the nature of time is perceived to be at the core of our understanding of the universe. However, scientists and philosophers have been perplexed in their efforts to postulate something on which time is dependent, through which the movement of time is possible but which, itself, is not a process. Isaac Newton saw time as absolute, flowing equably without reference to anything external. Yet process (or flow) and time are not identical. When the process stops, time does not. Heidegger has avoided treating time as a substance or entity. However, he invokes metaphors of motion and spatiality which suggest a flow where the self moves toward itself. And history, in Heidegger's account, does not capture the essence of time as a material entity but constitutes a representation of having-been-in-the-world.

If representation is a problem of mediating presence or being, then it is also a problem of presenting time. Time is just as elusive as being. Can time be re-presented? Or does it belong to the category of the unrepresentable? What is it, anyway? In a frequently quoted reference, St. Augustine said that if no one asked him the question, he knew; but if one required him to tell, he could not (Newton-Smith 1986, 24). In their book, *Descartes' Dream*, Philip J. Davis and Reuben Hersch respond: "Two millennia later, two revolutions in physics later, we can still sympathize with this answer" (1987, 189). Richard P. Feynman, the late Nobel laureate in physics, once remarked that he would rather not be asked what time was, although physicists work with it every day. He felt it was just too difficult to think about (Boslough 1990, 109). Throughout most of history, time was seen as a flow, a linear movement. Albert Einstein's theories of relativity, however, represented time as a dimension, thus imparting meaning to the context and order of events. There have been two conflicting views of time since antiquity. Parmenides and later Archimedes argued that time needed to be canceled or reduced to something like geometry. For Heraclitus and Aristotle the world could only be understood in its irreducible temporality. Augustine linked being to the present time. For the subject to exist meant to be present to itself, that is, to be coeval with itself.

In most philosophical debates, presentness seems crucial for an understanding of the notion of time. If the present moment were to be correctly identified, then the central metaphysical problem of time could be one vital step closer to a solution. Maurice Merleau-Ponty (1962, 424), for example, argues that although none of time's dimensions can be deduced from the rest, the present—in a broad sense, that is, the present enclosed by its horizons of the past and the future—is significant because it is the zone where being and consciousness coincide. However, the consciousness of the past in memory and the anticipation of future are always present in the present moment. In fact, Augustine views the present as consisting of three times: the past of present, the present of present, and the future of present. "The 'omnipresence' of past and future within the present uncovers an 'original' nonpresence at the very heart of the present," maintains Taylor, "past and future are not modalities of the present but signify irreducible absence. As identity possesses and is possessed by difference, so presence necessarily involves absence" (1984, 49). Such contradictions as the failure of identifying the present as the present or presence understood as absence, which lie at the heart of the problem of time, have led some thinkers to reject the reality of time.[5] Events cannot be identified as past, present, and future in any essential sense; they can only be encoded as differentiated temporalities by being assigned mutually exclusive relational attributes.

It is difficult to challenge the refutations of the reality of time, since time is available to consciousness only in terms of human representation and not as objective reality, and since it has no external referent. In turn, representations of temporality take on the form of measurement of time by identifying some periodic uniformity, like the earth's revolution around the sun. In a comprehensive study of time, Errol E. Harris maintains that, in the final analysis, if the nature of time is to be understood at all, such understanding can only be found in a structure or principle that accounts for time in and as a succession of change (1988, 37). Such accounts, to be sure, speak not of the essence of time but are representations or formal constructs. They are reconstructions of events that become temporal markers in the perpetual movement of time. In one of the numerous studies attempting to come to grips with the reality of time, Michael Shallis concedes that no scientific or philosophical inquiry can claim to discover the ultimate truth about time. The most any study can hope for, he maintains, is to identify how a particular culture's perception of time and how the prevalent assumptions of its scientific heritage affect and reflect its cosmology and are further explored in its scientific disciplines like physics and astronomy (1986, 63).

Obviously, this quick summary of a few selected speculations and articulations about the problem of time is meant to offer neither a systematic overview of nor a novel insight into one of the eternal mysteries of human experience. Rather, in keeping with Shallis's insight, I would like to investigate the perception of time in the context of a certain culture at a certain historical and philosophical juncture. The question to be addressed here is how the Romantic concern with representation involved the question of understanding time and history and how this involvement affected and is reflected in the philosophical, historical, and literary studies of German Romanticism. The concept of the full involvement of absolute being with time appears in various literary configurations in the texts of early Romanticism. These texts suggest that since no scientific principle or method can reveal the absolute or absolute time, the latter can only be indirectly understood through artistic representation. If being or essence is ineffable or unsayable except "allegorically," as Schlegel maintained, then time, which resists any form of direct representation, can only be understood or rather intuited as metamorphosis and metaphor. This assumes that all experience of time as memory (past), sensation (present), and anticipation (future) is lived and mediated through *Vorstellung* (imagination) and *Darstellung*. And it is this re-vision of the experience of temporality that is crucial for the inauguration of Romantic historiography, because it recognizes that the writing of history is predominantly the labor of aesthetic imagination.

In a certain sense, the tripartite structure of the Augustinian present offers a point of reference for the Romantic dilemma of representing the present. "All history is threefold," states Novalis, "past, present, and future" (1960, 3: 372, no. 598). The time in which the Romantics find themselves resists any transparent understanding. The Judeo-Christian eschatology represented time as the unfolding of salvation history, culminating in a divine telos. The French Revolution subverted this notion by wiping out the hope of salvation. The Enlightenment's view of history as the progress of humanity was an inadequate model for an age faced with unpredictable failures along the way. How could this particular time be represented, made critically present to itself? And what about time in general? "The notion of a past whose meaning could not be thought in the form of a (past) present marks the *impossible-unthinkable-unstatable* not only for philosophy in general but even for a thought of being which would seek to take a step outside philosophy" (Derrida 1978, 132). The Romantic answer was to present the present as its other, that is, either as the past or the future. Schlegel maintains that "a limited representation merely based on the present does not exist in the human mind" (1958, 13: 231) and that "remembrance or memory and imagination are thoroughly indispensable" in the generation of concepts, for memory recalls past representations in consciousness and imagination anticipates the future (ibid., 13: 253). "All remembrance is the present," writes Novalis, and it appears as "a necessary pre-text of the poetic [*nothwendige Vordichtung*]" (1960, 2: 559, no. 157). If memory provides the text of poetry and if poetry, as Novalis said, represents the unrepresentable then the past and future components of time, as transcendental entities, can only be available to consciousness through *Darstellung*. This, in turn, radically redefines methods of historiography. Ultimately, in early German Romanticism, the philosophical problem of representation reappears as the textual project of writing about time and history. The enduring product of this project is the recognition of poetic historiography as a legitimate disciplinary discourse.

If historiography is seen as a form of poetic representation, then it can participate in the rhetorical strategies reserved for literature. One of these is the art of "making strange" (*befremden*). Novalis sees in all artistic undertaking the gesture of embracing the strange or the unknown: "The author or artist has an unknown [*fremd*] purpose" (ibid., 3: 365, no. 571). "Making strange" often takes the form of exoticizing, that is, presenting something as distant in time or space. Thus, Romantic writing displays a predilection for the representation of histories not available to recent memory. Romantic histories re-member fragments of distant pasts and foreign places and present them in the familiar form of poetic conventions. The textual revival of antiquity, the reconstructed literary memories of ancient Orient and Greece, and the reinvention of the Middle Ages as the symbol of a new national unity all constitute attempts to understand the self by understanding otherness or to understand the present by understanding the past. Making strange, distancing, and exoticizing are, paradoxically, poetic operations of making an other familiar.

In the act of "making strange" or poetization, otherness and history become coextensive with the self and the present, respectively. However, the historical flux generated by the French Revolution occults visions of the future and renders any unproblematic or linear projection of today into tomorrow impossible. In this sense, Romantic consciousness is a consciousness of radical temporality, that is, a continuum of disjunctive moments. In *Delayed Endings* Alice Kuzniar shows that Romantic visions of the future are informed by a strong sense of indeterminacy. Kuzniar focuses on strategies of describing the future by Novalis and Friedrich Hölderlin and recognizes in their work the awareness of the difficulty in re-presenting something that was never present. Faced with this aporia, these writers indefinitely delay in language any vision of the apocalypse and hide it behind various figural strategies. Kuzniar locates the theoretical and historical context of such rhetorical ploys as narrative suspension and rupture in the unsettling aftermath of the French Revolution. The future can only be intimated in forms that mimic its uncertainty and discontinuity.

In his Jena lectures on transcendental philosophy (1800–1801), Schlegel singles out allegory as the trope of endlessness or endless consciousness which represents infinity in finite, sensory form (1958, 12: 3–43). Allegory fixes the reality that presents itself to consciousness in the form of images. The temporal progress of allegory toward absolute knowledge and its symbolic relation to it coincide with the concept of *Bildung* (educaiton, formation) in Romantic criticism. *Bildung* refers to the concept of the infinite perfectibility of the subject. "Allegory is nothing other than *Bildung*," (ibid., 12: 40) states Schlegel. It is also "the appearance of the ideal" (ibid., 12: 19). In other words, just as *Bildung* is a progressive approximation of the ideal, so is allegory that of infinity or of infinite and varying reality.

As a trope that negotiates analysis and synthesis, fragmentation and restoration (re-membering), allegory resembles memory. "The fruit of remembrance in every aspect is *Geschichte* [both history and story], and *Geschichte* of every sort is what lends our consciousness coherence and foundation" (ibid., 12: 402). In Novalis's *Heinrich von Ofterdingen* (Heinrich of Ofterdingen), we are told that memory invests events with coherence and meaning through poetic reconfiguration. In a certain sense, then, the early Romantics prefigure Georg Wilhelm Friedrich Hegel, who sees in the operations of memory the path to absolute knowledge. The Romantics went beyond Hegelian metaphysics by assigning the fragments of memory a distinctly material, albeit reinvented, history and form. Knowledge buried in memory could only be made present to consciousness by a machinery of formal representations. The search for artistic tools of representation and exotic icons of expression sends the Romantics on textual voyages to every corner of history. The expeditions to libraries, archives, museums, mausoleums, and ruins underline the Romantic desire to face the crisis of representation by creating a new mythology. This desire is also at the heart of the Romantics' encyclopedia project, an undertaking of colossal proportions which aimed to unearth, weld together, or reconstruct fragments of what was considered to have been a unified body of human knowledge.

Athenäum was not only the center for the collection of material for this universal encyclopedia but also the editorial collective that critiqued, revised, and rewrote Romanticism's cultural inheritance. In a sense *Athenäum* served as a combination library-laboratory where research centered around an examination of the sociocultural crises that mark the end of the eighteenth century. Its editorial policy was a critique in the broader Kantian sense, an attempt to investigate the conditions of the production of epistemological, moral, and aesthetic values, their historical contingency and limits, and the reasons behind the bankruptcy of some of these values. As Lacoue-Labarthe and Nancy contend, "literature or literary theory will be the privileged locus of expression" in this context (1988, 5). Literary criticism takes on the colossal task of holding up the mirror to an age in great need of self-reflection. The journal lasted not quite two years, yet managed to rewrite the critical history of the vast period that preceded it. Although in the *Romantic School,* Heine somewhat unfairly criticizes the work of the Schlegel brothers for lacking a philosophical ground, it is, in fact, the common penchant for situating literature and criticism in a philosophical context that joins the work of Friedrich Schlegel and Novalis in a close bond. Both Schlegel and Novalis double stitch their literary pieces with philosophical thread: "If one could establish the principles of poetry in the way our philosophical friend has tried to," says Lothario in Schlegel's "Dialogue on Poetry," "then the art of poetry would have a foundation lacking neither in solidity nor range" (1958, 2: 349). Novalis considered philosophy the theory of poetry. The rehabilitation of the problem of representation in Novalis and Schlegel is neither a merely disinterested exercise of imagination nor the ambitious and possibly self-indulgent attempt to finish the job philosophy left incomplete. The will to imagine the unimaginable and to represent the unrepresentable maps the path that takes Romanticism to a new frontier where the very foundation of accepted forms of knowledge is radically challenged.

"Philosophy's central concern," writes Richard Rorty, "is to be a general theory of representation, a theory which will divide culture up into the areas which represent reality well, those which represent it less well, and those which do not represent it at all" (1979, 3). In the discourse of early Romanticism, these three degrees of representation are subsumed under symbolic representation. Under this rubric, texts were not tested for accuracy of representation, since they referred not to the natural world of essences or the noumenal world but to worlds that were accessible to us through other constructed images, words, and symbolic systems. Elsewhere Rorty sees the spirit of "nineteenth-century idealism" embodied in "twentieth-century textualism" (1982, 139–159). Philosophers of the last century, claims Rorty, believed only in the existence of ideas, while some critics in our century believe only in the existence of texts. Among these textualists Rorty names literary critics Harold Bloom, Geoffrey Hartman, J. Hillis Miller, post-structuralist French thinkers Jacques Derrida and Michel Foucault, historian Hayden White, and social scientist Paul Rabinow. Thanks to the work of the textualists, philosophy is presently reliving its past, albeit reincarnated as literary theory. By some error of the "spiritual sciences" (a literal translation of the German term *Geisteswissenschaften,* a rough equivalent of the imprecise English term *humanities*) the spirit of philosophy now inhabits the same body as its other, that is, the corpus of metaphor which it had previously shunned. Like many contemporary philosophers, Rorty is acutely aware of this corporeal colonization of philosophical territory by literary criticism. Although idealism is "a philosophical doctrine" and textualism is "an expression of suspicion about philosophy," they are united in their initiation of comparable paradigm shifts. Whereas idealism "wanted to substitute one sort of science (philosophy) for another (natural science) as the center of culture, twentieth-century textualism wants to place literature in the center, and to treat both science and philosophy as, at best, literary genres." In a similar vein, on the critical canvas of German Romanticism all knowledge is presented to consciousness through poetic representation. Indeed, Rorty sees Romanticism per se as "what unites metaphysical idealism and literary textualism" (ibid., 141–142).

The current status of philosophy in relation to literary theory emerged as a result of the conceptual blockbusting generated by the aporetic questions philosophy raised. It was, after all, philosophers who problematized the relations between sign and representation, meaning and intention, and self and the other. These dualities are the property of metaphysics, not of literature. Philosophical authority has traditionally tried to banish those rebels and trespassers known as free play, figuration, and connotation from the epistemologically stable land of analytic and scientific loyalties. Meanwhile, literary criticism has turned the tables on philosophy by showing that the latter has consistently relied on metaphors, analogies, fictional paradigms, rhetorical ploys, in short, all the stock in trade of literature in its quest for truth and certainty. Romanticism constitutes the first modern challenge to philosophy's denial of its textual and ultimately metaphorical condition. Schlegel refers to the mission of European philosophy as "*the fruitless search for the highest knowledge*" (1958, 19: 20, no. 180; the emphasis is Schlegel's). The seeds of Romantic discontent about philosophical certainty come to full fruition in Nietzsche who embodies the textual interlinkage between early German Romanticism and late modernity. Such conceptual figures as free play, connotation, diversity, and chaos, which have all along inhabited the margins of German Idealistic philosophy and provided alternative terms for reason, unity, presence, or some other first principle, constitute the regulative metaphors of contemporary literary theory. The material "reality" of figural representation took its radical leap to the center of critical attention in early German Romanticism. The concept of free play of cognitive faculties not restricted to a definite conceptual rule was first formulated in the context of German Idealism by Kant in an attempt to define the status of aesthetic judgment. In Kant's schema, aesthetic understanding is realized in the free play of the mind's signifying capacity. Here imagination freely synthesizes the manifold of intuition and understanding to form a universally communicable judgment. Schiller translates the notions of free play and representation into strictly aesthetic terms. This new aesthetic, in turn, forms the basis of modern *Bildung,* which literally means (form)ation or figuration. And in early Romanticism, form and figure literally constitute the body of the work of art. In other words, the literary work becomes the embodiment or sensory representation of knowledge.

Thus, in an effort to link the conceptual history of early Romanticism to the larger cultural project of modernity, the Romantic paradigms of representation, temporality, and alterity will be studied in the larger context of German Idealism. This will involve a reexamination of the writings of Kant, Fichte, and Schiller in Romantic terms. A brief discussion of Schleiermacher's hermeneutics shows how his project complements Schlegel's and Novalis's views on linguistic representation. Although Schelling figures prominently in the Romantic discourse on representation, I do not go into a detailed discussion of his role, since in his work the problematic status of representation reaches a closure. In the final analysis, artistic representation becomes identical with reality and philosophy, therefore, culminates in art. In Schlegel and Novalis, however, the energy of the crisis of understanding is sustained. This is what ultimately makes their work more relevant to modern critical consciousness. It is probably correct to state that the fine line of distinction or continuation between modern and postmodern discourse can be understood in terms of a transition from a fascination with representation to a problematic confrontation with it. In *The Postmodern Condition,* for example, Jean-François Lyotard maintains that the production and distribution of information in the modern era was controlled by "metanarratives." These were a set of stories of a mythological or rational nature which represented authoritative accounts of the growth of knowledge and culture. The challenge to the legitimacy of these representations as unifying forces of cultural history culminated in the postmodern critique of knowledge. Postmodern knowledge is represented as a language game. The goal of the game, where participation takes the form of speaking and writing, is an ongoing reconceptualization of cultural accounts. The Romantic crisis of representation and postmodern language games provide a pre-text and a postscript, respectively, to Nietzsche's provocative views on language and representation, which will be discussed in detail in the final chapter. Nietzsche becomes the ultimate point of reference and reverence in the story of modern critical pilgrimages. His own story makes sense only when read in the larger context of his Romantic predecessors' history. They, like Nietzsche, had taken the representational conceit of traditional metaphysics to task. This story needs to be read sequentially (historically) as well as synchronically (in relation to its current methodical implications), in just the way Nietzsche himself read the story of Greek tragedy.

The process of *Bildung* in its broadest sense as formation, education, and diversification, that is, as the move from a unified subjectivity to the multiplicity of experience, finds its concrete expression in the novels and novellas of German Romanticism. "A classical text must never be entirely understood," remarks Schlegel, "but those who are cultivated [*gebildet*] and who cultivate themselves [*sich bilden*] must always want to learn more from it" (1958, 2: 149, no. 20). For Schlegel, a classical text is not a work defined by strictly aesthetic, generic, or historical criteria but an intertextual body.[6] It refers not only to other books but also to works of art, systems of thought, and social norms and practices. The process of *Bildung*, then, is an act of formation whose product is a text, which can take on the form of a history, an encyclopedia, or a novel. In other words, it always embodies the spirit of Romantic poesy (*romantische Poesie*), which is a free combination or association of forms and genres. Schlegel observes, for example, that exemplary novels are often "compendia" or "encyclopedias" of the intellectual life of an outstanding individual. Even if such a life story were to be written in a genre other than the novel, such as drama, the result would still be a novel (ibid., 2: 156, no. 78). In the literary tales of Novalis, Hölderlin, and Arnim, which we shall read with an eye on this pedagogical imperative, the concepts of Romantic idealism leave the domain of abstract thought and take on life in the "practical" world of fiction. Philosophy and pedagogical fictions are engaged in a dialectical exchange.

Poetic narratives lend philosophy a compelling presence, and philosophy, in turn, compensates for the absences or gaps in *Bildung* and, by implication, in poetry. "Philosophy must correct the mistakes of our education," states Novalis, "otherwise, we wouldn't need it" (1960, 2: 155, no. 132). Novalis's *Heinrich von Ofterdingen* and Hölderlin's *Hyperion* are in a sense *Bildungsromane*. In each, the hero embarks upon a quest for self-knowledge that comes as a result of encounters with the other. The other takes on the form of another time, place, and culture; it is the exoticized other. In each case the protagonist reinvents himself in a new mode of self-representation that is only a veiled representation or an allegory of alterity. The ultimate encounters with the exotic are perhaps most vividly exemplified in Achim von Arnim's novella *Isabella von Ägypten* (Isabella of Egypt). Here, all conventional knowledge about nature, history, and geography is subverted, fragmented, and reconfigured in imagination. The result is, as Schlegel would have said, an allegory of allegory. All three texts enact their allegorical stories through reduplicated narratives of their own critical tasks. The allegorical and contingent claims of these tales are subjected to critical analysis not to seal them in their own image but to open them to reinterpretation and reintegration into our modern literary sensibilities.

Our present institutions of criticism see themselves as facing another crisis of representation. Although deconstruction has provided the impetus for a reevaluation of all values in literary theory, it has also become locked in the toils of an endless demystification constantly raising doubts about its own methods. It has pushed the limits of all forms of understanding by its relentless demonstration of how language collapses under the strain of its own contradictory (or metaphorical) logic. To be sure, the recognition that philosophical language hides its defects behind a rhetorical veil is an important critical insight. However, as a mere diagnostic insight, it lacks any feasible conceptual mechanism to adequately differentiate the various ideological underpinnings of discourses controlled by the contingencies of temporality and alterity. By looking back at moments of conceptual blockbusting in the history of ideas we may be able to look beyond the present conflict and crisis. Perhaps deconstruction needs to relive its past through the restless spirit of Romanticism to exorcise its demons.

The present study aims at two related objectives. It hopes to reclaim for contemporary literary theory important critical concepts of an intellectual history that has been eclipsed either by fashionable jargon or buried by prejudice against the German Idealistic tradition that is often perceived as too abstruse, dense, or Teutonic. The dichotomy between Anglo-American and German critical positions has traditionally been informed by misunderstandings and a mutual sense of distrust, interrupted by rare moments of genuine exchange. The drift has become more pronounced in contemporary criticism, since, as Geoffrey Hartman points out, "Anglo-American critics did not see through French culture to German lines of thought" (1980, 44). The interdisciplinary orientation of the present account may render more accessible a discourse that has been conveniently long forgotten and whose critical rigor can direct our current intellectual curiosity into fruitful lines of inquiry. The study also aims for a critical relinking of questions raised by our modernity with a vital cultural legacy. It recalls and partially recovers forgotten strategies of understanding in order to more clearly reformulate modern critical concerns. Of course, conceptual explosions do not come about in the suspended tranquility of a space beyond time. Therefore, without venturing into the domain of *Ideologiekritik* (critique of ideology), I have tried to suggest that the preoccupation with representations of time and otherness in German Romanticism is linked to an ideology of adventure, of repossessing another time and space in the quest for self-identity. The nostalgia of Romanticism can border on a form of self-worship through veneration of relics associated with its own development. Or such nostalgia can be a vital link to a history facing the threat of being forgotten. For the Romantics, a history eaten away in time by forgetting amounts to death, that is, the loss of being in time.

My own project of writing this study is caught in the paradox of attempting to impose a certain structure and closure on what apparently resists closure. I realize I faced the rather ironic challenge of systematizing critically astute but fragmentary texts that resist any notion of systematic closure. The temptation to write a fragmentary text composed only of quotations, as Benjamin once intended to do, was great. However, the constraints of academic writing made this impossible. In spite of the formal closure, that is, a final sentence on the last page, this work remains, in the Romantic spirit which it has attempted to represent, a fragment of sorts, an incomplete commentary which will hopefully challenge others to fill in its gaps. I have tried to identify one significant critical question, that of representation, as it was defined by German Romanticism and as it defined German Romanticism, and attempted to synthesize its historical, theoretical, and literary implications. This book itself is only a representation and, as such, subject to losses in the form of gaps between historical "facts" and their interpretation and between the established critical value of works studied and their reconfiguration in theoretical imagination. In an apt and witty formulation, critic W. J. T. Mitchell summarizes the problem of representation as the reversal of "the traditional slogan of the American Revolution: instead of 'No taxation without representation,' no representation without taxation. Every representation exacts some cost, in the form of lost immediacy, presence, or truth" (1990, 21). Against these odds, I have tried to suggest something of the richness and complexity of the history of a critical discourse which has managed in record time to reconceptualize the discipline of literature. Finally, the progress of the present account of Romanticism's fortunes is not in the direction of a telos. Rather our story is one more testimony to Benjamin's insightful observation that in the course of its history, philosophy has always been "a struggle for the representation of a small number of words which are always the same—of ideas" (1972–, 1.1: 217).

2. From Transcendental Philosophy to Transcendental Poetry

> The poem of understanding is philosophy.
> Novalis, "Logologische Fragmente," no. 29

> Poetry is a part of the philosophical technique.
> Novalis, *Das allgemeine Brouillon,* no. 688

Under the gaze of the German Romantics the veiled world of the Orient was transformed into a textual space where the I/eye, like Hyazinth in Novalis's *Die Lehrlinge zu Sais* (The novices of Sais) in pursuit of a revelation by Isis (Sais), discovers its own reflection behind the veil of the elusive Oriental goddess. The search for Isis is occasioned by a crisis in understanding. Hyazinth's serene life is plunged into turmoil when one day a foreigner appears in front of his parents' house, befriends him, and gives him a book written in an unknown language. The first glimpse into the possibility of a radically alien mode of representation, the exoticism of another language, baffles and intrigues us. The initial shock of this heteronomy urges us to examine our own problem of understanding and leads, after recovery from the close encounter, to the eventual familiarization of the unfamiliar. The investigation and appropriation or appropriative representation of otherness constitutes the essential gesture of Romantic hermeneutics. "One studies foreign systems," observes Novalis, "to find one's *own system*" (1960, 3: 278, no. 220). In a very basic sense, self-understanding is the first prerequisite for the act of understanding. Positing an otherness by representing a split in subjectivity is the first step in self-understanding. The subject acquires its understanding of experience through its reflection on the posited object and through the self-reflexion occasioned by the difference of the object.

The challenge to understanding posed by the mystique of another system of thought heightens awareness of the problems inherent to representation. Representation goes from a concrete object of perception to its final verbal account via a system that combines memory, the desire to grasp the totality of experience, and exchange of the object for the linguistic sign. Each of these terms fails to maintain the mechanism of identity necessary to recuperate the object and points to the figural space of representation. This space is, in effect, the site of the unrepresentable. The critical imagination of Romanticism assigns this space to poetry. This assignment constitutes a revision, reconstruction, and reinvention of the concept of representation envisioned by Kant and Fichte. The Romantics considered representability as the condition of all knowledge. "Representability, or graspability," (*Darstellbarkeit oder Denkbarkeit*) writes Novalis, "is the criterion of the possibility of all philosophy" (ibid., 2: 217, no. 305). The preoccupation with representability maps the path to new crossroads where accepted notions of knowledge, art, and history face critical challenges.

Rethinking the Legacy of German Idealism

Kant's "second Copernican revolution" heralds a radical change in the understanding of representation. Kant uses this elegant metaphor to illustrate his concept of a revolutionary shift in the history of perception. If intuition is to conform to the constitution of objects, argues Kant, there can be no ground for the assumption that we can know anything of these objects a priori. However, if objects must conform to the constitution of our faculty of intuition, then the possibility of knowing objects is given a priori to the human mind. In other words, the a priori conditions of the possibility of experience constitute the source from which all universal laws of nature must be derived. Kant demonstrates the assumed link with Copernicus by arguing that the latter could discover the force that holds the universe together only when he shifted the locus of the observed movements of celestial bodies from these bodies to the spectator. Thus, in the sphere of metaphysics, instead of measuring the content, meaning, and truth of intellectual forms by some extraneous thing which is supposed to be reproduced in them, we must find in these forms themselves the measure and criterion of their own truth generated by the faculty of reason:

> As for objects which are solely and necessarily thought through reason but which can never (at least not in the way reason thinks them) be given in experience, the attempts to think them (for they need to be thought) will henceforth provide an excellent example of what we are accepting

as our new method of thought, namely, that we can recognize of things *a priori* only that what we ourselves put in them. (1983, 3: 26)[1]

In Novalis's words, "Kant places the *firm,* resting, legislative power a priori *in us*—the older philosophers placed in outside ourselves. In this way, he validated the counter position in philosophy—as in astronomy" (1960, 2: 391, no. 47). Astronomy initially posited the centrality of the earth with the celestial bodies circling it. In an analogous fashion philosophy placed the object in the center and considered the subject to be a moving spectator. "The revolutionaries in both sciences" have turned these misconceptions around (ibid). In other words, in arriving at knowledge via reason, the subjective mind does not try to reconstruct an external reality but (re)presents perceptions through a formal synthesis generated by a priori concepts of understanding. The synthesis lends the observed phenomena their recognizable content. The phenomena can only appear in space and time which are the pure forms of our intuition or our sensibility. Time and space are the only formal categories that sensibility presents a priori. "Time is not a discursive, or a so-called general concept, but a pure form of sensible intuition. Different times are only parts of the same time," (Kant 1983, 3: 79) and "space is nothing but the form of all appearances of external sense, that is, the subjective condition of sensibility that alone makes external intuition possible for us" (ibid., 3: 75).

The Kantian schema marks a decisive shift from the Aristotelean notion of form as an entity to a new understanding of form as a condition or functional-relational structure. Because of this redefinition of form Kant was able to maintain the view that knowledge of amorphous data is possible insofar as these are integrated into formal networks of relations. All particular laws of nature in this system manifest themselves as specifications of universal principles of understanding. Different times are different forms of the one and the same time. Or a particular geometric form, for example, constitutes a specific representation of space. Thus, all scientific laws transform the perceptions by which the world of experience is presented to us into a system. The scientific theory of nature is not the product of a mechanical agglomerate but a structural whole, a self-sustaining method which owes its unity to the configuration of relations built into it. The task of the transcendental critique is an understanding of the unity of this method and its explanation in terms of universal principles analogous to pure mathematics. In other words, transcendental knowledge denotes, in Kant, the a priori conditions of knowledge that make knowledge possible.

As can be seen from this briefly outlined schema, formal representations of perception, which are not reflections of external phenomena but self-constructing syntheses, are elements of knowledge. A representation by itself does not constitute knowledge. In order to know something we need to go beyond representation to recognize another representation linked to it. Knowledge is a system, a synthesis of representations. This synthesis can be a posteriori, based on experience, or a priori, assigning properties to an object not given in representation. The latter is inherent to a higher faculty of knowledge, that is, to the speculative interest of reason. Faculties such as sensibility, understanding, reason, and imagination denote specific forms of representations. Intuition is a formal representation which is directly linked to an object of experience and has its source in sensibility. Concepts relate indirectly to an object of experience through other representations and are regulated by understanding. Ideas, which are located in the faculty of reason, go beyond experience and, as such, are unrepresentable in a formal sense. Here the notion of representation runs into complications and needs to be reformulated in terms of the transcendental principle. This is the principle "by virtue of which experience is necessarily subject to our *a priori* representations" (Deleuze 1984, 13). The transcendental question concerning the conditions of the possibility of knowledge is fundamentally the question of the representation of objects for cognition. Cognition is bound to intuition, for the concept of the object is given only in the forms of intuition. What happens when no intuition is given for the concept, as is the case with the concepts of reason?

In his discussion of the transcendental schema in the *Kritik der reinen Vernunft* (Critique of pure reason), Kant articulates the need for a "third term" (*ein Drittes*) that can mediate between sensibility and reason. The transcendental schema is this third term which Kant calls the "mediating representation" (*vermittelnde Vorstellung*) and which partakes of the intelligible and the sensible (1983, 3: 189). Schemata can express pure concepts of understanding, that is, the categories in sensible form. On the other hand, concepts of reason, that is, ideas cannot be translated into forms intuitable to sense. They do not lend themselves to direct representation. In the *Critique of Judgment,* a measure of reconciliation is enacted between sensibility and reason in a typical Kantian compartmentalization. In paragraph 59 of the *Critique of Judgment,* Kant delineates two types of *Darstellung*: schematic when the corresponding intuition is given for the concept a priori and symbolic when no sensory intuition commensurate with the concept is available and the lack is compensated by an analogy. Thus, schematic representation operates directly and the symbolic indirectly:

> All *hypotyposis* (representation, *subjectio sub adspectum*), as sensible illustration is twofold: either schematic, when the corresponding intuition is given to the concept *a priori*; or it is symbolic. In the latter, to a concept only thinkable by reason and to which no sensible intuition can be adequate, an intuition is supplied that is in accordance with the procedure of judgment analogous to what it observes in schematism, that is, analogous merely to the rule of this procedure, not to the intuition itself; and consequently merely to the form of reflection and not to its content. (ibid., 8: 459)

Here Kant objects to the misuse by modern logicians of the term "symbolic" as an antonym to "intuitive," for the latter is composed of "schematic" and "symbolic" modes of representation. Kant stresses that both terms involve a representation and are not mere mimetic signs or expressions for the concept. In other words, representation, whether schematic or symbolic, affirms something more than what is contained in the represented object. Schemata present the concept by demonstration and symbols by analogy. In symbolic representation, the faculty of judgment performs a double function. First it supplies an object of sensory intuition for the concept. Reflection upon the intuition generated by this first symbolic object is then applied to a totally different object. As illustration Kant gives the unpretentious example of how a monarchic state is represented symbolically by a living body, if it is ruled according to popular law, and by a mere machine, if ruled by individual absolute will (ibid., 8: 460). Judgment emerges as the faculty of *Darstellung,* particularly that of symbolic representation. In a strict sense, however, symbolic representation constitutes only an approximate rendering of the ideas of pure reason. Fichte later attempts to solve the problem by asserting that sensible and intellectual representations are reconciled in schemata conceived by the imagination.

Having inherited the legacy of this problem—the incompatibility of the idea and its sensible representation—the early Romantics reinvent the concept of *Darstellung* in ways that increasingly invest it with rhetorical operations that constitute a critique of philosophy's search for absolutes. They cancel the distinction between schematic and symbolic representation and point to the lack of continuity in all representation. Novalis captures the essence of the problem in this formulation: "All representation rests on making present what is not present" (1960, 3: 421, no. 782). By ingeniously formulating the act of representation in terms of successive time, Novalis invalidates the distinction between the schematic and the symbolic. All representation involves the impossible project of making the absent (past) present, of re-presenting what is no longer present. Seen in this light, the relation between representation—as form—and what is represented can only be one of radical alterity and reciprocal transformation. Signs and symbols are continuously appropriated and reformulated by their referents: "Each symbol can be symbolized anew by what it symbolized." An ignorance of the unstable relation between the symbol and the symbolized and the belief in the possibility of total representation inform the source of all our misconceptions: "On the confusion of the *symbol* with the symbolized, on their identification, on the belief in true and complete representation, and the relation of the picture to the original . . . rest all the superstitions and mistakes of all times, people and individuals" (ibid., 3: 397, no. 685). This insight would only allow for indirect representation (Kantian symbolic representation) as legitimate representation. Thus, such figures and tropes as the arabesque and irony, which challenge the notion of total representation, become the formal staples of Romantic narratives of human experience. They imply a dialectic of discontinuity, open-endedness, and productivity that match the uncertain boundaries of fields and forces not given to empirical experience:

> This artificially ordered confusion, this attractive symmetry of contradictions, this wonderful, eternal alternation of enthusiasm and irony, which lives even in the smallest units of the whole, appear to me to be an indirect mythology. The organization is the same and certainly the arabesque is the oldest and the most original form of human imagination. Neither this wit nor a mythology can exist without an original and inimitable presence that is totally irreducible and through which after all the metamorphoses its original nature and force shine and where the naïve profundity lets the appearance of the absurd and the mad, of simplicity and stupidity, to shimmer through. For this is the beginning of all poetry, to cancel the course and laws of rationally thinking reason and transport us once more into the beautiful confusion of fantasy, into the original chaos of human nature for which I know no more beautiful symbol than the colorful crowd of ancient gods. (Schlegel 1958, 2: 318–319)

Reason is no longer able to grasp the paradox and the plurality of experiences that remain unrepresentable. The unfulfilled desire of reason migrates to the shelter of Romantic forms. One of these forms is the fragment, which Schlegel calls the *Naturform*. Fragment negates the philosophical postulate of continuous representation and induces cracks in the fundament of the idea. This gesture of disruption enacts the paradox that haunts philosophy: "Could there be a more beautiful symbol for the paradox of philosophical life than those crooked lines which can, with obvious constancy and regularity and hurriedly, always appear in fragments, for their one center lies in endlessness?" (ibid., 415). Similarly, Novalis calls the "crooked line" (*krumme Linie*) the "victory of nature over the rule" (1960, 2: 257, no. 485). Thus, nature itself mimics the nonlinear thrust of the fragment. Furthermore, the fragment intercepts and arrests reflection to delimit the idea. Figural forms lend the idea the representational space where hermeneutic currencies are exchanged. In his Jena lectures on transcendental philosophy, Schlegel illustrates how the structuring intuition given to the human mind regulates the formlessness of sensory data and casts it into figural form: "It is the characteristic of chaos that nothing can be distinguished within it; and what cannot be distinguished cannot enter consciousness. Only form comes into empirical consciousness" (1958, 12: 38). Schlegel presents aesthetic form as an agent of cognition by posing the philosophical question "on whose answer everything depends." The question is, *"why has the infinite come out of itself and made itself finite?*—that is to say, why are [there] particulars [*Individua*]" (ibid., 12: 39)? The play of nature could have taken place in a split second and prevented the formation of any perception. What ensures the perception of objects at the intersection of form and formlessness?

The endless is arrested in time and space by poetic form. In Schlegel's words, only "the picture or *representation, allegory*" can account for the transformation of the endless field of perception into specific, recognizable forms (ibid.). Thus, figural representation now subsumes sensibility and understanding, for it constitutes a synthesis of that which is presented to consciousness. The proper topos of understanding is constituted in the multiplicity and the free play of particular forms. The structuring consciousness of Kantian synthesis provided the Romantics with a text whose letters they freed from the confines of a priori categories and transformed into the spirit of poetry. In this figural domain a series of Romantic amendments allowed experience a free play of representations. Questioning the lack of diversity that characterizes pure forms of intuition determined by Kant, Schlegel muses, "isn't *movement* perhaps the third [category] complementing time and space?" (ibid., 18: 332, no. 99). He is also disappointed in not finding in Kant's family tree of original concepts the category "almost" (*beinahe*), a category that "has surely accomplished, and ruined as much in the world and in literature as any other. In the mind of natural sceptics it colors all other concepts and intuitions" (ibid., 2: 157, no. 80). Schlegel's deregularization of the categories and liberation of representational forms from reference to determinate concepts recall the unregulated and free relation of faculties in Kant's *Critique of Judgment*.

In the Kantian scheme imagination is the source of syntheses that generate knowledge. The act of imagination subsumes both the manifold of intuition and the reproduction of the forms of intuition, that is, the particular manifestations of space and time. In the *Critique of Pure Reason,* Kant assigns the faculty of understanding a dominant role. Understanding acts as a legislative faculty by enacting the decrees to which all phenomena are subject in terms of their form. Acting on a synthesis of imagination, understanding fulfills its transcendental function by subjecting experience of phenomena to our a priori representations. All faculties, including reason, abide by the principles of understanding: "Pure reason leaves everything to the understanding which then refers to the objects of intuition, or rather to their synthesis in the imagination" (1983, 4: 330). Gilles Deleuze argues that in Kant's *Critique of Pure Reason* and *Kritik der praktischen Vernunft* (Critique of practical reason), the faculties enter into variable relationships regulated by one particular faculty. However, in the *Critique of Judgment,* which drafts the inaugural project of Romanticism, faculties are capable of interacting in a "free and *unregulated*" fashion (1984, xi). It is in this free play of the faculties that intersubjective readings of a given representation are possible. In his discussion of the faculty of judgment, Kant calls upon imagination to synthesize the manifold of intuition and understanding to supply the unity of concepts that links representations in order that the ground of judgment be universally communicable:

> The cognitive powers, which are deployed by this representation [a given representation which in subjective judgment links our representative powers to "cognition in general"] are here in free play [*in einem*

freien Spiele] because no definite concept limits them to a definite rule of cognition. Hence the state of mind in this representation has to be a feeling of the free play of the representing powers in a given representation with reference to a cognition in general. To a representation, by which an object is given that is to become a cognition in general, belongs *imagination* for the assemblage of the manifold of intuition [*Mannigfaltigen der Anschauung*], and *understanding* for the unity of the concept joining the representations. This state of *free play* of the cognitive faculties in a representation by which an object is given must be universally communicable, because cognition as the determination of the object with which given representations (in whatever subject this may be) are to agree, is the only kind of representation which is universally valid (1983, 8: 296).

Imagination does not relate to a determinate concept of understanding. It relates, however, in a free fashion to the faculty of understanding in general, to unspecified, unrepresented concepts of understanding. It is a "productive faculty of cognition" (*produktives Erkenntnisvermögen*; ibid., 8: 414) and a "creator of arbitrary forms of possible intuition" (*Urheberin willkürlicher Formen möglicher Anschauungen*; ibid., 8: 324). Imagination can go beyond all concepts of an object because it is profoundly capable of "creating another nature from the material that real nature gives it" (ibid., 8: 414). Furthermore, imagination forms the source of symbolic representations which relate "aesthetic ideas" to the ideas of reason in an inverse fashion. The aesthetic idea is a representation to which no concept is adequate. Consequently, it "cannot be completely accessed and made intelligible by language. . . . It is the counterpart (pendant) of a *rational idea,* which conversely is a concept to which no *intuition* (or representation of the imagination) can be adequate" (ibid., 8: 413–414). In the Romantic translation of this view, the aesthetic idea is embodied in the "potentiated" language of poetry and denotes language to the second power, that is, a language that expresses what is inexpressible in the rational idea.

In Kant, judgment always involves several faculties and the free accord between them, and the universality of aesthetic pleasure is explainable by this unregulated relationship. In the judgment of the beautiful, reason plays no role. Only imagination and understanding interface. In the judgment of the sublime, however, the pleasure generated by the freedom of imagination turns to pain by the force that strains the limits of imagination. Kant's analytic of the sublime and its subsequent reinterpretation in Schiller probably anticipate most accurately the Romantic anxiety concerning the possibility of total representation. The notion of the sublime formulated in these texts subsumes Schlegel's image of chaos, of unrepresentable and unreproducible infinity that is beyond sensibility. The feeling of the sublime is generated when imagination is confronted by the formless or the unbounded: "The beautiful in nature is focused on the form of the object, which involves defining boundaries. The sublime, on the other hand, can also be found in a formless object, as long as in it or by occasion of it *boundlessness* [*Unbegrenztheit*] is represented, and yet its totality is also taken into consideration" (ibid., 8: 329).

The apprehension of the sublime is divided into two categories: the mathematical sublime and the dynamic sublime. What is apprehended in the first case is a boundlessness of magnitude, in the second, a boundlessness of power. In his discussion of the mathematical sublime, Kant shows that imagination is involved in two operations when it has to receive magnitude by intuition:

> *apprehension (apprehensio)* and *comprehension (comprehensio aesthetica)*. With apprehension there is no difficulty, for it can go on into infinity but, comprehension becomes increasingly difficult the further apprehension advances, and soon reaches its limit, that is, the greatest possible aesthetic base measure for the estimation of magnitude. (ibid., 8: 337)

In other words, imagination has no limit as long as it has to apprehend parts of a magnitude in succession. However, as soon as it has to retain previous parts while acquiring succeeding ones, a limit is imposed on its simultaneous comprehension:

> For when apprehension has gone so far that the partial representations of sensible intuition initially apprehended begin to disappear in the imagination, while this pursues the apprehension of others, then it loses as much on the one side as it gains on the other; and in comprehension there is an absolute beyond which it cannot go. (ibid., 8: 337–338)

Before discussing the eventual reconciliation of imagination and reason in the Kantian sublime, we should perhaps pause to reflect on the implications of the latter in Romantic poetry. We attribute the magnitude whose comprehension eludes imagination to nature. Kant defines sublime as "an object (of nature) *whose representation determines the mind to think the unattainability of nature regarded as a presentation of ideas*" (ibid., 8: 357). Kant argues that ideas cannot be presented in a strictly logical sense. Reason demonstrates to imagination its limits by representing the inaccessibility of the idea and stressing this very inaccessibility as a condition of sensible nature. The awareness of the unrepresentability of the rational idea launches imagination toward a "supersensible destination and obliges us, subjectively, to *think* nature itself in its totality as a representation of something supersensible, without being able to realize this representation *objectively*" (ibid., 8: 358). The abolition of sensible structures invests the imagination with a dizzying freedom. "The imagination, although it finds nothing beyond the sensible to which it can attach itself," writes Kant, "feels itself unbounded by this very removal of its limitations: hence this very separation is a representation of the infinite [*Darstellung des Unendlichen*], which for this reason can be nothing other than a mere negative representation but which, nevertheless, expands the soul" (ibid., 8: 365).

Thus, when the imagination confronts its own limit, it goes beyond this limit by representing to itself the unavailability of the idea. Schlegel locates the intuition of the infinite in the indirect, nonmimetic representations of Romantic poetry: "Poetry, which only implies the infinite, does not yield determinate concepts but only intuitions. It [the infinite] is an endless abundance, a chaos of ideas which [poetry] strives to represent and to bring together in a beautiful whole" (1958, 11: 114). Tropes like allegory and irony represent the endless in a manner that mimics the negative operation of the sublime. One definition of irony in Schlegel is "the clear consciousness of eternal agility, of an infinitely full chaos" (ibid., 2: 263, no. 69). The sublime constitutes a resignation to explain nature by the rules of understanding and makes this very incomprehensibility the basis of judgment.

When faced with the immensity of the sublime, imagination experiences its own inadequacy, and "in striving to surpass it, recoils upon itself" (Kant 1983, 8: 338). At first we attribute this overwhelming sensation to the objects of nature, but it is reason in effect that forces imagination to present the unlimitedness of the sensible world as a unified whole. Reason requires totality "for every given magnitude—even for those that can never be entirely apprehended, although (in sensible representation) they are judged as entirely given—and consequently requires comprehension in *one* intuition and *representation* [*Darstellung*] of all members of a progressively increasing series and does not exclude even the infinite (space and past time) from this requirement" (ibid., 8: 340–341). The encounter between reason and imagination leads to an uneasy alliance. In judging a thing as beautiful, the faculty of judgment relates the imagination in its free play to understanding. In judging a thing as sublime, the same faculty refers to reason "in order that it may subjectively agree with the *ideas* of reason (not determined), i.e. that it may produce a state of mind conformable to them and compatible with that brought about by the influence of definite (practical) ideas upon feeling" (ibid., 8: 343). In other words, the confrontation with the sublime authorizes reason to sober up the imagination.

In the final analysis, however, the sublime is not an external force. The power of the sublime is not released in a violent encounter. The object of the encounter itself is not, properly speaking, sublime. Its form (in magnitude and power) "is inappropriate for judgment" (*zweckwidrig für unsere Urteilskraft*) and appears to violate the imagination. Here a contradiction emerges. As an aesthetic judgment, the judgment of the sublime should display a purposiveness with respect to the faculties. As it stands, it is not harmonious with the latter. Kant resolves the contradiction by stating that the object of the encounter itself is not "the authentic sublime" (*das eigentliche Erhabene*). It is only fit for the "representation of a sublimity" (*Darstellung einer Erhabenheit*). Sublime proper "cannot be contained in any sensible form but concerns only ideas of reason which, although no adequate representation is possible for them, are conjured and called to the mind by this very inadequacy which can be sensibly represented" (ibid., 8: 330). The sublimity thus represented is not inherent to the objects of nature. The site of the authentic sublime is the subject. What appears to be sublime in the nature is withdrawn into the subject. The subjective relationship between reason and imagination in the case of the sublime is not one of free play but one of discord, although Kant portrays this conflict as a reconciliation of sorts. What the mind represents to itself is the form of the unrepresentable. Reason helps an overwhelmed imagination become aware of its fragmented capacity and presents this incapacity as the unrepresentability of sensible nature. Reason frees imagination of its pain, so to speak, by uncovering the cause of its anxiety and allowing imagination to come to terms with the source of its fears.

Although the analytic of the beautiful and the sublime anticipate the status of representation in Romantic discourse, the major impetus for the formulation of that problem comes from Fichte's attempts to hold up a critical mirror to Kantian philosophy. The implication of the self as the absolute point of departure for philosophy in Kant's grand design provided the analytic framework of Fichte's *Science of Knowledge.* Kant's system had not completely satisfied the desire for the unity of human knowledge. It provided no compelling deduction of the pure forms of intuition and posited an independently existing and totally unknowable thing-in-itself inaccessible to the faculties. But for Fichte the major critical weakness of Kant's philosophy lay in its failure to represent the self to itself. The Kantian self is the site of the faculties and their interaction but lacks the facility for self-representation. In other words, it lacks a posited consciousness or otherness that can reflect on itself. In his attempt to develop a system with an inherent self-critique, in other words, a transcendental system which is at the same time the system of a system, Fichte deduces the categories from the activity of the self, the *Ich.* This system is informed by the determination to accept no fact, law, or motion not deducible from the self. Fichte's theory of knowledge, which is required to display absolute totality and "give all the sciences their form," has to be based on an absolute first principle (1962–, 1.2: 128). Thus, the *Wissenschaftslehre* begins:

> We need to *discover* the primordial, totally unconditioned first principle of all human knowledge. This can be neither *proved* nor *determined,* if it is to be an absolutely first principle.
>
> It should express that *Act* [*Thathandlung*] which does not and cannot appear among the empirical states of our consciousness, but rather lies at the basis of all consciousness and alone makes it possible. (ibid., 1.2: 255)

This request for a spontaneous and unconditional point of origin for all consciousness implies an originally undifferentiated totality that would guarantee a systematic unity of conception, a single principle from which the multiplicity of experience may be deduced. Fichte sought to place the possibility of knowledge in the unity of human mental activity and as emanating from a point of origin.

Thus, the self posits itself as an object of cognition. Such positing is an act of representation: "The Act of the self, whereby it posits its own existence, is not directed to any object, but returns in upon itself. Only when the self presents itself to itself [*wenn das Ich sich selbst vorstellt*], does it become an object" (ibid., 1.2: 293). The act of positing imposes a limit on the infinity of the self and makes reflection possible by causing the self to turn upon itself. The moment of reflection inheres in the condition of a self-limiting self. In the *Wissenschaftslehre,* reflection is the mode of cognition. What is more important, especially from the viewpoint of Romantic aesthetic theory, is that reflection itself is a form of representation (*Vorstellen*).

In the 1794 edition of "Über den Begriff der Wissenschaftslehre oder der sogenannten Philosophie" (Concerning the concept of the *Wissenschaftslehre* or the so-called philosophy), a general treatise on the concept of philosophy, Fichte eloquently illustrates how the absolute first philosophical activity, the activity of the human mind, is presented to consciousness in representation (*Vorstellen*):

> The form of reflection which rules in the whole of *Wissenschaftslehre,* in so far as it is a science, is *a representation*. It certainly does not follow from this that everything that is reflected *upon* is a mere representation. In the *Wissenschaftslehre* the I [*das Ich*] *is represented*. It does not follow, however, that it is represented *as* merely representing, as mere mind. There may very well be other qualifications in this I. As philosophizing *subject,* the I is indisputably merely representing. The I, as *object* of philosophizing could very well be something more. Representation is the highest and the absolutely first act of the philosopher per se; the absolutely first act of the human mind could well be something else. . . . What definitely follows from the above discussion is that all activities of the human mind, which are supposed to be fully covered by the *Wissenschaftslehre,* come into consciousness in the form of representation, in so far as and in the way that they are represented. (ibid. 1.2: 149)

When the self op-posits itself, its endlesssness is deflected and returns to the absolute self where it is captured in the representation of the representing being. The point of unconditional departure in Fichte's system of knowledge is our direct and suprasensible relation—which he calls "intellectual intuition" (*intellektuelle Anschauung*)—to an infinite and absolute self. The self is regulated by two opposing drives. The theoretical drive guides the self to reflect upon itself. The practical drive, on the other hand, incites the self to expand into infinity. Each drive presupposes the other, and both form the condition of self-activity and representation.

> Without infinitude of the self—without an absolute productive faculty thereof that reaches beyond the unlimited and the illimitable, we cannot even explain the possibility of representation [*Vorstellung*]. From the postulate that a representation must exist, which is contained in the principle that the self posits itself as determined by the not-self, this absolute productive creativity is hereafter synthetically derived and demonstrated. (ibid., 1.2: 361)

The tension between the expansive drive of the self and the limiting drive of the not-self is resolved in imagination (*Einbildungskraft*), which unites opposing principles (*welche widersprechendes vereinigt*).[2] The subject which posits itself cannot be without the existence of an object thus posited. As Fichte adds, the determination of the self, its reflection on itself is only possible under the condition that it limits itself "by an op-posited" (*durch ein entgegengesetztes*; ibid., 2: 361).

From Fichte's transcendental schema, Schlegel derives the critical position of transcendental poetry. The primary schema of all reflection takes on the form of a knowledge of knowledge:

> Fichte's *Wissenschaftslehre* is a philosophy about the subject matter of the Kantian philosophy. He does not say much about the form, since he is a master of it. However, if the essence of the critical method inheres in the fact that the theory of the determining faculty and the system of determined affective states therein are intimately bound like objects and ideas in a prestabilized harmony, then it may very well be that he is a Kant raised to the second power and the *Wissenschaftslehre* far more critical than it appears to be. Above all, the new representation of the *Wissenschaftslehre* is always simultaneously philosophy and philosophy of philosophy. (1958, 2: 213, no. 281)

In a similar vein, Schlegel sees in the critical sensibility of poetics an aesthetic reflection on the work of art which he calls "poetry of poetry" (*Poesie der Poesie*) or "transcendental poetry." In a proper analogy to transcendental philosophy, this poetry represents "the producer along with the product" and represents itself in all its representations. It unites "the transcendental elements and preliminary drafts of a theory of poetic creativity" and is always simultaneously "poetry and the poetry of poetry" (ibid., 2: 204, no. 238).

In his *Fichte-Studien* (Fichte studies) of 1795–1796, Novalis recasts the principles of *Wissenschaftslehre* in a new language. To this end he seeks to transform Fichte's notion of self-activity into a creative or poetic principle. Novalis interprets the endlessly free activity of the self as "appropriation" (*Vereigenthümlichung*). The self appropriates whatever comes into its sphere. In this act of appropriation Novalis sees the transformative, creative power of the self which makes the object its product (1960, 2: 274, no. 568). The self "represents merely to represent—to represent in order to represent is a free representation [*freyes Darstellen*]" (ibid., 2: 282, no. 633). Novalis's analysis of the *Wissenschaftslehre* begins by a challenge to the threadbare analytic in the sentence of identity A = A. The identity of sameness and difference inherent in this formula is problematic, because all representation is packed in the self and divested of diversity. "Has Fichte not placed everything in the self too arbitrarily?" (ibid., 2: 107, no. 5) asks Novalis. In Fichte's analytic sentence the self seems to represent only the self. The difference of the terms goes unnoticed because of their apparent sameness. When the self posits a not-self, it re-presents itself. However, such an obvious gesture of self-representation oversimplifies and limits the concept of representation: "We think of representation [*Vorstellung*] too much in terms of that which represents. . . . We can easily imagine the representation of the self—since everything is representation, any representation can easily be the material for another representation" (ibid., 2: 255, no. 477).

Novalis's project is to remove representation from the abstract plane where it is embedded and place it in a poetic medium where it can be expanded. Identity as a pure analytic proposition of sameness cannot be represented, unless it is op-posited to something that it is not. Therefore, "we leave the *identical* in order to represent [*darstellen*] it," (ibid., 2: 104, no. 1)[3] states Novalis. He posits the relation between the two terms in A = A as a representation of the nature of consciousness which is "a being other than the being in being" (*ein Seyn außer dem Seyn im Seyn*). That other is "an image [*Bild*] of the being in being" (ibid., 2: 106, no. 2). Thus, consciousness is a representation or an image of the self by something outside the self. In other words, Novalis posits the necessary existence of an eye for the representation of the I. As he states, the analytic self "posits itself for itself by positing a *picture* of its founder and thus reproduces the action of its own founding" (ibid., 2: 140, no. 53).[4] In this way, the analytic self takes on a synthetic or reproduced character. "In the synthetic self the analytic self looks at itself. . . . The synthetic self is at the same time the mirror of reality" (ibid., 2: 141, no. 63). Representation begins with a split or division (analysis) and ends in a reproduction (synthesis). Novalis calls synthesis the "highest *representation* [*Darstellung*] of the ungraspable" and "positing of contradiction as non-contradiction" (ibid., 2: 111, no. 12).

In order to understand the conditions for the production of meaning, Novalis situates the theory of representation in the larger context of a semiotic theory or what he calls "the theory of the sign" (*Theorie des Zeichens*). What is necessary in order to perceive being is a "theory of representation or of the not-being in being" (*Theorie der Darstellung oder des Nichtseyns im Sein*) (ibid., 2: 106, no. 2). By synthesizing the moments of an absolute activity prior to consciousness, Novalis develops a theory of representation and sign from the analytic sentence of identity. The latter is only an "apparent sentence" (*Scheinsatz;* ibid., 2: 104, no. 1). The self and the not-self are necessary heuristic fictions for the representation of Fichte's theory of knowledge. Elsewhere Novalis calls Fichte's *Ich* "Robinson [Crusoe], a scientific fiction for the simplification of the representation and development of the *Wissenschaftslehre,* thus, the beginning of the story, etc." (ibid., 3: 405, no. 717). Representation operates through signification which rests neither with the subject nor with the object but is a freely creating activity. In other words, the self cannot posit itself and a not-self as fixed points of reference. In explicating self-positing and op-positing in terms of sign and signification, Novalis underlines the representative operation of the relation between the self and the object and refers to this operation as the "basic schema" (*ursprüngliches Schema*):

The necessary relation of a sign [*Zeichen*] to a signified [*Bezeichnete*] should inhere in the signifying agent [*Bezeichnende*]. In *this* [the signifying agent], however, both [the sign and the signified] are freely posited. Thus, there must be a free necessity of the relationship between the two in the signifying agent. It is to be free with respect to this signifying agent—thus, it can be necessary only with respect to *the nature of the signifying agent* or to the other signifying agents. Free necessity could be called self-determination—consequently, self-determination would be the very nature of *the signifying agent in general* and of the other signifying agents—the nature of self-determination would, accordingly, be synthesis—absolute positing of the sphere—thesis—defined positing of the sphere—antithesis—non-defined positing of the sphere. Each of these three is all three and this is the proof of their belonging together. The synthesis is or can be thesis and antithesis. The same is true of thesis and the antithesis. Basic schema. One in all. All in one.

Each *comprehensible* sign must, therefore, be in a *schematic* relationship to the signified. (ibid., 2: 109, no. 11)

In this representational relationship the self reconciles necessity with freedom. The freedom inheres in the synthetic process of representation which derives from the reciprocal play between the elements of the tripartite schema of the signifying agent (self), the signified (object), and the sign (form of representation).

Novalis's move from the sphere of philosophical representation as construction to aesthetic representation as a process of signification informs the spirit of Romantic criticism. His rudimentary theory of semiotics anticipates the modern understanding of sign systems. In "Myth Today" (1972, 109–159), a provocative analysis of signifying practices, Roland Barthes demonstrates that the three-dimensional pattern composed of the signifier, the signified, and the sign operates with enhanced generative capacity in the domain of myth (which in this context refers to the intricate system of images and traditions that govern the conditions for the production of meaning) and in the manifestation of myth in literature.[5] Myth is a peculiar construct, for it functions as a *"second-order semiological system"* (ibid., 114) based on a preexisting system of signification which is language. The relation between the signifier and the signified in language is finite in its signifying capacity, since it is governed by conventionally prescribed rules. A bunch of roses, Barthes states, can be used to signify passion. In this instance, the bouquet constitutes the signifier, passion, the signified. The relation between the two generates a third term, the bunch of roses as a sign. Or a black pebble can be made to signify a death sentence in an anonymous vote. It should be noted, however, that as signs the roses and the black pebble are quite different from the same horticultural and mineralogical objects as signifiers. Since it is governed by socially prescribed norms, the primary mode of signification in language is limited in expressive range. Now, in the "second-order semiological system" the sign of the rose is emptied of its fullness, that is, relieved of its first signifying baggage and becomes a new signifier or image in the symbolic realm of myth.

Language lends itself readily to transfiguration of its signs, argues Barthes, since it does not assign them determinate meanings from the outset. Myth is characterized by a "disproportion between signifier and signified" (ibid., 120).[6] Therefore, its concepts are open to multiple contingencies. Barthes's semiological model explains almost ideally Novalis's concept of "language to the second power" (*Sprache in der Zweiten Potenz*) which is characteristic of myth and fable or what Novalis calls the "expression of a total [system of] thought." This system finds its expression in "hieroglyphics to the second power" (*Hieroglyphistik in der Zweiten Potenz*) and constitutes "in itself a complete production of the *higher faculty of language*" (1960, 2: 588, no. 264). The "higher faculty of language" is the realm of the free self constructed in all its synthetic diversity in representation.

The self, argues Novalis, cannot posit itself unless another self or not-self is given. In the "basic schema" the self represents the signifying agent. The agent, the signified, and the sign are in a dialectical relationship in the schema. The first signifying agent finds in a second one a basic schema and selects from the latter its communicating signs. The first agent is free in its selection of signs. The second signifying agent "is only free in so far as it is necessary and, conversely, it is necessary in so far as it is free—in short—it is *necessarily free*." Novalis then asks how the first agent could have recognized the schema from which it selected the sign. The answer is, "the first signifying agent will have covertly painted its own picture in front of the mirror of reflection, and it should not be forgotten that the picture is painted in the position it painted itself" (ibid., 2: 110, no. 11). Thus, the first signifying agent recognizes itself in the second one, which is its own representation. In the concept of "free necessity," Novalis demonstrates that the objects of consciousness are freely posited as signs by which we understand the world. Both signifying agents refer to one another in their determination of the signified. Both have to be free to represent effectively.

By positing two freely representing agents in his basic schema, Novalis negates the idea of a primordial absolute self that posits a not-self. Instead, he develops a schema of signifying selves in the representational medium of language. However, all powers or faculties in the schema have to stand under the sign of the "absolute synthetic" (ibid., 2: 111, no. 11) which, in its reconciliation of irreconcilables, constitutes the highest form of representation. Here the self is free because it represents freely. "Philosophizing" (*Filosofiren*), as Novalis sees it, negates all absolutes in order to legitimize the infinitely free activity of the productive self: "All philosophizing aims at emancipation." All first principles have to originate in free representation in a metaphysical system that names freedom as its highest goal: "The highest principle must not be simply given but be freely made, invented or imagined, in order to establish a metaphysical system that begins with freedom and goes to freedom" (ibid., 2: 273, no. 568).

Freedom and infinity are the informing principles of the representation of the self. Since in its capacity of representation the self appropriates the objects of consciousness, it ensures itself an infinitely free faculty. The self "represents freely" because it determines the ground of activity. In its representing activity, the self mediates between the subject and the object and presents the unconditional with the conditional. Novalis defines this activity of the self as an "*oscillation* [*Schweben*] between opposites" and, like Fichte, understands this oscillation to be the gesture of the "productive imagination." Novalis explicitly states that "freedom" is the term for the "*oscillating* imagination" (*schwebende* Einbildungskraft; ibid., 2: 188, no. 249). "Being free is the tendency of the self," writes Novalis, and "the faculty of being free is the productive imagination" (ibid., 2: 266, no. 555). "Being, being (one)self, being free, and oscillation" (*Seyn, Ich seyn, Frey seyn und Schweben*) are synonymous in aesthetic practice. They are "predicates of the single concept [of the] self" (ibid., 2: 267, no. 556) which dance in a free play. In a bold analogic turn, Novalis visualizes the universal metaphysical system as an oscillation without closure, "a system of manifold unity, of the endless expansion—a compass of freedom, neither a formal nor a material system" (ibid., 2: 290, no. 649). Novalis infinitely postpones the closure of Fichte's system by opening it up to the endlessness of representational forms, of "transcendental images": "Philosophy is . . . [the] transcendental *picture* of our consciousness" (ibid., 2: 136, no. 46).

In two essays dating from 1795 and 1798 that focus on the origin of language and the concept of drives, respectively, Fichte presents a sort of prefatory postscript to the Romantic reception of the question of representation formulated in his own philosophy. In different ways both essays demonstrate how imagination constitutes the source of our representations of self and otherness and how sensible representation intimates the suprasensible concept. In "Von der Sprachfähigkeit und dem Ursprung der Sprache" (Of language ability and the origin of language) Fichte starts with the apparent objective of formulating an a priori history of language. He defines language "in the broadest sense of the term" as "the expression of our thoughts by arbitrary signs [*willkürliche Zeichen*]." In these arbitrary signs, the signifier and the signified need not have a necessary connection: "Whether or not these [signs] bear a natural resemblance to the signified is here of no consequence" (1962–, 1.3: 97–98). These signs serve for us no other purpose than to represent an object. The question that engages Fichte's interest is how humans came upon the idea of expressing their ideas by arbitrary signs. Every human is a "being capable of representation" (*ein vorstellendes Wesen*) argues Fichte, and therefore strives to reconcile the personal representation of things with the human drive for reason, that is to say, every human tries to represent everything in a rational (*vernunftmäßig*) way, to make the reality correspond to the ideal (ibid., 1.3: 100–101). In the drive for reason lies the desire to realize language. Language, as representation, reduces the otherness of the outer world and denies it any radical alterity that can challenge the self-identity of reason. In a way, language constitutes the self-representation of reason. Reason, however, is represented even beyond language, as demonstrated in a note Fichte appends. Thought is possible in images projected by imagination: "I do not prove here that the human being cannot think without language and have general abstract concepts without it. He can certainly do that by means of images that his imagination casts for him [*vermittelst der Bilder, die er durch die Phantasie sich entwirft*]" (ibid., 1.3: 103).

The characteristic that marks any subject as possessing reason is the ability to adjust its actions to the purposes of others. In other words, when one subject perceives the actions of another in such a way as to freely change its own course of activity to agree with these, it exhibits reason. The activity of the subject is informed by both purposiveness and freedom, and the "reciprocal effect" (*Wechselwirkung*) between purposiveness and freedom is the site of reason. Of necessity humans want to find a "rationality" (*Vernuftmäßigkeit*) outside of themselves and, therefore, often attribute reason to lifeless things. There is ample evidence of this in our mythologies and religious beliefs. This drive to impose reason on the world urges humans to communicate their ideas to others so as to prevent any misunderstanding of their actions which would thwart their expectations and place them in conflict with their own purposes. Thus, they use signs of language to effect a reciprocal action between their ideas and those of others. However, linguistic signs pose difficulties in the expression of mental concepts. Not surprisingly, Fichte cites, in this context, the example of the word 'being' (*Sein*), the primordial participle of his philosophy. This word represents for him "the *permanent* as opposed to the *changing, or the sensible concept of the substance*" (ibid., 1.3: 111). It is not permanence, however, but change that is the object of our perceptions. Nevertheless, we need to relate all change to permanence. This permanence can only be a product of imagination. In other words, only imagination can lend substance or sensibility to a mental concept that originally lacks a sensible referent, and the substance manifests itself in the representation, or sign, that is language.

The invention of signs for suprasensible concepts is carried out by the schemata conjured by imagination. States Fichte:

> These signs for suprasensible ideas are very easily found in the ground lying in the human soul. For there is in us a unification of sensible and suprasensible representations through the schemata brought forth by the imagination. Designations for mental concepts are derived from these schemata. That is, the sign that the sensible object, from which the schema was derived, already had in language, was itself carried over to the suprasensible concept. (ibid., 1.3: 113)

However, these derived signs are informed by ambiguity or illusion. A case in point is the representation of "the soul, the I" (ibid.) which must be thought of as ethereal or incorporeal, since it is op-posited to the bodily world. However, if we wish to represent this concept as something outside ourselves, it has to be represented in space, which, paradoxically, is the site of the sensible object. In order to resolve this contradiction humans originally used as metaphors those elements which were not visible but partially attributable to the suprasensible concept, in order to designate that concept. For example, since air and spirit are invisible signifiers, they were metaphorically used to designate the soul. This kind of designation became more refined as the concepts became more eloquent. Thus, without the metaphorical operations of the imagination there could be no designation of suprasensible or mental concepts and the philosophical text would cease to exist. In other words, imagination is the pre-text of philosophy.

In "Über Geist und Buchstab in der Philosophie" (On the Spirit and the Letter in Philosophy), an epistolary essay fragment published in 1798, Fichte establishes three categories of the concept of drive (*Trieb*) which constitutes the highest principle of self-activity. These are the cognitive drive, the practical drive, and the aesthetic drive. Drive is "the one thing in human beings which is independent and utterly incapable of being determined from outside. . . . This alone transforms us into independent, observing and acting beings" (ibid., 1.6: 340). Drive is the force behind the human capacity for representation:

> Only through drive is the person a representing being [*vorstellendes Wesen*]. Even if, as some philosophers would have it, we could through objects provide humans with the material of their representations, letting images flow to them from all sides through things, they would still need self-activity to be able to grasp them and transform them into a representation that the lifeless creatures in space around us do not possess, although they must be flooded with the images floating through the whole universe as we are. (ibid., 1.6: 340)

Thus, the first principle of all human activity is the ability to represent. When the self posits a representation of the sensible world, all that it is aware of is its perception of this world. The only way it can become conscious of its own activity through representation is to entertain a representation of its own activity of representing the sensible world. Now the self reflects upon its own activity which is present in its own representation. This is for Fichte the very essence of transcendental philosophy, that is, not directly engaging in representation but representing the process of representation itself. Such is the activity that leads to knowledge.

The three categories of drive Fichte establishes are separate forms of representation that differ in terms of their relation to the object represented. The cognitive drive aims at knowledge simply for the sake of knowledge. In the purview of this drive, representation has no other task than to conform fully to the object. The practical drive, on the other hand, focuses not on the mere knowledge of things as they are but on the conditions of their production, change, and development. In the case of the cognitive drive, an object independent of the subject is presupposed and the drive proceeds to represent an image that is in full conformity with the characteristics of this object; whereas inherent to the practical drive is a basic representation freely created by the self. This drive seeks to call forth an object in the sensible world that conforms to the given representation. These two drives presuppose each other. Fichte states that in both cases the drives aim neither at the thing nor at the representation alone but seek an agreement between the two. In the cognitive drive, the representation has to orient itself to the sensible object. In the practical drive, the object needs to agree with the representation.

The third drive, which Fichte calls the aesthetic, stands apart from the other two for it concerns itself not with any form of agreement between object and representation but solely with representation for its own sake. The interest of this drive lies not in re-presentation but in the creation of an independent image. As Fichte puts it:

> it is not the portrayal of something but a free form of the image which is called for. . . . Just as a representation whose very content is designed through absolute self-activity forms the basis of the practical determination, so a representation designed in the same way is at the basis of the aesthetic, only with the difference that the latter need not, like the former, correspond to something given in the sensible world. (ibid., 1.6: 342)

The task of both the cognitive and the aesthetic drives is to create a representation. The representation of the first type has to harmonize with an object, whereas the aesthetic representation is not subject to any conformity with objects. It is possible, Fichte asserts, that a representation (*Darstellung*) of the aesthetic image be called for in the sensible world, but this is not the function of the aesthetic drive "whose job is done with the creation of the image in the soul." Rather it is the practical drive which somehow "intervenes in the order of representations and sets up a possible external and extraneous objective for this representation [*Nachbildung*] in the real world" (ibid., 1.6: 343). The practical drive is engaged in *constructing* or *construing* the object of representation. It pursues an object external to the self. However, the concept of this object is formed in the self. When the concept of the object is created in the mind (*Gemüth*), the practical drive becomes conscious of it and attempts to create the conditions in which the object can become real. If the object is produced, the drive is satisfied. "The human spirit [*Geist*]," observes Fichte, "receives as it were something that belongs to it, an expression of its own activity outside itself, and it easily sees in the objects its own form, as if in a mirror" (ibid., 1.6: 345). As this visual metaphor implies, the practical drive constitutes an act of constructing an exteriority derived from an essential interiority.

The cognitive and practical drives participate in a dialectic of exteriority and interiority. Not so the aesthetic drive. It can only be self-referential: "No prior representation of its object is possible because its object is itself only a representation" (ibid., 1.3: 345). Fichte establishes the autonomy of the aesthetic object by freeing it from any possible referent. However, he then proceeds to argue that aesthetic representation originates in the experience directed toward cognitive knowledge. The practical drive is geared "in its baser expression" to the preservation and "external well-being of animal life." The cognitive drive at first serves the practical drive in order "to develop the faculty for an independent subsistence." These drives need to carry out their respective assignments, before the aesthetic drive can be fulfilled: "The cry of want from within must first be silenced, and conflict from without must be settled, before we can dwell on our contemplations, and devote ourselves during this leisurely and liberal contemplation to aesthetic impressions . . ." (ibid., 1.6: 348).

Once humanity achieves a certain stage of external well-being and security, the drive for cognitive knowledge is aroused for the sake of knowledge itself. Our "inner eye" (*geistiges Auge*) can now linger longer on objects, observe them from various angles without necessarily determining a practical use for them. We collect the "wealth of the spirit" (*Geistesschätze*) for its own sake and value it as its own currency (ibid., 1.6: 350). In this disinterested contemplation of objects, the aesthetic sense develops under the guidance of reality. However, after accompanying the latter for some distance, the aesthetic object goes its own way. It goes beyond the observable physical world "in order to complete and round off the beautiful whole that had been begun." It is imagination guided by the aesthetic sense that fulfills the realization of the suprasensible world. In this operation imagination achieves total freedom. It remains in the realm of the aesthetic drive, "even when this drive deviates from nature and represents forms not as they are but as they ought to be according to the dictates of this drive" (ibid., 1.6: 351–352). Fichte names this free "creative faculty" (*Schöpfungs-Vermögen*) "spirit" (*Geist*).

The Romantic aesthetic is anchored at the site where imagination and spirit become synonymous and flow as one into the open sea of "progressive universal poetry." The endless goal of our drive is the idea and when that idea is represented in a sensible image it becomes an ideal. The domain of imagination and representation, once annexed to the province of philosophy, becomes an independent state. This secession had already been recognized by Fichte when the Romantics took up residence in the new state: "Spirit leaves the boundaries of reality behind it, and in its own particular sphere there are no boundaries. The drive to which it is entrusted moves into the infinite; through it the spirit is guided onward from one vista to another, and when it has attained its objective new horizons open up to it" (ibid., 1.6: 352).

The Play Drive and Aesthetic Representation in Schiller

Credit for translating the philosophical problem of representation into strictly aesthetic terms goes to Schiller. Since Kant's first *Critique* all major German thinkers—including Kant himself—have sought to complete their philosophical systems by a treatise on art. The function of aesthetics in the larger philosophical framework has been seen by and large as arbitration between such dichotomous faculties as sensibility and reason, reason and imagination, and feeling and understanding. "The focus of the imagination is on changing its objects according to will, that of understanding on combining them with strict necessity," notes Schiller, "as much as these two interests appear to be in conflict with one another, there is, nevertheless, a point of unity between the two, and to find this [point] is the real service of *belles-lettres*" (1962, 5: 675).

"Philosophy originates in an infinite dissension of opposed activities," writes Schelling in *System des transzendentalen Idealismus* (System of transcendental idealism), "but this dissension is also the basis of every aesthetic production, and by each individual representation of art it is wholly resolved [*vollständig aufgehoben*]" (1979, 270). In other words, for Schelling the conflict of the faculties is sublated in the aesthetic product. This product embodies a closure, for it represents a finite form of the infinite (ibid., 266). Schiller also considers the aesthetic process as an act of reconciliation between the opposing activities of the mind. However, unlike Schelling, he does not see this pact as a final one that resolves all conflicts. Rather, aesthetic arbitration is seen as a play without binding rules, an ongoing process without apparent closure.

The beautiful, asserts Schiller in the long epistolary essay *Über die ästhetische Erziehung des Menschen in einer Reihe von Briefen* (On the aesthetic education of man in a series of letters), attempts to mediate "between matter and form, passivity and activity, feeling and thought" (1962, 5: 624). But the distance between these dichotomies or "op-posited states" (*entgegengesetzte Zustände*) is endless. This is the dilemma that the beautiful has to address. "If we succeed in solving this problem satisfactorily," writes Schiller, "we shall have at the same time the thread which will lead us through the whole labyrinth of aesthetics" (ibid., 5: 625). In *Aesthetic Education,* Schiller pursues the analytic of the beautiful along the path paved by Kant's *Critique of Judgment.* The opposing states, which he undertakes to define in meticulous detail, are cast in a twofold taxonomy of drives. Like Kant, Schiller attempts to reconcile sensibility (*Sinnlichkeit*) with reason in the realm of the aesthetic. However, this reconciliation in Schiller's discourse has far-reaching ramifications that relate to the social conditions of his time. Schiller sees modern humans being fragmented between the demands of the individual self and those of the state and claimed by the conflicting forces of reason and nature. In Schiller's triadic schema, which develops in a highly dramatic narrative, humanity is originally seen in a state of unity with nature. However, with the advance of civilization and the advent of logical reason, cracks begin to appear in the moral and intellectual foundations of the state:

> It was civilization itself that inflicted this wound upon modern humanity. Once the growth of experience and more exact modes of thought made sharper divisions between the sciences inevitable, and once the increasingly complex machinery of the state necessitated a more rigorous separation of ranks and occupations, then the inner unity of human nature was also torn apart, and a ruinous conflict set its harmonious powers at variance. The intuitive and the speculative understanding now took up hostile positions in their respective fields, whose frontiers they began to guard with jealousy and mistrust; and by confining our activity to a particular sphere we have created in ourselves a master who tends not infrequently to suppress the rest of our capacities.

While in the one a luxuriant imagination ravages the hard-earned fruits of the intellect, in another the spirit of abstraction stifles the fire at which the heart could have warmed itself and the imagination been kindled. (ibid., 5: 583)

In this statement on the state of contemporary affairs Schiller bases his argument on a Kantian premise. His point of departure originates in the split, introduced by Kant, between sense (*Stoff*) and form *(Form)*. Schiller names the parties in the conflict of culture the sense-drive (*Stofftrieb*) and the form-drive (*Formtrieb*). It seems at first that these two drives denote, respectively, the contingent (a posteriori) and the determinate (a priori) structures of human understanding. Schiller states that the first furnishes the cases (*Fälle*), and the second writes the laws (*Gesetze*; ibid., 5: 605). In other words, sense-drive legislates over man's actions in the physical world, oversees change, and points to a historical understanding of life while the form-drive establishes the permanence and the identity of selfhood. The latter's focus is theoretical rather than historical. It operates in the confines of objectivity and necessity. In short, it seems that here we are dealing with the opposition of self and world or formality and reality (or history). In fact, Schiller states that the sense-drive pushes for "absolute *reality*." It tries to transform all that is "mere form" into the sensible world. Conversely, the form-drive insists on "absolute *formality*" and tries to "destroy" everything that is "mere world" in order to systematize the random facts of the physical world (ibid., 5: 603).

On closer examination, we realize that these two drives have a very intricate relationship with temporality. On the one hand, the sense-drive tries to situate us in and confine us to the fortunes of physical time. This drive is referred to as a state or condition (*Zustand*), a term subject to and capable of change. The form-drive, on the other hand, cancels time and change. It "embraces the whole sequence of time," which means that "it annuls time and change. It wants the real to be necessary and eternal, and the eternal and the necessary to be real" (ibid., 5: 605). It insists on establishing what is true and right. This drive is represented by the self, which Schiller here calls *die Person,* and is informed by permanence in temporality. The self in this philosophical context symbolizes the ground of being. As long as humans merely feel, want, and act out of want, they are nothing more than "world," which means "the formless content of time." In order to transcend mere worldliness or sensuality they have to impart form to sense. And in order to transcend mere formality, they have to create time and counter permanence with change and the eternal identity of the self with the diversity of the world. From this encounter the two opposite claims on human beings, "the two fundamental laws of their sensuous, rational nature" issue forth (ibid., 5: 603).

As long as one drive rules over the other, humans will continue to be subjected to the conflicting demands of permanence and change and of feeling and reason. In order to free humanity from this struggle it is necessary for a "reciprocal action"[7] (ibid., 5: 611) to take place between the two drives. To initiate this action, states Schiller, is the duty of reason. Although Schiller assigns this duty, which he calls the idea of humanity, to reason, he is aware that reason itself does not constitute this idea. The idea of humanity can never be reached but only infinitely approximated. "On transcendental grounds" (ibid., 5: 615), reason requests that a unity be established between the two drives. Enter the play-drive (*Spieltrieb*). The sense-drive had expelled from its domain "all autonomy and freedom," and the form-drive excluded "all dependence, all passivity" (ibid., 5: 613). The play-drive transcends the competing claims of the sensible and the formal and establishes a permanence of free movement or free play that combines the fullness of existence with the highest autonomy. Schiller associates this drive with art. "The object of the sense-drive, expressed in a general concept, is called life, in the widest sense of the word," writes Schiller. This concept points to "all material being and all that is immediately present to the senses." Similarly, the object at large of the form-drive is form or figure (*Gestalt*), a concept that subsumes all the formal characteristics of objects and their relation to mental faculties. Consequently, the object of the play-drive is what Schiller calls a "living form" (*lebende Gestalt*). The latter defines "all the aesthetic qualities of phenomena [*Erscheinungen*] and, in a word, what in the widest sense of the term we call *beauty*." Since beauty is the "consummation" of our humanity, asserts Schiller, it can be neither mere life nor mere form (ibid., 5: 614–615).

By introducing the dramatic metaphor of play Schiller aims at an aesthetic reconciliation of philosophical irreconcilables. He states that linguistic usage justifies the term play in this context, for "everything which is neither subjectively nor objectively fortuitous,

and yet imposes neither outward nor inward necessity" is designated as play (ibid., 5: 616). In addition to representing the notion
of infinite perfectibility, play reconciles the simultaneous and the
sequential, being and becoming, by sublating time in time. Signifi-
cantly, the resolution of the temporal predicament, which afflicted
both the sense-drive and the form-drive, takes place in the play-
drive. Time is finally freed from all dictates and transcends its own
identity: "The play-drive . . . would be directed towards annulling
time *within time,* reconciling becoming with absolute being and
change with identity" (ibid., 5: 612–613). In resisting the confines
of traditional metaphysics, art presents us with the concepts of play,
performance, and dance, in other words, with dynamic and dialectic
structures of experience where our perception of the world is independent both of contingency and of closed structures.

In the play-drive, the conflict between the sense-drive and the
form-drive is resolved in the beautiful. Since Schiller situates the
beautiful and play in the same space, he wonders whether his ad-
dressee thinks that he is committing an error of reason by confining
the beautiful, which after all is considered "an instrument of culture," to "*mere play,*" and, conversely, by identifying play with the
beautiful. But there is no such thing as "mere play," for is it not
"precisely play and play *alone,* which in every human condition
makes human beings whole and unfolds both sides of their nature
at once?" Human beings fulfill their true selves only in play: "Humans only play when they are in the fullest sense of the word human
beings, and *they are only fully human beings when they play*" (ibid.,
5: 616–618). In *Wahrheit und Methode* (Truth and method), Hans-
Georg Gadamer draws out the implications of the role Schiller has
assigned to the play-drive by affirming that all play is intimately
linked to the movements of nature (e.g., the play of animals, of
water, and of light). It constitutes the essence of self-representation
(*Sichselbstdarstellen*; 1960, 100). And representation is the very nature of the work of art. Human play (*das menschliche Spiel*) fulfills
itself in art. Gadamer calls the translation of play into its highest objective, that is, into art, "*transformation into constructed
image*" (*Verwandlung ins Gebilde*; ibid., 105). Thus representation
and, more specifically, image construction derive from play. In the
final analysis, play is free representation of nature. In Schlegel's
words, "all the sacred plays of art are only distant imitations of the
infinite play of the universe, the eternally self-generating work of
art" (1958, 2: 324).

Since the free status of play can sustain its independence from a set of rules and absolutes, the concept provided a viable metaphor not only for Schiller's humanism but also for Nietzsche and the poststructuralists who refused to accommodate the desire for any teleology, categorical statements, or programmatic reason. In Schiller, as later in Gadamer, play becomes the ontological ground of all meaningful experience. Derrida opposes play to logocentrism, to the dictates of absolute reason in the Western metaphysical tradition,[8] whereas Schiller posits play as a higher manifestation of the centered self in the flux of sensible experience. The sphere of aesthetic play is "the state of supreme rest and supreme movement, resulting in that wonderful excitement for which the understanding has no concept and the language no name" (1962, 5: 619). The laws of the reasoning self and those of the sensible world shed their former identity and reappear as a unified third term in play. The Kantian transcendental schema has been recast in a cultural role which authorizes aesthetics to restore mankind to its forgotten freedom. The ailing faculties of reason and understanding will now be healed in the sanatoriums of the aesthetic state.

In "Kallias-Briefe" (Kallias letters), another epistolary essay, Schiller develops the concept of autonomy as the single most important characteristic of aesthetic representation. The essay is also a rigorous examination of the sensible form of the beautiful which informs works of art. Schiller's analysis begins with the relation of sense to form in terms of an analytic of the beautiful. "Beauty," states Schiller, is "only the form of a form and that which is called its sense [material] has to be merely a 'formed' [*geformt*] sense. Perfection is the form of sense; beauty, meanwhile, is the form of this perfection which is to beauty what sense is to form" (ibid., 5: 395). In other words, the beautiful form is the ultimate manifestation or representation of the sensible world. Every representation (*Vorstellung*) of nature is "a manifold [*ein Mannigfaltiges*] or sense [*Stoff*]; the art of connecting the manifold is its form. Sense [*Sinn*] produces the manifold; reason effects the connection (in the broadest sense), for reason is the faculty of connection" (ibid., 5: 396). As in Kant, it is reason that imposes a recognizable form on the manifold of perception. But the conditions for the production of form are regulated by the formal coordinates of imagination (*Vorstellungskraft*).

The different categories of reason refer to the ways it connects the manifold of perception. If it connects representation (*Vorstellung*) with representation for cognition, it is theoretical reason. If it connects representation with the will to action, then it is practical reason. When practical reason decides that an object of nature is self-determining, it ascribes this object freedom. But since reason merely loans this freedom to the object and since nothing can be free but the suprasensible, we can only talk of "*freedom in appearance, autonomy in appearance*" (*Freiheit in der Erscheinung, Autonomie in der Erscheinung*). The form of freedom in appearance is the beautiful. Thus, "beauty is nothing other than freedom in appearance" (ibid., 5: 400). Freedom in appearance, in turn, "is nothing other than the self-determination of an object insofar as it manifests itself in intuition" (ibid., 5: 401). A form presents itself as free when we do not look for its ground outside itself. In other words, an object "represents itself as free in intuition" (*in der Anschauung als frei dargestellt*; ibid., 5: 402–403), when its form does not require understanding to look for an explanation or reason for its existence. The beautiful is self-explanatory. Its form does not need the mediation of concepts to represent itself. A triangle, for example, is self-explanatory only in terms of a concept; a wavy line does not draw upon any concept to explain itself.

In short, beauty manifests itself in a certain form of representation (*Vorstellungsart*) that is self-determining. The self-determination or autonomy of the beautiful object is legislated by practical reason. However, the faculty which investigates the nature of this autonomy is understanding. Understanding reflects upon "the form of the object" (ibid., 5: 410).[9] The form is designated as technical or artistic (*kunstmäßig*) when it conforms to certain rules. Freedom can only be represented in sensible form by means of technical methods. At this point, Schiller summarizes his argument to demonstrate that "the ground of beauty is everywhere freedom in appearance. The ground of our representation of beauty is *technique* [*Technik*] in freedom" (ibid., 5: 411). In other words, the representation of the beautiful entails a freely regulated method of artistic creation. When we combine the condition of beauty with the representation of beauty, we can say that "beauty is nature in appropriate aesthetic representation" (ibid.).

Nature, states Schiller, is a term that situates freedom in the sensible world. In other words, nature invests the concept of freedom with its immediate visual and experiential reality. A bird in flight, for example, is "the happiest representation of the material harnessed by form, of the weight overcome by force. It is not unimportant to note that the capacity to triumph over weight is often used as a symbol of freedom" (ibid., 5: 414). In art as in nature, technique has to conform to the essential interiority of the object. The autonomy of the technique is "the pure harmony of the essential nature [of things] with form, *a rule at the same time observed and given by the thing itself*" (ibid., 5: 416). Consequently, in the sensible world, only the beautiful is a symbol of perfection, because it cannot be related like the purposive (*Zweckmäßige*) to something outside itself but only abides by its own freely created rules. In other words, the autonomy of the beautiful lies not in correspondence to an outside referent but in its internal coherence.

In the final part of the essay, subtitled "Das Schöne der Kunst" (The beautiful in art), Schiller combines the concepts of freedom, representation, aesthetic rule, and imagination in a drama that portrays the complex destinies of *Darstellung*. Schiller brings to bear upon the expository text the analytic transparency characteristic of his dramatic imagination and works. First Schiller presents us with an analytic of "freedom of representation." An object is represented when it is directly presented to imagination. An object is free as long as it is or appears to be self-determining. Freely represented, then, means the presentation to the imagination of a self-determining object. However, the execution of this ideal representation encounters difficulties on several counts. The nature of the object to be represented and the nature of the material of representation need to be reconciled by the artist. This is only possible if the form of representation can appear to have exchanged its nature completely with that of the represented object, that is, if both appear fully interchangeable. And only form (aesthetic form) can sustain this complete exchange. Although in the plastic arts and in theater the form of representation can be continuous with the object represented, in literature the relation between the two becomes problematic. The medium of the poet, the words, are abstract signs. There is no sensible similarity between words and things. This is not a major problem since such relationship is also lacking between a human being and a statue representing the former. But there is no formal similarity between words and things, either. "The thing and its verbal expression are merely accidental and arbitrary (with the exception of a few cases)" (ibid., 5: 431). Even this would not be a problem, if there were words or phrases which could conceivably represent the individual or unique character of things or the objective characteristics of the particular. Then it would not matter if the relation between things and words were arbitrary or necessary. Since language lacks direct and immediate expression of so many things and concepts, "the object to be represented has to make *a very wide detour* through the abstract region of concepts, where it loses much from its vitality (sensible force), before it is brought to imagination and transformed into intuition" (ibid., 5: 432).

The language presents everything to reason, and the poet presents everything to imagination. This last act Schiller calls *darstellen*. Poetry wants intuitions but language can only provide concepts. Thus, language robs the object which is entrusted to it of its sensibility (*Sinnlichkeit*) and particularity. The object, regulated or mediated by language, can no longer appear to imagination as free. How can, then, free representation be possible in language? Here, Schiller suggests the definitive approach to the dilemma of representation by asserting that the poet can overcome the generalizing tendency of language by presenting the object in poetic form. Thus, free representation is possible only when figural mobility transcends the boundaries of conceptual language. "The beauty of poetic representation [*Darstellung*] is the 'free self-activity of nature in the chains of language,'" (ibid., 5: 433) concludes Schiller. Thus, direct or mimetic representation occludes the freedom of the beautiful. Free representation is the autonomy of poetic figuration. It is the freedom of imagination. Schiller has led the way to the very core of Romanticism's understanding of *Darstellung* and its complex relationship with the idea of liberty.

3. Representation and History

Does *time* itself manifest itself as the horizon of *Being*?
Heidegger, *Being and Time*

"In the temporal world [*Zeitwelt*] being [*Seyn*] is a rhythmic relation" (1960, 2: 247, no. 456) is Novalis's prescient response to the closing question of Heidegger's *Being and Time*. Schlegel argues that space and time cannot be interpreted as mere phenomena in human consciousness or traced to some origin in being. They are constituted in such activities of the mind as remembrance, intuition, and presentiment. However, they take on concrete form only in imagination (1958, 12: 412). In Kant, time constitutes the a priori form of sensible intuition but does not belong to representation. Novalis sees time as the condition of all representation, since it is the prerequisite of all synthesis: "*Time* is the condition of all synthesis" (1960, 2: 154, no. 117), and "synthesis is realized in time, when I seek to realize its concept *successively*" (ibid., 3: 373, no. 603). In Fichte the activity of the independent self fulfills itself in time. Here successiveness is the necessary condition of self-positing. The philosophical and aesthetic articulations of temporality that inform the discourse of early German Romanticism occupy an important critical space between Kant and Fichte on the one hand and Hegel and Heidegger on the other.

The Romantic construction of temporality was subject to a complex negotiation of historical, philosophical, and aesthetic factors. The Romantics were aware that the mystery of time could not be decoded by any philosophic or scientific system. Therefore, their investigation of temporality was concerned primarily with how a particular culture understood time and how this understanding affected its self-representation in history. The immediate point of reference for the major shift in the understanding of history was the French Revolution. The volcano that erupted in 1789, that revolution which in Schlegel's words was "an almost universal earthquake, an immeasurable flood in the political world" (1958, 2: 247–248, no. 424) radically challenged the teleological vision of the Judeo-Christian history of salvation. The French Revolution deferred apocalyptic expectations. It assumed conflicting signifiers, pointing simultaneously to the end and the beginning of time. To the German Romantics the French Revolution remained inaccessible both in time and in space. The liberating force of the revolution could not be imported to the German soil. Since the physical impact of the revolution remained elusive, it began to acquire greater metaphysical and symbolic significance in the Romantic imagination. Schlegel referred to the French Revolution as an "outstanding allegory of the system of transcendental idealism" (ibid., 2: 366) and, reciprocally, regarded the discovery of idealism as a greater revolution (ibid., 3: 96) that recognized no telos.

The Judeo-Christian tradition represented time as the agent of sacred history, whereas the French Revolution became for the Romantics an allegory of radical change in time, of the elusiveness of time, and of the cancellation of telos. The Reign of Terror that followed the revolution dashed all hopes for a redemptive reversal of oppressive political conditions. The comforting vision of a linear or cyclical concept of history became a sad memory. Neither a chiliastic philosophy nor the Enlightenment's tenet of human progress were adequate paradigms for an age facing a historical experiment with unpredictable or explosive results. In reference to the French and their revolution, Schlegel makes the curious observation that the French are a "chemical nation and in them the chemical sense is most widely developed, and they always conduct their experiments—including those of moral chemistry—on a grand scale. Likewise, the age is a chemical one." He adds that revolutions are "universal and not organic but chemical movements" (ibid., 2: 248, no. 426). Schlegel, then, extends the chemistry metaphor to characterize the novel, criticism, wit, sociability (*Geselligkeit*), the new rhetoric, and history. The metaphor highlights the experimental and synthetic nature of time and history and implies that they are subject to unexpected combinations, reactions, and results. "A so-called investigation," observes Schlegel, "is a historical experiment. Its subject and result are a fact. Every fact must have a strict individuality, be both a mystery and an experiment. . . . Everything that can only be understood by enthusiasm and philosophical, poetical, or moral sensibility" is secretive and mysterious (ibid., 2: 249, no. 427). The Romantics faced this historical experiment with apprehension but with faith in poetic and moral sensibility. The past provided no insight, the present was chaos, and the future could not be visualized, since the recurring pictures of history were irreparably damaged. Thus, time became the unrepresentable. As such, it moved into the metaphysical space of the absolute, where art alone could claim to represent it, albeit nonmimetically.

For Schlegel, Novalis, and Hölderlin, the problem of temporality was intimately linked to the problem of narrative representation. Absolute time became human time in narrative.[1] In his Jena lectures, Schlegel had referred to form as the medium through which chaos— or infinite, unbounded time and space—was presented to consciousness in a graspable way. In a comprehensive survey about the concept of time in German Romanticism, Manfred Frank argues that the concept of "temporalization of self-consciousness" (*Verzeitlichung des Selbstbewußtseins*) informs the whole spectrum of Romantic philosophy (1972, 15). In the *Fichte-Studien* Novalis states that whereas space is governed by intuition (*Anschauung*), time is bound to representations (*Vorstellungen*; 1960, 2: 168, no. 218). Our notion of time is a representation of "the indeterminate finitude" (*das unbestimmte Endliche*). Space, on the other hand, represents "the definite infinity" (*das bestimmte Unendliche*). Thus, within the spectrum of occulted origins and delayed endings, the mind represents time in an infinite series of free forms. "The universal system of philosophy," writes Novalis, "must be like time. A thread that can run through endless determinations—It must be a system of manifold unity, of infinite expansion, a compass of freedom—neither a formal nor a material system" (ibid., 2: 289–290, no. 649).

The ambiguous face of time can only be etched in imagination. On the one hand, time is the absolute, the primordial condition of creation, of existence. On the other hand, it self-destructs all representations of itself by obliterating and destroying the past, refusing to sit still for the present, and blocking visions of the future. It is a suprasensible consciousness and the ontological ground of being as well as a sensible form of lived experience. Synthesized in imagination, time governs the destinies of all forms of representation. Representation is, as Novalis so acutely observed, a re-presentation, an act of making present what is no longer present, an act itself only possible in temporality: "That which exists out of time," observes Novalis, "can only be active or visible in time" (ibid., 2: 290, no. 650). Thus, temporality subsumes the acts of imagination, synthesis, and representability and is always coeval with them. And, because the notion of time is employed synonymously with these terms, it resists and postpones self-representation. When the Romantics realized that time would not sit still for their portrait, they resolved to capture it in discontinuous forms and tropes.

Exoticized History

The Romantics recognized their own extensions in time and, therefore, refrained from converting time's motion into absolutes. Therefore, in the discourse of the *Frühromantik,* time and history were not measured or accounted for on an absolute scale but were relativized, fictionalized, and exoticized. In other words, aspects of temporality were presented discursively in different perspectival frames. No aspect of time was available to individual or collective consciousness—or history—except in the form of a disjunctive continuum. Since temporality was representable only in fragmented form, history came to be regarded no longer as an archive of complete records but rather as a palimpsest of traces, obliterated notes, and memories. Time, as past, present, and future, could only be conceived in memory and anticipation and synthesized in imagination. Since narrative representation could only provide an oblique entry into the "truth" of history, the Romantics realized only too well that all historiography necessarily involved writing unfinished or incomplete accounts. Schlegel maintains that the insight into the fragmentary nature of the temporal constitutes the transcendental concept of historical understanding:

> The sense for projects—which one could call fragments of the future—differs from the feeling for fragments of the past only in direction: progressive in the former but regressive in the latter. What is essential is to be able to idealize and realize objects directly and simultaneously, to complete them and in part carry them out within oneself. Since transcendental is precisely that which refers to the union or separation of the ideal and the real, one could very well say that the sense for fragments and projects is the transcendental element of the historical spirit. (1958, 2: 168–169, no. 22)

The object of a critical history, then, becomes the inscription of the possible movements, jolts, ruptures (and raptures) of what no longer seems to be linear time. Just as critical philosophy is a "higher organ" of philosophy (1960, 3: 335, no. 463) or philosophy "to the second power," so is critical history transcendental, that is, it goes beyond what actually happened to what could happen. In *Being and Time,* Heidegger relates the transcendental dimension of history to representation: "Because . . . existence is only factually thrown, history will disclose the quiet power of the possible in greater depth, the more simply and the more concretely it understands the having-been-in-the-world in terms of its possibility and 'only' *represents* it" (emphasis mine; 1975, 2: 521–522). This history is not an accounting of facts but an inquiry into the conditions of happening (*Geschehen*). Schlegel prefigures this Heideggerean sentiment in an *Athenäum* fragment: "The subject of history is the realization [*Wirklichwerden*] of all that is practically necessary" (1958, 2: 178, no. 90). Time, for Heidegger, is not present either in the subject or in the object but, as Novalis had pointed out earlier, is the condition of their possibility: "'Time' is given neither in the 'subject' nor in the 'object,' neither 'inside' nor 'outside' and 'is *earlier*' than any subjectivity and objectivity, because it represents [*darstellt*] the condition of the very possibility of this 'earlier'" (Heidegger 1975, 2: 554). In a sense, then, time is only given to representation and only represents itself. In Novalis's words, "time is the surest historian" (1960, 3: 386, no. 256). Schlegel refers to history as "philosophy in the state of becoming" (*werdende Philosophie*) and to philosophy as "completed history" (1958, 2: 221, no. 325). In other words, history is a transcendental process, but it never reaches the ultimate transcendental signified. It cannot be rigidified in systematic categories. Like Romantic poetry, it is always in a state of becoming. Philosophy, on the other hand, is grounded in empirical history and locked into a system proven to work in the past. Time and history realize themselves in representation. Their freedom resides in the ability to extend themselves in all temporal dimensions.

Thus, a true understanding of history involves presenting events not only as they "really" happened as Ranke maintained but also as they could have happened.[2] A self-reflexive historiography mediates between the historical field of investigation and the possible scripts of its expression. It offers alternative views of experience often simultaneously displayed on the monitors of history. This is, of course, not a novel insight. In chapter nine of his *Poetics* Aristotle notes that the task of the poet is to record events not as they happened but as they could have happened, whereas a historian records merely what happened. In this sense, poetry emerges as the more meaningful and philosophical genre, for it represents the general as opposed to the particular which is the object of historiography. The distinction drawn between the two genres in terms of their respective preference for generality and particularity persisted well into the eighteenth century. This categorical dichotomy was seriously called into question by Johann Gottfried Herder and the Romantics, for it was seen as separating historiography from its necessary philosophical ground. As Hinrich Seeba has argued in an essay on Herder's contribution to the aesthetization of historiography, the second half of the eighteenth century witnessed, particularly in Herder's work, an attempt to expand and exploit the generic potential of history writing. This realization could only be possible if historiography would cease to be defined as a factual reporting of what happened and would be allowed to poeticize its narrative by speculating on "what could have happened." Thus, figural language assumed a highly important role in reconceptualizing the problematic of history writing. Seeba states that Herder credited poetic language with capturing the theoretically relevant pictorialness and the textual nuances of history. History which represents (*darstellt*) itself to the subject as image (*Bild*) and history which the subject produces (*herstellt*) in images are so tightly interwoven in Herder's conception of history that neither a strict objectivism of the Rankean "as it really happened" kind nor a solipsistic subjectivism can alone lay claim to the pictorialness of history. Therefore, Herder maintained that representation and reproduction of historical connections and the multiperspectival reality of the images of history could be realized only in the rich ambiguities of poetic language (Seeba 1985, 53–55).

The importance of perspective and position in recording historical events was suggested some thirty years earlier than Herder in the work of Johann Martin Chladenius. Chladenius's historical hermeneutics, which establishes the importance of point of view for understanding history, is a noteworthy preamble to the Romantic concept of historiography. Here, point of view refers to the position—historical, social, intellectual, and emotional—of the narrator of history, a position accountable for representing an event in one way and not in another. Thus, all historical typology presupposes a topology ([1742] 1969). And, some eighty years after the publication of Chladenius's work, in "Über die Aufgabe des Geschichtsschreibers" (On the historian's task), a lecture delivered in 1821, Wilhelm von Humboldt postulates another model of historical hermeneutics that attempts to reconcile the determinate nature of the object of inquiry and the possibilities of the historian's narrative. Humboldt starts his argument by observing that the "task of the historian is the representation of what happened [*Darstellung des Geschehenen*]" (1960, 1: 585). But an event "is only partially visible in the sensible world [*Sinnenwelt,*] and the rest has to be intuited, inferred, and guessed. The manifestations [of an event] are scattered, disjointed, isolated." The mode of representation that joins the disjunctive moments of an event is not given to direct observation and therefore cannot imitate "reality." Thus, the historian, like the poet, has to create a configuration where "everything depends on the fusion of the inquiring power and the object of inquiry" (ibid., 1: 588).

Both historical and artistic representation can be either mimetic or indirect whereby the idea of the whole is abstracted from the outer form of the object and reconfigured in imagination to yield a higher truth. Although both the artist and the historian imitate and represent, the artist is free to play with appearances of reality, whereas the historian has to plunge himself into reality, that is, establish the inner nexus of given events. Once again, in this endeavor artistic treatment is much more congenial to the spirit of history than philosophical dictates. "Philosophy dictates a goal to events," states Humboldt, "this search for final causes, even though it may be deduced from the essence of man and nature, distorts and falsifies every independent view of the characteristic operation of [historical] forces" (ibid., 596–597). Humboldt attempts in this essay to stake out another operational territory for the historian that would permit a creative and intuitive filling in of the gaps of memory.

In order to represent the invisible yet "labyrinthine" interconnections of the forces of history, the historian has to abstract the form from the events themselves. The apparent contradiction in this endeavor disappears when we consider that:

> all comprehension, as a condition of its possibility, presupposes in the understanding subject an analogue of that which will actually be understood later, an original, antecedent conformity between the subject and the object. Understanding is not merely an extension of the subject, nor is it merely a borrowing from the object, rather it is both simultaneously. Understanding always resides in the application of a given generality to a new particularity. (ibid.)

Humboldt concludes by stating that "the goal of history can only be the realization of the idea represented by mankind in every way and shape whereby the finite form may converge with the idea." Thus, in the final analysis, "the task of the historian, in its final but simplest solution, is the representation of the striving of the idea to acquire presence [*Daseyn*] in reality" (ibid., 605). The hermeneutical understanding of history as a representation of complex and intertwined destinies of events that cannot accommodate the vision of a telos informs the Romantic idea of historiography.

The criterion by which Romanticism re-membered fragments of history can be summed up as the coherence of imaginative and aesthetic reconstruction. The order of events has to be abstracted from evidence that is always fragmentary. Thus, the gaps in the overall picture, the inevitably missing parts of the jigsaw puzzle have to be filled in by what R. G. Collingwood in *The Idea of History* has called the "*a priori* imagination." In other words, the labor of imagination is the first principle in the construction of any account of the past. In Collingwood's words, it is "the historian's picture of the past, the product of his own *a priori* imagination, that has to justify the sources used in its construction. These sources are sources, that is to say, credence is given to them, only because they are in this way justified" (1946, 245). The historian's imagination justifies sources as sources by a creative investigation that involves an imaginary conversation with its object of inquiry, that is, with the past. The hermeneutic model always presupposes a partner or an other in a dialogue. In *Time and the Other* (1983), a critical examination of how anthropology temporalizes its object, Johannes Fabian has argued that, in the practice of a critical or reflexive history, the location of past experience is neither fixed nor irreversible for it designates an encounter with otherness that constitutes intersubjective understanding. Reflexivity enables us "to present (make present) our past experiences to ourselves" and "to be in the presence of others precisely inasmuch as the Other has become content of our experience. This brings us to the conditions of possibility of intersubjective knowledge. *Somehow we must be able to share each other's past in order to be knowingly in each other's present*" (1983, 91–92).

Past as the other of present constitutes an important dimension of Romantic experience. Schlegel calls the historian "a prophet facing backwards" (*ein rückwärts gekehrter Prophet*; 1958, 2: 176, no. 80). In other words, all historical understanding is located at a site where different visions and dimensions of time intrude upon one another. Novalis's *Die Christenheit oder Europa* (Christianity or Europe),[3] for example, seeks to envision, to enrich, and to establish a future state of mind, although it is apparently a treatise of a bygone age. By definition, the prophet's gaze is focused on the future. In *Christenheit*, Novalis as prophet-historian projects an ideal future based on a paradigmatic representation of the past. Mythologizing the Middle Ages provides Novalis with an allegory for his prophecies. In brief, Novalis argues that in the Middle Ages Europe was harmoniously united under the hierarchical structure of the Catholic Church. The Reformation destroyed this order by associating religion with nation states and by subjecting Christianity to the critical rigor of philology. The Jesuits reintroduced a hierarchical order, but the Enlightenment transformed its attack on Catholicism into an attack on religion, belief, enthusiasm, and poetry. Yet Christianity can once again initiate a new religion, a new humanity, and a new history and establish peace between feuding powers. This religious ritual, of course, is the repetition of a primordial action which becomes not a repetition but a recovery of that action through the healing powers of the ritual. In this way, past, present, and future interconnect and time ceases to have meaning as succession, becoming simultaneity instead. Written after Napoleon's return from Egypt to overthrow the first of the post-Revolution regimes, the Directory (1795–1799), and during the acceleration of the activities of the Second Coalition of European powers against France, *Christenheit* bears the spirit of the political burdens of an embattled Europe. Its self-consciously allegorical representation, however, extends beyond the confines of real time and space and offers no timely remedy but rather philosophical innocence and poetic solace.

Both Novalis and Schlegel see the present as the crossroads where past and future representations of time play out their philosophical and socio-political implications. Since accounts of time forgotten or not yet experienced are self-consciously representational, the Romantics deliberately allegoricize time. In other words, they construct an ideal, imaginary, and absent past and posit it as the other. Fabian asserts that "for the historian, otherness is remoteness in time" and "exotic otherness is the prerequisite of anthropological knowledge" (1983, 64, 121). This other is also a form of self-representation. In a philosophical sense, consciousness is the awareness of the self as the reflex of its eternal other. The self projects its experience of otherness as the knowledge of the world. Likewise, the experience of time—though not an experience of the physical world, the cosmos, or the historical anthroposphere yet inherent in them—projects itself as the reality of the world.

In Romantic hermeneutics, understanding the self involves understanding the other. Schlegel asserts that "there is no self-knowledge except historical self-knowledge" (1958, 2: 270, no. 139). Novalis often affirms that we need to understand otherness before we can understand ourselves. He sees Romantic poetry as the art of making an other strange yet alluring (1960, 3: 685, no. 668), in other words, of exoticizing. Similarly, Romantic history becomes allegoricized, exoticized time. It constitutes a source of allegorical representations with implications for the present and the future. Seen in this context, the Romantics' preoccupation with the Middle Ages appears less a reactionary gesture, as Heine claimed,[4] than an exoticized paradigm, a translation of an abstract metaphysics of history into concrete representational form. "In many old texts vibrates a mysterious pulse," writes Novalis, "and designates the site of contact with the invisible world" (ibid., 3: 469, no. 1096). Thus, in a paradoxical way, the exotic, perceived as distance in time and space, provides access to the absent. Novalis repeatedly stresses that knowledge is constituted in the appropriation and mastery of the foreign and, conversely, in investing the known with the unknown. "The generation of new ideas can be a useless luxury," he states, "the learned man knows how to appropriate the foreign and to render the known strange" (ibid., 3: 405, no. 716). Therefore, it should come as no surprise to discover an archaeology of old mythologies, the Middle Ages, and the ancient Orient as a recurrent item on the Romantic agenda. Romantic history thus reveals itself as a representation of a remotely known and exoticized time. However, it is important not to mistake this representation of otherness—in time—for a sentimental recourse to a lost golden age but to see it instead in its larger philosophical context as a heuristic use of historical memory. This memory refers to an immemorial past which can only be realized as a self-conscious narrative representation.

As is well known, the Romantic dilemma of knowing before knowing haunts Hegel's *Phänomenologie des Geistes* (Phenomenology of spirit). The subject learns and acquires its *Bildung* by studying a blueprint of remembered forms, traces of what is already known by the absolute spirit. Phenomenological recollection culminates in absolute knowledge. The narrative of *Phenomenology* unfolds as an act of remembrance. This memory not only recounts the development of spirit in history but also reconstructs metaphors representing forms of consciousness.[5] In the final chapter time emerges as the destiny and condition of the spirit. In the process of its becoming (*Werden*), the absolute spirit experiences its own history as a succession of spirits in time that Hegel calls "a gallery of pictures." When the spirit fulfills itself in absolute knowledge, it goes into itself (*Insichgehen*), leaves its being (*Dasein*), and hands over its form (*Gestalt*) to remembrance (*Erinnerung*; 1980–, 9:433). The Romantics prefigured the Hegelian idea of understanding through recollection. "The world constitutes a system of necessary presuppositions—a past" (1960, 3: 687, no. 679), writes Novalis. For him, all memory is a "poetic pre-script" (*Vordichtung*), but not necessarily a prescription of knowledge. The early Romantics saw history as a kind of memory, but this was not the reconstructive memory of the Hegelian system that insured the ontological status of representation. In fact, Romantic criticism stressed the relation between the problem of representation and acts of memory which replace presence with a dialectic of creation and dissolution. The latter is the site of Romantic irony.

Tropes of Temporality

The popular twin tropes of Romantic writing, allegory and irony, confirm the impossibility of the mimetic project. Their representational status disrupts any closure in the idea(l) and in time. In very general terms, allegory signifies an approximation and irony an implicit impossibility of the ideal. In *The Shape of German Romanticism*, Marshall Brown describes the linked destinies of the two tropes with deft economy: "Allegory is irony with a purpose; irony is allegory freed of the melancholy inherent in the inability to express its meaning directly" (1979, 99). In the Jena lectures Schlegel states that allegory is "the appearance of an ideal" (1958, 12: 19). Novalis observes that "ideals are also products of a transitional moment" (1960, 3: 414, no. 753). Thus, allegory as the semblance of an ideal is marked by transitoriness. Both allegory and irony signify the absence of an ultimate referent in terms of concept and time and recover it only as poetic representation. They are temporally detached from their origin and telos and signify by arbitrary and derived associations. In Romantic poetry, allegory constitutes the representation of an intercepted infinity. Although no clear critical definition distinguishes allegory from symbol in Romantic criticism and both terms are often used interchangeably, allegory consistently designates an ideal that coincides with an elusiveness characteristic of temporality.

Approximately a decade after the *Athenäum* period, Friedrich Creuzer introduces the category of time as a marker of the distinction between symbol and allegory. He emphasizes the constitution of the allegorical mode in temporal succession in contradistinction to the instantaneous quality of the symbol whose understanding fulfills itself in an unrepeatable moment of illumination.[6] Reviewing the work of Romantic critics Joseph Görres and Creuzer in *The Origin of German Tragic Drama,* Benjamin notes that their introduction of the concept of temporality into the semiotic comparison of symbol and allegory made possible a formal definition of the relationship between the two tropes. Benjamin maintains that both tropes involve a violation of linear time and a transfiguration of that violated moment. Whereas symbol glosses over this disruption of the moment in the transcendental image, allegory captures the shocked face of history in memorable form.[7] In other words, allegory manifests itself in a sustained image of captured time and "is represented by the idea of an unfulfilled infinite progression." On the other hand, "for the symbol the ideal of time is found in the fulfilled mystical instant (*Nu*)" (Wolin 1982, 66). Therefore, allegory is informed by a particular affinity to historical representation, for it dwells not only on the enigmatic question of the nature of human existence as such but also on "the biographical historicity of the individual" (Benjamin 1972–, 1.1: 343). It captures the shattered images of time in its re-collections. In the work of Benjamin and Ernst Bloch we see a recovery of the subtly differentiated use of symbol and allegory in German Romanticism.[8] Bloch's definition of the distinction between symbol and allegory perhaps comes closest to the spirit of their Romantic usage. He observes that, whereas allegory goes off metaphorically in all directions, symbol tries to be metaphorically grounded. The exchange of significations in symbol is minimal. Its restricted movement is dictated by a desire for totality. Allegory, on the other hand, is free to go through a large repertoire of temporal appearances to find analogical pictures without the restrictions of consistency (Bloch 1977, 13: 339).

Both Schlegel and Novalis see allegory as an indirect mode of reference, a metaphorical intimation of the absolute: "All beauty is allegory. The absolute, because it is unsayable, can be expressed only allegorically" (1958, 2: 324). In a letter dated March 1800 to his brother Karl, Novalis writes that poetry is not an imitation of nature: "Poetry is completely the opposite. At the most, the imitation of nature, of truth can only be carried out allegorically . . ." (1960, 4: 327). True poetry "can only have an *allegorical* meaning in general" (ibid., 3: 572, no. 113). The noncoincidence of sign and referent characteristic of modern allegory signifies the impossibility of unmediated truth. The allegorical form forever mourns the death of truth and re-collects its temporal relics. For Schlegel, allegory constitutes the philosophical ground of all poetry which "only implies the endless, does not provide definite concepts, but only intuitions" (1958, 11: 114). Allegory points to the "impossibility to reach the *highest* positively through reflection" (ibid., 19: 25, no. 227; 19: 5, no. 26). Thus, allegorical knowledge is the formal expression of our inability to grasp the absolute. It is also a marker of time or a conceptual icon of temporalization. In the Jena lectures Schlegel had asked why the "play of nature" did not run in an "instant" (*Nu*) with the result that nothing came into being. The answer required the introduction of an intermediate concept. Schlegel posited the concepts of "endless substance" and "particulars." To explain the transition from one to the other, to mediate between the eternal and the experiential, we need the concept of "*the picture or representation, allegory*" (ibid., 12: 39). Schlegel defines "the endless substance" as the source of all form, in other words, as consciousness or spirit. Allegory is that form the primordial consciousness takes in its movement through time. Manfred Frank states that for Schlegel allegory represented "the temporalization [*Verzeitlichung*] of the absolute" and that his whole philosophical undertaking could only be understood in terms of his conception of allegory (1972, 44, 30). Similarly, Hegel later illustrated in *Phenomenology* that the world is made up of images (or allegories) representing the successive stages of the absolute spirit in time.

Allegory mediates in a temporal context between an elusive revelation of being and the sensible finitude of poetic representation, between unrepresentability and representability. It constitutes an empirical re-presentation of the world of experience in image. "Every allegory means God," writes Schlegel, "and one cannot speak of God save allegorically" (1958, 18: 147, no. 315). And "to realize godhood is the endless work of nature." The site of allegory is where "the appearance of the finite and the intimation of the infinite flow into one another. Each work of art is an intimation of the infinite" (ibid., 18: 416, no. 1,140). In a certain sense, allegory performs a "scientific" task by endlessly synthesizing the flowing images of life and nature in time. In fact, Schlegel calls allegory "a science" (*eine Wissenschaft*) and irony "an art" (*eine Kunst*; ibid., 18: 232, no. 465). The methods of this science, however, can only constitute an "approximation" of its ideal. Therefore, "*all truth is relative. All knowledge is symbolic*" (ibid., 18: 417, no. 1,149). Allegory mimics the act of synthesis which yields a cumulative effect realized in time. "Time is nothing but the process of activity" (ibid., 18: 410, no. 1,072). Irony, on the other hand, subjects this synthesis to the de-structuring effect of time. As a rhetorical ploy, irony goes the analytic route. It originates in the critical examination of the presumed totality of representation. In their respectively synthetic and analytic activity, allegory and irony duplicate the work of reason itself. As Schlegel comments, "reason is an *eternal* determination through eternal separation and connection" (ibid., 18: 304, no. 1,318).

Like allegory, irony points to the inherent fragmentariness of any vision that aspires to totality. Irony "is the form of paradox" (ibid., 2: 153, no. 48). Both irony and allegory forever pursue a temporal void where representation could ideally catch up with the represented. They are "linked in their common demystification of an organic world postulated in a symbolic mode of analogical correspondences or in a mimetic mode of representation in which fiction and reality could coincide" (de Man [1969] 1983, 222). They self-consciously substitute for the absent body and voice of philosophy. "Philosophy does not have its own form and language in a real sense," states Schlegel, "the actual idea and recognition of the *highest, the endless* can never be represented adequately" (1958, 12: 214). Therefore, "irony is the duty of all philosophy that is yet neither history nor system" (ibid., 18: 86, no. 678). In fact, "philosophy is the real homeland of irony, which one would like to define as logical beauty; for wherever philosophy appears in oral or written dialogues—and is not yet fully systematized—there irony should be demanded and supplied" (ibid., 2: 152, no. 42). In other words, like allegory and irony, the philosophical pursuit can only proceed paradoxically and disruptively. In its philosophical and aesthetic role, irony performs an experiment of "self-creation" and "self-destruction" (ibid., 18: 11, no. 988). Furthermore, the operative principle of irony coincides in Schlegel's analysis with that of critical thought. "Is there perhaps another name for my irony," he asks, "and is it not actually the innermost mystery of critical philosophy" (ibid., 18: 285, no. 1,067). The dialectic of invention and deconstruction does not lead to a synthesis. Irony is "an absolute synthesis of absolute antitheses, the continually self-generating exchange of two conflicting ideas" (ibid., 2: 184, no. 121). At the site of this productive play of intellectual forces irony reigns supreme (ibid., 18: 393, no. 878). The free play of irony, which traverses the path between the finite and the infinite, leads to the freedom of poetic creation.

The rhetorical consciousness that informed the critical praxis of early German Romanticism problematized the relation between the natural object and its formal representation. However, the uncertain status of the sign, its inability to recover the presence of the object, ironically fed an intense desire to search, re-locate, collect, and appropriate figural forms hidden and preserved in texts. The absence of the object made the heart grow fonder toward the poetic form that fleshed out the abstract skeleton of metaphysical idealism. As elusive modes of representation, allegory, irony, catachresis, metalepsis, and ellipsis find their physical home in the fragment and the arabesque (or the grotesque). Arabesque houses a multiplicity of changing forms. "Arabesques and dialectical attempts go into infinity" (ibid., 18: 354, no. 403), states Schlegel. The motif of infinity represents the ideal of nonclosure Schlegel attributed to the Romantic work of art. In fact, Karl Konrad Polheim treats the idea of Friedrich Schlegel's innovative poetics itself as an expression of the arabesque. He maintains that Schlegel sees the arabesque as the "real" paradigm for the "ideal" Romantic form in the same league as the novel, novella, and fairy tale.[9] The arabesque enables the creation of an infinity of forms within the larger unity of poetry (Polheim 1966, 23–34). Indeed, the ideal of perfection in a work of art is the ability to accommodate a free play and generation of forms: "A work is cultivated [*gebildet*] when it is everywhere sharply delimited, but within those limits boundless and inexhaustible; when it is completely faithful to itself, totally homogeneous, and yet exalted above itself" (1958, 2: 215, no. 297).[10] Furthermore, the Arab and Moorish origins of the design lend the arabesque the right amount of exoticism required by the Romantic imagination. The grotesque, on the other hand, is an untrammeled variation on the theme and in the form of the arabesque. It is arabesque to the second power. It "loves the illusion of the random and the strange and coquettes with unconditional arbitrariness" (ibid., 2: 217, no. 305).

Like the poetic form, the philosophical form is not immune to the random combinations of the arabesque and the grotesque: "If each purely arbitrary or purely random connection of form and matter is grotesque, then philosophy, like poetry, has its grotesques; only it knows less about them and has not yet been able to find the key to its own esoteric history" (ibid., 2: 238, no. 389). While the arabesque mimics an unending spiral, fragment enacts both interruption and subversion of closure. In narrative form, the fragment resists all claims to truth and desires of system building. Therefore, "as a fragment, the incomplete appears in its most bearable form" (Novalis 1960, 2: 595, no. 318). The fragment intimates the unrepresentable presence of philosophical idealism. All forms of Romantic writing claim to be fragmentary: "A dialogue is a chain or a garland of fragments. An exchange of letters is a dialogue on a larger scale, and memoranda constitute a system of fragments" (ibid., 2: 176, no. 77). If memoranda are fragments, however, then they resist being integrated into systematically coherent narratives. Schlegel also maintains that a fragment, like a miniature art work, should be self-referential, "entirely isolated from the surrounding world and be self-contained like a porcupine" (1958, 2: 197, no. 206). In these definitions, the fragment is located both inside and outside systems of signification. Schlegel states that fragments provide relief from "intellectual laziness" and are notes on the margins of the discourse of the age (ibid., 2: 209, no. 259). Writing fragmentarily is writing across the borders of time, beyond the confines of the moment. "Many works of the ancients have become fragments," writes Schlegel, "many modern works are written as fragments" (ibid., 2: 169, no. 24). As Novalis correctly observes, the preference for the fragmentary form in Romantic texts is based on its interpretive possibilities: "The basis of all effective opinions and ideas of everyday life are fragments" (1960, 2: 593, no. 302). The fragment, the arabesque, and the grotesque self-consciously duplicate the apparently contradictory pursuit of the absolute and challenge philosophy to reflect on its own "esoteric history."

In order to document the literary history of poetic forms that "represent the unrepresentable," Schlegel and Novalis authorized a search for these forms in ancient and exotic texts and in the vast memory of libraries. For the Romantics the world appeared accessible only as a text. Since the world as text would not cease beyond the library shelf, life and history metamorphosed into a universal library. On the one hand, Novalis felt that the Romantics were "beyond the time of generally valid *forms*" (ibid., 2: 649, no. 479). Schlegel argued, on the other hand, that all old forms could be recovered and reconfigured: "All forms, even the most unusual ones, must come back and gain a new significance" (1957, 50, no. 342). The Romantics' new mythology initiated a long-term search for lost or forgotten forms and texts of literary history. The materiality of the text approximated the physicality of the "real" world. Keenly aware of the impossibility of an ideal coincidence between object and word, the Romantics tried to compensate for the loss, so to speak, by an ardent emphasis on the materiality of poetic form. "In terms of the actual nature of materialism, there can only be *one* science: *physics,* for everything belongs to nature," comments Schlegel. Materialism, however, is informed not only by a priority of the physical over the mental but also by a rich and bold fantasy that grasps nature in all its diversity. Therefore, "the poetic representations of materialism" definitely have an edge over its philosophical representations. "The original method of materialism," adds Schlegel, "appears and expresses itself in the best and most powerful fashion in poetry, by far better than in all other systems" (1958, 12: 123). Similarly, in "Intentional Structure of the Romantic Image," Paul de Man argues that in Romantic poetics the awareness of the loss of the object is often accompanied by

a return to a greater concreteness, a proliferation of natural objects that restores to language the material substantiality which had been partially lost. At the same time . . . the structure of the language becomes increasingly metaphorical and the image—be it under the name of symbol or even of myth—comes to be considered as the most prominent dimension of style. ([1970] 1984, 2)

The early Romantics went beyond Hegelian metaphysics in assigning the fragments of memory a material history and form for they realized that

memory is not a simple past that can be willed to presence, nor are its objects ordinary objects perceptually identifiable. They need to be reconstructed to become objects of ordinary perception; they will then, and only then, exist as linguistic or pictorial representations. (Donato 1978, 576)

Schelling had already gone beyond *Darstellung* to a pure revelation of the absolute which could not be perceived in any form. The Romantics attempted to restore representation and memory to material consciousness. The prerequisite of philosophical construal was the allegorical realization or object-ification of the absolute. *Athenäum* fragment 116 states that Romantic poetry strives to "fill and saturate art forms with every kind of solid formative material" (Schlegel 1958, 2: 182). The Romantic concept of recollection is closely linked to collection and production. For Novalis "processing" the collection constitutes "a higher degree of activity" (1960, 3: 405, no. 716). The Romantics looked for figural artifacts in the vaults of memory banks in order to script their own history, to reproduce themselves symbolically. Their recovery of lost, forgotten, or unrecorded texts and figural forms is underwritten by an archaeological epistemology. The quest for form generated in the philosophical domain reemerges in the archaeological field.

An entry in Novalis's encyclopedia project, *Das allgemeine Brouillon,* defines archaeology as "galvanism of the ancients, their *material*—revivification of antiquity" (ibid., 3: 248, no. 52). Archaeology constitutes a labor of displacement and reconstruction in a space where the relics of another culture lie. It is the "definition of antiquity. An antique *representation* of antiquity" (ibid., 3: 255, no. 84).[11] The exotic finds are rearranged to support the foundation of theoretical fictions generated prior to the excavation. However, the Romantic project of textual archaeology goes beyond a theoretical interest in the reconstruction of literary histories. To a certain extent the Romantics' attempt to lend the history of consciousness a formal property prefigures Karl Marx's critique of German ideology that had all along ignored and forgotten the material basis of ideas. In *Die deutsche Ideologie* (The German ideology), for example, Marx and Engels write that it had never occurred to the German philosophers "to inquire into the connection of German philosophy with German reality, the relation of their critique to their own material surroundings" (1969, 20). Viewed apart from history, empty talk about consciousness has no value as knowledge (ibid., 26). Of course, the Romantics' concern with material expressions of consciousness is not directly related to the idea of the production and exchange of goods. However, they understand language as a material medium of exchange. Just as money enables the exchange of goods, language enables the exchange of meaning. As Marx and Engels argue, the idea of language as a form of material consciousness and material representation of history is precisely what had escaped the critical attention of German philosophy: "The production of ideas, of representations [*Vorstellungen*], of consciousness is directly interwoven with the material activity and the material intercourse of human beings, with the language of real life" (ibid., 27).

Textual Expeditions

The search for familiar and exotic forms in which to cast their experience of the world booked the early Romantics on textual voyages to the past and the Orient. Once again, Schlegel emphasizes the materiality of poetic forms by referring to them as "capital." In the "Dialogue on Poetry," one of the discussants, Andrea, remarks that "the masters of all ages and nations have paved the way for us [*haben uns vorgearbeitet*] and left us an immense capital" (1958, 2: 307). The desire for the recovery of this capital harbors an ideology of collecting and appropriating the past and mastering it as an object of investigation. This ideology is motivated by the fear of losing to the imperfections of memory metaphorical artifacts by which human beings as agents of history defined themselves. Furthermore, transforming the site of exotic finds into familiar territory is, in Novalis's view, the basic impulse of philosophical hermeneutics: "Philosophy is actually homesickness [*Heimweh*]—*the drive to be home everywhere*" (1960, 3: 434, no. 857).

In the larger context of the Romantic project the recovery of lost or forgotten histories constituted an act of revisiting one's own history. The travels to past and distant topoi were undertaken in the universal library. The textual remains of forgotten times, which were rediscovered on the vast stacks of this library, served to confirm, institute, and legitimize comparative models of knowledge already drafted by the theoretical imagination of Romanticism. In *The Oriental Renaissance* (1984), a landmark study on the Orient of modern Western imagination, Raymond Schwab argues that the Oriental renaissance in Europe was predominantly a recognition

and revaluation of difference that generated such comparative
studies as philology, literature, and ethnography, whereas the first
Renaissance had a unifying thrust that implicitly affirmed Europe's
cultural identity and dominance. In the context of German Romantic history, the reconstructed culture of the Orient served as a pre-
text for theoretical orientation and self-examination. The India of
German Romanticism constituted in a way a pre-history of Romantic forms of self-representation. "In the usual representational form,
this Oriental characteristic appears in great boldness and in the ex-
travagant cloak and pomp of images along with the related predilection for allegory," writes Schlegel (1958, 8.1: 311). The German
intellectual tradition, as Schwab argues, required an enormous alternative to hold Cartesian absolutism at bay (1984, 482). Dissat-
isfied with the stifling rationalism of their Enlightenment heritage,
Schlegel and Novalis urged upon their countrymen and fellow Euro-
peans a study of India and Sanskrit as an antidote to the materialism
and mechanism in which the Western world seemed to be trapped.
"What new source of poetry could flow towards us from India,"
remarks a discussant in Schlegel's "Dialogue," "if a few German
artists with their universality and profundity of mind, with their
unique genius for translation, had the opportunity [to appropriate
the cultural riches of India] which a nation, which grows increasingly limited and brutal, understands little of" (1958, 2: 319–320).

The allegory of the other, which constitutes one of the major
regulative concepts of Western metaphysics, has variously been represented as the unknown, the absent, the void, and the unconscious.
The various representations of the other as manifestations of the
exotic are posited by the self as emphatic terms of an alternative
to the cognitive ego, presence, closure, or some other first principle.
The Romantic image of the Orient evoked a consciousness that had
constantly eluded the rational paradigms of Western thought. What
awaited the Western investigative mind in the Orient was the other
as the great untapped unconscious of humanity. At the site of this
unconscious the Romantic imagination engaged in a prepsychoana-
lytic excavation and reconstruction. The retrieval of antiquity (an
ancient Orient, in this case) meant salvaging and resurrecting both
buried artifacts and texts.[12] In *Die Sprache und Weisheit der Indier*
(The language and the wisdom of the Indians) Schlegel attempts to
reconstruct a history of Romantic poetry from the recovered textual
fragments of ancient India.

The objective of Schlegel's Romantic Orientalism is to unearth "the hitherto unknown regions of the earliest antiquity . . . and to offer in the process not negligible treasures of poetic beauty and philosophical profundity" (ibid., 8.1: 317). The Romantic desire for a lost language protected from the curse of mediacy fulfills itself in the colonization of the exotic—be it Sanskrit, Arabic, Persian, or Provençal poetry—by a literary archaeology.[13] The allegorical wisdom of the ancient Orient guards the treasures of human imagination no longer available to Western consciousness. Novalis called the Orient the land of poetry and located the immediacy of experience and knowledge in the poetic operations of Oriental languages. "In the Orient, the true mathematics is at home," he writes, "in Europe it has degenerated into mere technic" (1960, 3: 594, no. 241). In its Romantic representation, Oriental thought conformed in full measure to the panoply of poetic traits accredited by Schlegel in fragment 116 of the *Athenäum*. The modes of its signification were motivated and generative, the wealth of its imagery eluded interpretive reductionism, and its insights were preserved in allegorical form. "If only the treasures of the Orient were as accessible to us as those of antiquity," muses Schlegel's narrator, Ludoviko, "in the Orient we must look for the highest form of the Romantic [*das höchste Romantische*] . . ." (1958, 2: 319–320).

In order not to underplay the relation between image and ideology we need to emphasize that the Romantics reinvented Oriental texts as a way of affirming the identity of their new cultural history. In this context, Roland Barthes in *L'empire des signes* makes a revealing statement. He puts into practice the concept of inventing an alterity by isolating "somewhere in the world (*faraway*) a certain number of features (a term employed by linguistics)" and from these creating a signifying system radically different from our own, which he calls Japan. This system does not in any way claim "to represent or to analyze reality itself (these being the major gestures of Western discourse)." Barthes writes:

> I am not lovingly gazing toward an Oriental essence—to me the Orient is a matter of indifference, merely providing a reserve of features whose manipulation—whose invented interplay—allows me to "entertain" the idea of an unheard-of symbolic system, one altogether detached from our own. (1982, 3)

Like Barthes's Japan, German Romanticism's India constitutes the recovery and reinvention of an occulted system of representation that gives Western imagination access to an alternative and unexplored path of signification. Schwab, for example, argues that although the French get the credit for creating the values of a new and free society, Germany provided these innovative ideas "with their philosophical detonator" (1984, 483). This involved among other things the invention of an alternative order of knowledge and system of signification.

In the German Romantic imagination India emerged as one of the historically suitable sites for this conceptual project. Hinduism, for example, as an imagistic religious tradition, where the divine presents itself to the world in representational form, agrees with the concept of *Darstellung* where the highest or religious truth presents itself allegorically.[14] The diversity of deities and their representations also accommodates the Romantic notion of the work of art as one formal manifestation of the infinite. Although there are several orthodox philosophical traditions in India, which embrace a diversity of perspectives on divine truth and knowledge, each considers the other's viewpoint as valid as its own. Thus, philosophical discourse takes the form of an ongoing dialogue, a free exchange of perspectives on knowledge whose ultimate aim is liberation (Eck 1985, 25). This insight coincides almost ideally with Novalis's assertion that the highest principles of knowledge are not given but freely made in order to establish a metaphysics of freedom (1960, 2: 273, no. 568). Novalis saw in the "mystic dogmatism of the Orient" an indirect form of action, a passive resistance which generated "a higher revelation of knowledge" (ibid., 3: 441, no. 902).

The early German Romantics saw the realization of their ideals of freedom in the practical life of poetry where the human mind remained immune to oppression. The revolutionary intellectual and political project of late eighteenth-century Germany, inspired greatly by the vision of idealistic philosophy, was nothing more radical than a desire for the unification of politically oppressed and restless states. The Orient, as an uncharted domain of the poetic, as the topos of unified consciousness, and as the site of humanity's encounter with its mythical heritage and lost language, became the metaphor of transcendental freedom. In a fragment on the language of music, Novalis writes of the freedom the spirit achieves in the experience of music. This elation takes the spirit briefly to its "Indian homeland" (ibid., 3: 283, no. 245). The so-called secrets of the Orient lent Romanticism a renewed awareness to listen more attentively to the many voices of nature and to break the fossilized forms of perception and discourse in which the West seemed caught up. Faced with the aggravations of a less than ideal society and the transience of phenomena, the Romantic memory salvaged ancient and exotic forms from the unconscious of time and reinscribed itself through these artifacts in history.

The flip side of this picture remains nevertheless ideologically problematic. The appropriation of another time and space gives the subject a definitive edge and mastery over its object of investigation. The knowledge of the other is a necessary component of the subject's history. In fact, Michel de Certeau has argued that "memory is a sense of the other," and that it "develops an aptitude for always being in the other's place without possessing it, and for profiting from this alteration without destroying itself through it" (1984, 87). Novalis often reaffirms the necessity of intersubjective knowledge through an understanding alterity.[15] From another perspective, however, one can argue as Johannes Fabian eloquently does that this appropriative ideal masks an ideology that promotes scavenging exotic otherness. This ideology, he maintains, is the major motivation behind the project of modern anthropology. The birth of anthropology as an academic discipline coincided with the rise of colonialism. Colonialist expansion converted so-called primitive societies into objects of investigation, which could only be achieved by denying them coevalness. In other words, the subject and the object could not share the same time. The Western subject assumed priority in time. Anthropology, Fabian argues, "is a discourse whose referent has been removed from the present of the speaking/writing subject." The methodological framework of anthropology placed the West's other in a less advanced stage, for it "needed Space to occupy" and "Time to accommodate the schemes of a one-way history: progress, development, modernity (and their negative mirror images: stagnation, underdevelopment, tradition)" (1983, 143–144). In this context Novalis's assertion that "history is applied *anthropology*" (1960, 3: 690, no. 688) carries an unselfconscious irony. In the final analysis, one can argue that Romanticism's exotic Orient remained just that, a faraway time and place whose traditions and symbolic wealth the Romantics excavated, carried off, and converted to their own currency without attempting to understand its historical present. Furthermore, escape into another time before time assured the subject a kind of theoretical innocence by sublating the ideological bonds of one's own history.

The view that the historical other is trapped in frozen time finds its ultimate expression in Hegel's philosophy of history. Hegel refers to the Orient as "the childhood of history" (1970, 12: 135). Although "the outward physical sun" rises in the *Morgenland* (literally, the morning land, that is, the Orient) and sets in the *Abendland* (the evening land, the Occident), "the inner sun of self-consciousness" rises in the West, a sun which "diffuses a nobler shine" (ibid., 134). In the Oriental world the world spirit had not started on the journey that was to eventually discipline the uncontrolled natural will and lead from general to subjective freedom. Although a rational vision is not lacking in the gorgeous edifices of Oriental empires, it conceives of the individual as merely accidental. Thus, everything revolves around a center, a sovereign. "The glory of the Oriental conception is the one subject as that supreme being to which all belongs, so that no other subject has a separate existence, or is reflected in its subjective freedom," states Hegel. "All the riches of imagination and nature," he adds, "are appropriated to that subject in which subjective freedom is essentially merged" (ibid., 12: 136). No dialectic operates in this phase, since the subject has not realized its antithesis and overcome it. As such it occludes the linear development or progress of history. This period consists of two parts. One of these is characterized by stability and durability, which signifies being out of time and only in space. To this phase belong the Oriental empires of the "space" of "unhistorical history," such as China where the state is based on rigid familial structures and where "infinity and ideality" have not asserted themselves (ibid.). In the other phase, time and space stand in opposition. That is, the empires undergo no change but constantly shift positions toward one another resulting in conflict and destruction. Hegel's Orient, in short, is a land where time, which is the ground of all representation and self-knowledge, stands fully paralyzed.

Many recent works of criticism and anthropology take issue with the intellectual colonization or self-centered reconstructions of others' histories. Fabian, as mentioned above, challenges the subject's denial of coevalness to its "primitive" other. Edward Said's *Orientalism* (1979) is a critique of the Occident's epistemological representations of the Orient. Said sees the institutional appropriation of Oriental studies in the West as an act of assimilating, interpreting, and distributing knowledge of the Orient. One can however argue in defense of the German Romantics that their representation of the Orient, unlike that of Hegel and the nineteenth-century Orientalists, was not motivated by a desire for cultural hegemony or for marking the progress of Western history. Hegel's Orient is trapped in irretrievable time, in Occidental fictions of history, never to be restored to modern consciousness. The textual Orient of early German Romanticism instead serves as an exemplary pre-text for the open-ended, uncertain status of Romantic or modern discourse itself. In "the so-called Oriental character" Schlegel sees "that bold allegorical pictorialness" which compensates the modern imagination for the loss of "old mythology" (1958, 8.1: 311). For the Romantics, the paradigmatic metaphor of the Orient—the textual India of Schlegel as well as the poetic Arabia of Novalis—represented the force of transfiguration or indefinition, the re-membered dream of a "new mythology." As an uncharted territory open to endless exploration and ready to reveal the poetic secrets of a lost time, the Orient provided the perfect space of defense against rational thought as an absolute.

What gradually fills in the spaces of abstract theorizing and representation with words, poems, songs, hieroglyphs, images, and maps is a force within history which Romantic archaeology discovers in relics and fragments and re-presents in allegory and irony. Collecting the past salvages things from unrepeatable time, but irony refers them back to their historical and contingent fate. It tests language by language, fiction by fiction. It maintains the tension between the material evidence of history preserved in texts and radical doubts about philosophical and historical representation, between the appropriation of another culture and constructions of subjectivity. Novalis argued for a true philosophical insight that would introduce systemlessness (*Systemlosigkeit*) into a system. Only such a system whose literary expression is irony and physical manifestation, the fragment, "can avoid the mistakes of the system and be related neither to *injustice* nor to anarchy" (1960, 2: 289, no. 648). Irony, allegory, and criticism all operate in a context of similar self-intercepting moves. They regulate system with systemlessness. Under their regime the familiar meets the foreign, and the hermeneutic project of appropriating the other clashes with the allegorical desire to preserve the alterity. At the site of this clash the Romantics signed a protocol allowing critical investigations—those of philosophy, rhetoric, and archaeology—to be undertaken. One product of these labors was the fragmentary first outline of a universal ency-

4. Representation and Criticism

> If some mystical art lovers who regard every criticism
> as a dissection and every dissection as a destruction of
> pleasure were to think logically, then "wow!" would be
> the best criticism of the worthiest work of art. Certainly,
> there are criticisms which say nothing more but only say
> it in a more rambling manner.
>
> Schlegel, "Critical Fragments," no. 57

The fragmentary impulse of allegory and irony prevents the interpretation and analysis of Romantic texts in terms of their narrowly defined documentary purposes. Representation is inseparably
bound to the question of commentary. In agreement with Kant's
view that understanding in a universal sense is the ability to define
limits, Novalis sees criticism as a process of translation where an
abstract language or mode of signification is redefined in terms of
concrete poetic employment: "*Criticism* shows precisely the necessity of limitation, determination—pause—and points to a definite
purpose and transforms *speculation* into a useful and itself poetic
instrument" (1960, 3: 442, no. 906). Criticism as the analytic of
representation constitutes a willed invention of rhetorical theory
that inscribes itself in the interstices of various disciplines. As an
interdisciplinary activity, criticism, as Roland Barthes observes,
does not aim

> to rediscover the 'essence' of the work, for this essence is the subject
> itself, that is to say an absence: every metaphor is a sign without a sub-
> stance, and it is this far-off quality of the signified that the symbolic
> process, in its profusion, designates: the critic can only continue the
> metaphors of the work, not reduce them. . . . It is sterile to bring the
> work down to pure explicitness, since then *immediately* there is nothing
> more to say about it . . . but it is hardly less vain to seek in the work
> what it might be saying without actually saying it and to suppose that
> it has a final secret, to which, once discovered, there would equally be
> nothing to add: whatever one says about the work, there always remains
> in it something of language, of the subject, of absence, *just as there was
> at the moment of its inception.* (1987, 87)

The ambiguous status of representation resides in this residue of
"language, of the subject, of absence." Here reason cannot pene-

trate the mystery of language. In an essay on irony, "Über die Unverständlichkeit" (On incomprehensibility), Schlegel argues that the welfare of humanity depends in the final analysis on the possibility of that mystery:

> But is incomprehensibility really something so thoroughly contemptible and evil? I think the salvation of families and nations rests on it. . . . Even the most precious thing a human being has, inner happiness itself, depends, as anyone would easily know, in the last analysis, on some such point that must be left in the dark, but that nonetheless carries and supports the whole and would lose this strength the moment it were subjected to reason. Truly, you would fare badly, if as you demand, the whole world were to become totally comprehensible in earnest. And isn't this endless world itself formed by the understanding out of incomprehensibility or chaos? (1958, 2: 370)

In every form of mediation in language a gap remains, an absence which, as both Schlegel and Barthes show, is where representation represents its own impossibility. The realization of this paradox constitutes "the final stage of intellectual formation [*Geistesbildung*]." It involves the ability to posit the very "sphere of unintelligibility and chaos. The understanding of chaos inheres in this recognition" (ibid., 18: 227, no. 396). The realization of this paradox is the self-reflexive gesture of representation. Norbert Bolz maintains that the hermeneutic practice of early German Romanticism is not an attempt to "make intelligible the unintelligible" (*ein Verständlichmachen des Unverständlichen*) but an elicitation and elucidation of what Schlegel calls the "hidden unintelligibility" (ibid., 2: 371; Bolz 1979, 107).

What this self-reflexive practice demonstrates is that in Romantic hermeneutics the act of understanding becomes its own object of inquiry. This is analogous to Kant's philosophical critique where the presentation of philosophy constitutes an investigation into the conditions and limits of philosophy and to Fichte's elevation of philosophy to a philosophy of philosophy. The intensified reflective status of interpretation in Romanticism establishes criticism as reproduction or as doubled production of the work of art. If writing is a mode of construction then reading and criticism are strategies of reconstruction. Consequently criticism is a reflection on construction and therefore qualifies as a potentiated form of writing.

Criticism is perceived as an ongoing activity or production. As such the value of the work of art is no longer dependent on its adherence to a set of externally determined criteria but on its potential to generate reflection.[1] "The critics always talk of rules," notes Schlegel, "but where then are the rules which are really poetic, not merely grammatical, metric, logical, or applicable to all works of art?" (1957, 44, no. 286). The most important aspect of criticism is, in Schlegel's words, the ability to present "a reflection of the work, to impart its characteristic spirit, to represent the pure impression in such a way that the form of representation itself verifies the artistic civic rights of its originator." Criticism is not merely "a poem on a poem," nor is it "merely the impression that a work made yesterday or today on this or that person but that which it should make on all educated people [*alle Gebildete*]" (1958, 1: 499).

Since representation always points to the absence of full truth, criticism takes on the task of demonstrating that the word does not designate a determinate referent. "The letter is the bound spirit," Schlegel writes, "reading is freeing the bound spirit, in other words, a magic action" (ibid., 18: 297, no. 1,229).[2] The "magic" of criticism is often couched in metaphors of alchemy, for it is an attempt to transmute a baser activity into a higher form of understanding, into a universal solvent. Metaphors of chemical processes and experiments serve as convenient analogies for acts of testing language and freeing it from fixed meaning. Schlegel, for example, compares philosophy to chemistry, because neither is "a means of invention of truth" but rather "of purification and combination" (ibid., 19: 38, no. 349). In other words, philosophy and its product, criticism, are not in the business of inventing truths but analyzing and synthesizing them. Furthermore, the Romantic idea of endless transformation of form accommodates as does chemistry the principle of contradiction: "Those who have a sense for the infinite and know what they want to do with it see in it the result of eternally separating and uniting powers, conceive of their ideals at least as being chemical, and utter, when they express themselves decisively, nothing but contradictions" (ibid., 2: 243, no. 412). Schlegel sees the philological analysis of the text as the "enthusiasm for chemical knowledge; for grammar is certainly only the philosophical aspect of the universal art of dividing and joining [*Scheidungs- und Ver-*

bindungskunst]" (ibid., 2: 241, no. 404). And the masterful work of criticism requires "the ability for *absolute* synthesis and *absolute* analysis" (1957, 41, no. 251).

The idea of the text as a field where conflicting forces of fusion and diffusion are in full play implies that the act of writing itself is informed by the chemical processes of synthesis and analysis. Schlegel delineates two model texts based on two different approaches to writing:

> The analytic writer observes the reader as he is; he then makes his calculations and sets up his machines in order to make the proper impression on him. The synthetic writer constructs and creates a reader as he should be; he doesn't imagine him calm and dead, but alive and responsive. He lets whatever he has created take shape gradually before the reader's eyes, or he urges the reader to discover it himself. He does not try to make any particular impression on the reader, but enters with him into the sacred relationship of the most profound symphilosophy or sympoetry. (1958, 2: 161, no. 112)

The reader of the synthetic writer is the transformative model of the text itself. Schlegel's typology corresponds to Barthes's famous distinction between the *lisible* (readerly) text designed for passive consumption and the *scriptible* (writerly) text, where the writer and the reader jointly tease out a diversity of meaning. The idea of the text as a field of encounter between analytic and synthetic activity dislodges that center which in traditional texts arrests and grounds meaning. This decentering gives rise to a plurality of meanings. In Barthes's words:

> the text is not coexistence of meanings but passage, traversal; thus it answers not to an interpretation . . . but to an explosion, a dissemination. The Text's plurality does not depend on the ambiguity of its contents, but rather on what could be called the *stereographic plurality* of the signifiers that weave it. (1979, 76)

Romantic idealism creates the conditions for the possibility of this dissemination. "True idealism," states Schlegel, "does not merely state that we make the object; rather it constructs the universe and shows *how* we make it; it constructs infinitely many objects and worlds" (1958, 18: 140, no. 219). The creative reading of a text, a genuine aesthetics of reception has to be, in Schlegel's words, "the solution of a critical equation, the result and representation [*Darstellung*] of a philological experiment and of a literary research" (ibid., 2: 241, no. 403).

The Romantic concept of the text as a context for the formation, dissolution, and re-formation of meaning is the object of Novalis's miniature essay "Monolog" which analyzes the conflicting dictates of representational autonomy and referential validity in language. In order to be able to discuss the critical potential of this essay, I quote it in its entirety:

> Speaking and writing are fundamentally very peculiar things; real conversation is a mere play of words. One can only be amazed at the ridiculous error of those who think that they speak for the sake of the things said. Precisely that defining characteristic of language that it is merely concerned with itself, no one knows. That is why it is such a wonderful secret, that when one speaks merely to speak, he says the most wonderful, most original truths. But when one intends to speak about something specific, then capricious language makes him say the most ridiculous and contradictory stuff. From this arises also the hatred that many serious people feel for language. They are aware of its mischievousness but are not aware that idle chatter is the infinitely serious aspect of language. If one could only make people understand that it is with language as it is with mathematical formulae—they constitute a world for themselves—they play only with themselves, express nothing but their own wonderful nature, and are, therefore, so expressive—precisely because of this, the strange play of relations is reflected in them. Only because of their freedom, are they links of nature, and only in their free movements does the world soul express itself and makes of them a delicate measure and fundament of things. The same is also true of language—whoever is sensitive to its use, its measure, its musical spirit, whoever feels the delicate effect of its inner nature, and moves his tongue and hand accordingly, will be a prophet; on the other hand, whoever knows but has not adequate ear or sense, will write truths like these, but will be tricked by language and mocked by people, like Cassandra by the Trojans. If I believe that I have hereby given a most accurate account of the nature and function of poetry, I nevertheless know that no one can understand it, and that I have said something quite silly, because I wanted to say it, and in this way no poetry comes into being. But what if I had to speak? and this drive to speak were a sign of the inspiration and effectiveness of language in myself? and what if my will also wanted everything that I had to do, then this could, without my knowledge and belief, be poetry after all, and could make a secret of language understandable? and so I would be called a writer, for a writer may very well be a person inspired by language? (1960, 2: 672–673)

Novalis puts to task the crude understanding of representation attributed to language. The representational status of language is not built on a system of correspondences with the objects of the world but, following Fichte's theory of knowledge, on language's ability to reflect on itself. Language guarantees no referential security. It simply represents itself to itself. This activity is not controlled by an agency even if the agent is the speaker. Language defies the referentiality and intentionality conceived by the subject. Novalis's own reflection on language demonstrates that he can speak of language in language only ironically. The operative trope of the essay is irony. This form of irony is, in Schlegel's words, "the tone and style of analytic philosophy" (1957, 60, no. 453). The first part of the essay argues that language rejects all mimetic links to the world of experience and exists in a state of free play with it. If the speaker attempts to fix meaning by suspending language in time, meaning will elude the speaker every time. Once language extends beyond the conscious control of the subjective agency, it speaks wondrously. Novalis argues that language resembles mathematical formulae in so far as it creates its own world.

Because language refers only to itself, it is able to reflect the strange configurations of things. This is a paradox, but such is the real nature of things. Language is a self-generating activity. In Fichte the activity of the self is manifested in free representation. Both mathematics and language reflect in their freedom of expression the ever-changing spirit of life and nature. Once Novalis demonstrates the elusive disposition of language that duplicates the flux of experience, the text performs its own conceptual play in a final staging of irony. If language is to reflect on language and if meaning defies permanence, then Novalis's eloquent description of poetic language itself becomes a hollow formula. This paradox, nevertheless, does not claim to negate or transcend representation. Language itself, couched in irony, constantly brings up the question of representation. However, the danger posed by the unstable ground of representation is diminished in aesthetic enthusiasm. Novalis believes that this danger does not deter the poet, "a person inspired by language" (*ein Sprachbegeisterter*). Language itself inspires the poet to language, even though the absolute eludes language. "The poet must have the ability to imagine other thoughts and represent ideas in all forms of their consequences and in manifold expressions," writes Novalis elsewhere, ". . . he must invent conversations, letters, speeches, tales, descriptions, passionate expressions full of all kinds of possibilities by thousands of different persons in various circumstances, and put these on paper in suitable words. He must be in a position to speak of everything in an entertaining and meaningful way and speaking and writing must inspire him to speaking and writing" (1960, 3: 689, no. 685).

The paradoxes of language eloquently articulated in "Monolog" strive toward a resolution in the concept of dialogue. A long, critical fragment by Novalis dating from 1798–1799 maps out the route that leads from Kant's systematic formulation of critique through Fichte's undifferentiated field of self-activity to the Romantic view of hermeneutics as an ongoing social conversation where the subject-object dichotomy yields to an epistemology that links the participants. Since this fragment situates Romantic hermeneutics in a well-defined historical and philosophical context, it deserves closer critical inspection:

In effect, *criticism*—or the method of *exhaustion*—which includes the method of interchange, the theory that refers us, in our study of nature, to ourselves, to inner observation and experiment, and in our study of ourselves, to the external world, external observations and experiments, is, in a philosophical sense, the most productive of all *indications*. It lets us perceive nature, or the *external world,* as a human essence—it shows that we can and should understand *everything* only in the way we understand ourselves and our *beloved,* understand us and *you.*

We see ourselves in a system, as *a link* in ascending and descending lines, from the infinitely small to the infinitely large—*human beings* of infinite variations.

Naturally, we understand everything strange only through self-*estrangement, self-change,* self-observation.

Now we see the real bonds of connection between the subject and the object, see that in us there is also an outward world which is in an analogous relation with ourselves as the outward world is with our outward selves, and that the former and the latter are connected like our inner and outer selves.

That is, we can only perceive the inner self and the spirit of nature through ideas, as we do the external self and the body of nature through sensations.

Now the so-called transcendental philosophy—the reference to the subject—*idealism,* and the categories—the relation between object and representation appears in a completely new *light*. *Demonstration* why something belongs to external and internal nature—demonstrability of each existence and its modification. Nature is the *ideal*. The true ideal is possible, real, and necessary at the same time.

The principle *I* is simultaneously the true social and *liberal* and universal principle—it is a unity without being a *limit* and determination. Rather it makes all determinations possible and sound—and gives them absolute context and meaning. Selfhood is the ground of all *knowledge*—as the ground of permanence in change—and the principle of highest diversity—Thou. Instead of Not-Self, Thou [*Statt Nicht-Ich-Du*]. Generality and specificity. Everything can be Self [*Ich*] and is Self or should be Self. (ibid., 3: 429–430, no. 820)

Critical practice aims at "exhausting" all the formal relations between the self and the world of experience. Any form of commentary represents an alterity, that is, it distances itself from a given text, becomes its transfiguration through critical reflection. Criticism is the other, the mirror reflection of the ideal, of self-positing, of the external world, or of art, just as history is the other of the present. The pre-texts of criticism, however, eventually become forms of self-representation, for "everything strange" can only be grasped through "self-observation." In itself, nature is incomprehensible, because it is external to us. In the final analysis we can understand only that which is a part of ourselves. But we can understand something alien or external, like nature, by relating it to the self, by intuiting it, so to speak, analogically. Conversely, we comprehend our inner selves in analogy to the external world. Through critical and intuitive reflection, the encounter between the self and the foreign other results in self-understanding, which is the prerequisite of understanding in a universal sense. The world is no longer a differentiated sphere of experience in the Kantian sense, nor is it posited by the self as Fichte construed it; rather, it represents a potentiated form of self-understanding. This concept plays an important role in the later development of hermeneutical theory.

These relations point to the practical implications of transcendental philosophy "in a totally new light." The light issues from the lantern of "magical idealism." In a letter written in May 1798 to Friedrich Schlegel, Novalis uses the term "magischer Idealismus" to designate the "very great, very fertile idea, throwing a ray of light of the highest intensity on the Fichtean system" (ibid., 4: 254). Novalis grounds the concept of reality not in observable facts but in the idea of the poetic self and the productive imagination which is an integral part of this empirical self. This poetic (or practical) understanding, which presents Fichtean idealism in a new light, reveals that the "genuine ideal is possible, real, and necessary at the same time." In this poetic epistemology, necessity and freedom are reconciled. Transcendental poetry now reveals itself as an empirical experiment of an inverted order. It does not "demonstrate" the world—as an experiment confirms a hypothesis—but arrives at a symbolic synthesis of it.

Unlike Fichte's theoretical *Ich,* Novalis's poetic Self admits of no restriction imposed upon it by a posited world. Novalis defines selfhood as "the ground of all knowledge," of "permanence in change," and as "the principle of highest diversity." For Schelling, the reconciliation of opposing modes of human understanding— idealism and realism, permanence and change, knowledge and action—was only possible in art that represented the pure essence of things beyond the confines of time, because in representing them for all eternity it took them out of time. On the other hand, Novalis's concept of the self as poetic subjectivity is temporally marked, for it represents an ironic and allegorical consciousness of reality. One of Schlegel's many definitions of irony underlines the eternal mutability of this trope (1958, 2: 263, no. 69). Schlegel also argues that each subject understands something external to it through a sense for diversity which comprises not only "a comprehensive system" but also "a feeling for the chaos outside that system, like humanity's feeling for something beyond humanity" (ibid., 2: 262, no. 55). Furthermore, each sequence in the act of understanding represents a mutation in time, each successive stage in the generation of knowledge marks a temporal jolt: "The life of the universal spirit is an unbroken chain of inner revolutions" (ibid., 2: 255, no. 451). Similarly, Novalis sees understanding as temporally not ontologically grounded, since it is constituted in a dialogic relationship between the self and the world, which now appears as "thou" rather than as an objective third person. This dialogue is an open-ended activity; it flows continuously through time. Only in this temporality do the self and the other reach reciprocal understanding and knowledge.

Novalis no longer sees identity as a primordial principle that engenders a subject-object split. It is now the joint activity of equal partners in a communicative enterprise. Furthermore, in Novalis's writing Fichte's *Ich* is transformed into a social body. The full privileges of the first principle are now directly transferred to society. The spaces between the self and the world, I and thou, and objects and representations shift from the theoretical to the practical domain informed by a dialogic and textual reality. There is no longer an escape from language; we are enmeshed in a web of words that define our very being. Referential validity cannot be external. It inheres in the dialogue between the self and its partner. The implications of this notion reach into the core of all critical activity. Criticism can only be understood as a dialogue with the original text. As such, poetry and criticism have to share the same language: "One cannot really speak of poetry save in the language of poetry," writes Schlegel (1958, 2: 285). This critical sentiment is frequently reiterated by both Novalis and Schlegel.[3] Romantic criticism transgresses the boundary between poetry and commentary. The latter becomes the self-representation of poetry. Once more the opposition between a first principle and its other is canceled, and representation subsumes them both.

By breaking down the barriers between different forms of knowledge and merging philosophy, rhetoric, criticism, science, and religion, the Romantics transformed the world into a universal text.[4] As Bolz observes, the world represented for them a gigantic book where life was recorded in every detail (1979, 89). As such, life became an act of writing and reading the world of experience. This notion of the progressive textualization of the world challenges the categorization of works in terms of period, oeuvre, and genre, thus undermining what Foucault has called the "discursive unities." The significance of a text constructs itself only in the context of a complex set of relations it has to other discourses, such as philosophical and scientific heritages, works of art and literature, readers' horizons of expectations, beliefs, and social practices and customs. This network of relations challenges the notion of boundaries that define, for example, the "unity" of a book. Such boundaries can never be universally applicable. As Foucault observes, "the frontiers of a book are never clear-cut: beyond the title, the first lines, and the last full stop, beyond its internal configuration and its autonomous form, it is caught up in a system of references to other books, other texts, other sentences: it is a node within a network" (1974, 23). In other words, the unity of a work as scripted by a certain author or belonging to a certain period or genre loses its self-evidence.

The Romantic penchant for the textualization of life found one of its most explicit expressions in the project of a universal encyclopedia.[5] This project involved the compilation of all forms of philosophic discourse, all disciplines of natural sciences, and all genres of literature. As early as 1797 Novalis envisioned the unification of the arts and sciences that had been separated by diverse traditions and discourses: "We owe the greatest truths of our age to those combinations of the long separated parts of total knowledge" (1960, 2: 368, no. 27). In this reconfiguration of knowledge Novalis considered each idea in relationship to its overall context as a "philosopheme." Everything strange or foreign could be explained and appropriated by a "*total* encyclopedic scientific observation" (ibid., 3: 306, no. 365). To the question "what is nature?" Novalis responds, "an encyclopedic, systematic index or plan of our spirit [intellect]. Why should we content ourselves with the mere catalogue of our treasures? Let us examine them ourselves and process and use them in manifold ways" (ibid., 2: 583, no. 248).

The major paradox that the encyclopedia project as a systematizing principle faced was the question of its form. In an entry in *Das allgemeine Brouillon*, the draft of the universal encyclopedia, Novalis states that he plans to write to Friedrich Schlegel regarding the form the Romantic encyclopedia should be cast in: "Should it be a study (or an essay), a collection of fragments, a Lichtenberg commentary, a report, a recommendation, a story [or history], a treatise, a review, a speech, a *monologue* (*or fragment of a dialogue*)?" (ibid., 3: 278, no. 218). There is something inherently contradictory about the content and form of the project. It aims at a totality and a coherent system. However, set in the larger framework of Romantic discourse, it is best presented in fragments, perhaps as a dialogue. In fact, Schlegel considers the style of the fragment most applicable to the encyclopedia (1958, 19: 36, no. 332). If, for example, the most appropriate form of the project is the "fragment of a dialogue," then we can assume that all forms of knowledge can only be represented as a kind of conversation. This conversation is possibly interrupted, exists in a temporal reality, and is disseminated across time. It is therefore impossible to determine knowledge for all time as if it were an atemporal and invariable given. An encyclopedia constitutes an endless book, a text that subsumes all knowledge-generating activity. For Schlegel the allegorical model of the encyclopedia is the Bible:

> Even what we call the Bible is actually a system of books. This is, after all, no arbitrary turn of phrase! Or is there another word to differentiate the idea of an endless book from an ordinary one than Bible, the book as such, the absolute book? . . . In a similar way, in a perfect literature all books should be only a single book, and in such a book that is eternally in a state of becoming, the gospel of humanity and education will be revealed. (ibid., 2: 265, no. 95)

Similarly, in *Das allgemeine Brouillon* Novalis considers the study of the Bible not a mere reading of the Scripture but an understanding of a system of self-extending books. This system resembles a *"complete, well-ordered library*—the schema of the Bible is also the schema of the library" (1960, 3: 365, no. 571). In reference to his incomplete (but infinitely *scriptible*) novel *Heinrich von Ofterdingen,* Novalis states that his book "must contain the critical metaphysics of *reception,* of authorship, of experimentation, of observation, of reading, writing, etc." (ibid., 3: 361, no. 552). In other words, it should be "a scientific bible—a real and ideal model—and the seed of all books" (ibid., 3: 363, no. 557). The Bible serves as the extended metaphor of the open-ended Romantic text whose visions become re-visions in its varying receptions over time. Schlegel believes, however, that the infinite progressivity of the Bible in reception was given somewhat short shrift by Martin Luther. It was beautifully predisposed to being a "national novel that could have been *endlessly serialized*; it was Luther's mistake to fix it and to cut off the legends" (1957, 60, no. 458).[6] In fact, the novel, where all genres mix and mingle, is itself an encyclopedic project. It is related, as Schlegel notes, to philosophical dialogues, travelogues, confessions, conversations, anecdotes, and biographies (ibid., 71–72, no. 581). In the same encyclopedic vein all the novels of an individual author, for example, constitute a system of works which repeat and complete one another (ibid., 59, no. 447). Thus the encyclopedia, the Bible, and the novel all constitute material representations of the ideal Romantic text.

The concept of the text as a strategy of conceptualizing the world cuts across traditional lines of writing and reading. "There are so many writers," observes Schlegel, "since reading and writing are now only different in degree" (1958, 2: 399, no. 10). The text moves away from the work, which is a concrete structure, into the hermeneutic field of activity. Here the reader or critic engages in a dialogue with the text that results in its re-presentation. "Interpretation [*Auslegen*] is not infrequently an insertion [*Einlegen*] of something that is desirable or expedient, and many deductions [*Ableitungen*] are actually traductions [*Ausleitungen*]" (ibid., 2: 169, no. 25). Novalis explicitly refers to reading as the continuation of writing:

> The true reader has to be the extended writer. . . . And when the reader assays the book according to his idea, then the second reader would explicate [*läutern*] it even more, and in this way the reworked material would be cast into molds of fresh activity and finally become an important part, an organ, of the effective spirit. (1960, 2: 470, no. 125)

In this way criticism becomes the ultimate ideal of Romantic poetry. It is a progressive act which expands to take in all modes of epistemic and aesthetic activity. Schlegel noted:

> the good critic and characterizer must observe correctly, conscientiously, and thoroughly like the physicist, measure acutely like the mathematician, carefully arrange in columns like the botanist, dissect like the anatomist, separate like the chemist, feel like the musician, imitate like an actor, embrace practically like a lover, review like a philosopher, study cyclically like a sculptor, acutely like a judge, religiously like an antiquarian, and understand the moment like a politician. (1957, 76–77, no. 631)

Critical re-vision attempts to account for all past paradigms of understanding and incorporates them into new narratives. Literary history thus finds a new avenue of representation in the Romantic "new mythology," which in turn is ushered in by idealism, "that great phenomenon of our age" (1958, 2: 313). Consequently, Romantic criticism constitutes an encyclopedic paradigm: "*Rhetoric* belongs to criticism, as does compilation. Genuine rhetoric is *interpretive*, popularizing. This and compilation and archaeology together [constitute] *literature*—linked to encyclopedia" (ibid., 18: 491, no. 191).

Ernst Behler has argued that in contrast to Hegel's *Enzyklopädie*, which from the onset reveals a strictly systematic orientation, the

Romantics' encyclopedia has a more fluid movement that follows the path of "infinite perfectibility" (1982, 17: 180). Thus, both in conception and in form, the Romantic project represents a challenge to the idea of absolutes and hierarchies of knowledge. It presents knowledge not as a uniformly applicable and acceptable body of facts but as an asystemic system of historical and aesthetic contingencies. "A systematic encyclopedia" has to be historical, maintains Schlegel (1958, 18: 352, no. 377). He also states that next to poetry it is history that most fully incorporates the encyclopedic character (ibid., 18: 380, no. 717). The fragmentary nature of the encyclopedia suggests a resistance to and questioning of attempts at system building and as such represents a critique of totalizing modes of knowledge. It operates in the mode of Romantic irony by generating as well as by dissecting, disputing, and doubting. Therefore, the encyclopedia becomes an apparatus of critical interpretation. In its use of fragmentary and elliptical forms and through its operation in the tropological mode, the encyclopedia project of early Romanticism stakes out territories that pose problems of knowledge and contextualizes them in the larger problem of literary representation. Schlegel sees the encyclopedia as both "the totality of ideas" and "constitutive reason" and "revolutionary imagination" (ibid., 18: 434, no. 80). The Romantic encyclopedia represents a complex and expansive equation whose solution, as one may expect, is ultimately given in the poetic mode: "The realization of the encyclopedia," writes Schlegel, "requires that all art and knowledge and criticism be resolved, in the final analysis, in poetry" (ibid., 16: 419, no. 34).

The Contemporary Relevance of Schleiermacher's Hermeneutics

Critical *ideas* are practical mathematics, *absolute* analysis and *absolute* hermeneutics.
          Schlegel, *Literary Notebooks,* no. 564

Wilhelm Dilthey maps the path of hermeneutics as starting at the point of artful interpretive skill, progressing through the rules for a canonical interpretation, and reaching a decisive station when the act of understanding itself becomes the subject of reflection and theoretical investigation in Romanticism (1914–1977, 5: 317–

331). Hans-Georg Gadamer describes a similar development that reaches a major turning point, when in Romantic hermeneutics interpretation becomes a critical reflection on interpretation itself (1960, 162–185). Friedrich Schlegel's notebooks *On Philology*, which constitute the first documents of a new hermeneutics, date from 1798, when he shared living quarters in Berlin with his friend Friedrich Schleiermacher.[7]

It is in the work of Schleiermacher—whose name literally means veil-maker—that the problem of language and texts is most systematically unveiled. He is due the credit for defining for the first time the question of understanding as a strictly philosophical problem. In his hands hermeneutics, long ago cast as a minor branch of biblical studies, expanded its purview, reaching out to take in all manner and means of interpretive activity and theory. True to the Romantic spirit, Schleiermacher's critical enterprise systematically reflects on it own premises. Like Novalis's grand-scale conception of the universal encyclopedia, Schleiermacher's hermeneutic project locates the domain of human cognition in the framework of the transcendental critique where the general and particular constituents of knowledge alternately define and expand each other's boundaries: "Everywhere complete knowledge is in this apparent circle where each particular can be understood only from the general whose part it is and vice versa. And each instance of knowledge is scientific only when it is formed in this fashion" (1977, 95).

Schleiermacher's *Dialektik*[8] is an attempt at transforming Kant's critical philosophy into a transcendental dialectic of knowledge. Knowledge is posited in relation to the rational order of the universe, and being encompasses the rational order. The structures of knowledge are not founded solely on a priori principles of cognition nor are they based on the priority of practical reason. Rather, they are grounded in the general coherence of a system which reveals itself in knowledge and is reflected in the products of knowledge. The first argument for this system of knowledge concerns the agreement of all thinking subjects in the process of knowing. The primordial drive for knowledge contains two transcendental presuppositions, which themselves cannot be objects of knowledge, but determine all knowing. These are the two moments of sensible and suprasensible cognition. They constitute the agreement among all thinking subjects and the interdependence of thought and being. Both these elements, the sensory and the intellectual, the real and the ideal, are correlated as the transcendental presuppositions of all human knowledge. The thinking subject does not experience it-self simply as a nexus of accidental perceptions and unconnected thoughts. Rather, that which is given in sense perception is formed and transformed in thought.

This transcendental dialectic figures prominently in Schleier-macher's formulation of hermeneutic principles. The analytic of understanding and interpretation, which subsumes the question of representation, is the ongoing concern of Schleiermacher's earlier lectures and writings in *Hermeneutik und Kritik*. The precondition for all interpretive activity is the correspondence between thought and language and grammar and hermeneutics:

> The alliance of hermeneutics and grammar rests on the fact that each speech is comprehended on the presupposition of the understanding of language. Both have to do with language. This leads to the unity of lan-guage and thought. Language is the way and means for the realization of ideas. . . . Since hermeneutics should lead to the understanding of thought, and since thought is only real in language, then hermeneutics, as the knowledge of language, rests on grammar. (ibid., 77)

Furthermore, in acknowledgment of the diachronic or historical coordinate of language, Schleiermacher contends that "each speech can only be understood further by the knowledge of the historical totality that it belongs to or the knowledge of the history related to it" (ibid.). Thus, Schleiermacher locates the axis of understand-ing at the intersection of the structural and historical paths of language. Furthermore, since the human spirit and by extension lan-guage are greatly influenced by biological and physical aspects of humans and the earth, hermeneutics is also based on physics. In this larger context hermeneutics moves beyond descriptive analysis to the broader question of the conditions for the production of mean-ing in language. This modern hermeneutical concern transforms language and text into a field of investigation that cuts across the traditional lines of subject and sign, speech and writing, and physics and history.

Schleiermacher's innovation rests not so much on linking thought and language and diachronic and synchronic forms of un-derstanding as it does on the cancellation of their differences to produce something new: an explosive, generative text where no language is privileged over the other. This text marks the site of inter-disciplinary activity in hermeneutics. As Barthes put it:

> *Interdisciplinary* activity, valued today as an important aspect of re-search, cannot be accomplished by simple confrontations between vari-ous specialized branches of knowledge. Interdisciplinary work is not a peaceful operation: it begins *effectively* when the solidarity of old disci-plines breaks down—a process made more violent, perhaps, by the jolts of fashion—to the benefit of a new object and a new language, neither of which is in the domain of those branches of knowledge that one calmly sought to confront. (1979, 73)

Schleiermacher lays the foundation of modern hermeneutics as an interdisciplinary project by fusing the traditional lines of thought into a new field of understanding without relinquishing the subject. This is the utopian ground of subject and language in the hermeneu-tic circle. One of Schleiermacher's more important critical insights, one that links his work to early Romanticism's concern with rep-resentation, is the recognition of the multi-referentiality of lan-guage. His critical reflections on language are informed by a clearly articulated awareness of the fallacy of total representation. All rep-resentation stands under the sign of mediacy: "There exists no word in living speech or writing of which one could say that it could be represented [*dargestellt*] as pure unity" (1977, 108). Thus, under-standing can only be situated at the approximate intersection of the paradigmatic and the syntagmatic, the semiotic and the intuitive: "Art can develop its rules only from a positive formula and this is 'the historical and divinatory (prophetic), objective and subjective reconstruction of the given speech'" (ibid., 93). In this perception the object of understanding as speech (*Rede*) or writing (*Schrift*) moves from a formal or organic whole to a methodological field, that is, a field of activity, construction, and transformation.

Although Schleiermacher does not explicitly distinguish between understanding and interpretation, he reserves the methodologi-cal procedure for the interpretive process. The process comprises "grammatical" and "psychological" (also designated as "techni-cal") analyses. Initially Schleiermacher situates understanding in the concept of the hermeneutical circle. Here understanding and cogni-tion are contained in an apparent circle, so that every object of in-quiry can only be understood in relation to its general context, and the whole is only graspable as the common denominator of all its parts. The hermeneutical circle excludes the possibility of direct and total representation. Schleiermacher translates this philosophical concept of the circle into concrete interpretive praxis by introducing the methods of grammatical and psychological interpretation. Neither method is prior to the other, for "understanding is only a fusion [*Ineinandersein*] of both these moments." The two moments of the interpretive act "are totally equal, and one would only unjustifiably call the grammatical interpretation lower and the psychological higher" (ibid., 79).

Schleiermacher posits two "canons" or classes of grammatical interpretation. The first places language within a system, as part of a network of synchronically shared rules. The second canon rests on the notion that every word has a whole sphere of possible meanings and that the appropriate meaning must be determined from the context. The interaction between one grammatical canon and the next and between grammatical and psychological interpretation proceeds dialectically. The psychological (or technical) interpretation involves the understanding of the individuality of the text and therefore addresses the question of style: "The whole objective is to be defined as the complete understanding of style" (ibid., 168). The grammatical interpretation with its emphasis on language as a system had relegated the subject to the background. The psychological interpretation restores the subject to its place in language. It is probably more correct to say that language and subject simply exchange roles in an ongoing play of interpretive categories, since neither has a prior status in Schleiermacher's schema. He is quick to point out, however, that relegation or displacement of either language or subject can occur, if both categories are treated separately as opposed to being employed complementarily:

> Grammatical. The person [subject] and his activity disappear and appear only as an organ of language. Technical. The language in its determining power disappears and appears only as an organ of the person [subject] in the service of his individuality, just as in the former, personality was in the service of language. (ibid., 171)

It is noteworthy that Schleiermacher anticipates critical positions that parallel those of structuralism and poststructuralism. In the former, as in grammatical interpretation, the subject disappears and is replaced by the sign (language), whereas the latter, like technical interpretation, questions the priority of the sign and restores the question of subjectivity or the subject in language. The ideal interpretive position grants both subject and sign legitimacy by its operative dialectic. The emphasis on the reflective and dialectic operation of critical activity prevents Schleiermacher's project from becoming a hermeneutics of closure but does not necessarily produce a hermeneutics of indeterminacy. Furthermore, by carefully separating and defining the respective interpretive operations of the grammatical and the technical or the psychological, Schleiermacher demonstrates that figural language is not a mere extension of grammatically explainable forms and that an unproblematic and unquestioned continuity between grammar and rhetoric cannot be assumed.[9] Whereas the grammatical rests more or less on the certainty of direct representation, the rhetorical or the figural problematizes that very certainty.

On the whole, Schleiermacher uses the terms psychological interpretation and technical interpretation interchangeably but sometimes points to a minor technical difference between them. The psychological interpretation proceeds by comparative and divinatory methods. The concept of the divinatory, which has been the unfortunate and unwitting source of various misconceptions in the reception of Schleiermacher's work, makes in fact perfect sense in the larger framework of both Schleiermacher's proposed interpretive method and of Romanticism's concern with the problem of direct representation. In the divinatory method the interpreter seeks to understand directly, attempting to transcend the sensible form or limits of *Darstellung*. The divinatory is probably best understood as the perception of a suprasensible representation in imagination. Schlegel considers "divination" synonymous with "hieroglyphics and allegory," in so far as it represents a mystified scepticism or the impossibility of expressing the infinite (1958, 19: 5, no. 26). Schleiermacher also repeatedly stresses that the divinatory derives its coherence and certainty only from its other half, the comparative. In a certain way the divinatory and the comparative constitute the modus operandi of intersubjective understanding. Although language is a system of codes designed for communication, the codes are convertible and form zones of resistance to understanding. In other words, the codes are representational and therefore polyvalent. By imagining the invisible beyond the boundaries of sensible representation and consulting the context of meaning in figural lan-

guage, the psychological interpretation points to a potentiation of
understanding in reception:

> The task is expressed as "to understand a speech just as well and then
> better than its originator." Since we do not have a direct knowledge of
> what is in it, we need to try to bring much that can remain unconscious
> in it to consciousness. . . .
>
> Presented in this way the task is endless because what we want to
> see in the moment of speech is an endlessness of the past and the future.
> (1977, 94)

The concept of understanding an author better than he understood himself is introduced at the beginning of the "First Book of
the Transcendental Dialectic" in Kant's first *Critique* as justification
for his deviation from Plato's doctrine of ideas. "It is not at all unusual," observes Kant, "that in comparing the thoughts which an
author has expressed about his subject, whether in ordinary speech
or in texts, we understand him better than he has understood himself. As he has not sufficiently determined his concept, he has occasionally spoken or even thought, in opposition to his own intention" (1983, 4.2: 322). Kant's statement most likely refers to an
author's lack of self-reflection and is intended as a questioning
or correction of authorial intention. Fichte develops a similar notion in his *Einige Vorlesungen über die Bestimmung des Gelehrten*
(Some lectures on the vocation of the scholar), when in his observation of certain contradictions in Rousseau he assures his audience
that they will be able to solve the contradiction and understand
Rousseau better than he understood himself (1962–, 1.3: 61). The
task of resolving the contradictions of a text by reading it according
to its spirit rather than its letter authorizes the reader to recreate
the text in a productive way.[10] Schleiermacher goes beyond Fichte's
idea of the infinite perfectibility of understanding and defines the
task of the reflective interpreter as bringing into consciousness what
remains unconscious in the text.

This creative task of interpretation involves yet another difficult
methodological feat. It becomes a self-correcting program that can
only operate in a genuinely reflective and systematic hermeneutical
mode. Schleiermacher sums up this dialectical method:

> *Addition.* General methodological rules: a) beginning with a general
> overview; b) simultaneous conceptualization in both directions, the

grammatical and the psychological; c) only when both coincide in a single place can one proceed further; d) necessity of going back, when they do not agree until one finds the mistake in calculation. (1977, 97)

Today we see such self-correcting methods in artificial, computer languages. This sophisticated methodological insight certainly exorcises the demons of mystification often associated with hermeneutical understanding. What Schleiermacher draws here is the structural model of a spiral—rather than a circle—as a picture of the endless signification process of language. The model grants no temporal or logical priority to any one operation but defines the process of understanding as a dialectically progressive one. And in the ruthlessly analytic spirit of deconstructive criticism, which insists on questioning the notions of originary truth and time-worn assumptions embedded in language, Schleiermacher rejects the idea of a point of origin in language: "We have great spaces of time in front of us in which a language lived, and we can move backwards from any point but not to the origins, for these are not given anywhere in time" (ibid., 109).

In contrast to Schleiermacher, who situates criticism within the larger framework of universal hermeneutics and outfits it with sophisticated interpretive methodology, Schlegel understands criticism as the infinitely perfectible self-representation of the literary work which constitutes a special branch of hermeneutics. "Art," writes Schlegel in an early essay, "Über das Studium der Griechischen Poesie" (On the study of Greek poetry), "is infinitely perfectible, and an absolute maximum in its steady development is not possible; only a conditional, *relative maximum,* an insurmountable *fixed proximity* [*fixes Proximum*]" (1958, 1: 288). In the work of criticism, the work of art infinitely re-presents itself: "The question of what the author intends can be settled," states Schlegel, "not, however, the question of what the work is" (ibid., 18: 318, no. 1,515). As Walter Benjamin correctly observes, Romantic criticism has, "in total contrast to the present understanding of its character, not judgment as its central purpose but perfection, completion, and systematization of the work on the one hand, and solution in the absolute on the other. Both processes coincide in the final analysis" (1972–, 1.1: 78).

Criticism, in other words, is no longer the handmaiden of literature but its self-representation. However, criticism also declines to be a handmaiden of philosophy by refusing to use its rigid grammar and syntax: "Critical prose has to be fluent (flowing) and floating and fight against a rigid terminology, for then it would acquire an illiberal look, as if it only served philosophy" (Schlegel 1957, 81, no. 685).

5. The Site of Instruction
Literary Tales

Like the heart, reason has its epochs and its fortunes, but its story is told much less frequently. One appears satisfied with elaborating on passions and their extremes, mistakes, and consequences without taking into account how closely they are linked with the thought systems of the individual.
Friedrich Schiller, Philosophische Briefe

Like Minerva from the head of Jupiter, philosophy springs from the poetry of an infinite, divine being.
Friedrich Hölderlin, Hyperion

All language is of a successive nature; it does not lend itself to a reasoning of the eternal, the intemporal. . . .

Denying temporal succession, denying the self . . . are apparent desperations and secret consolations. . . . Time is the substance I am made of. Time is a river which sweeps me along, but I am the river; it is a tiger which destroys me, but I am the tiger; it is a fire which consumes me, but I am the fire.
Jorge Luis Borges, "A New Refutation of Time"

The literary tales of German Romanticism choreograph the rise and fall or the condition and limits of logos, word, and reason against the background of an individual's life. In the true Romantic spirit each life constitutes a text weaving disparate strands of time, memory, knowledge, and intuition into a poetic reality. This reality is more an aesthetic form of self-reflection than a reflection of an epistemic or historical truth. The path of the fictional traveler proceeds from a unified subjectivity to a diversity of experience and understanding. The skeleton of abstract ideas is fleshed out in the body of fiction.

The tales of literary Romanticism discussed here present in the physical body of poetic texts the metaphysical concerns of Romantic idealism. Their interest is decidedly historical. The characters and events are drawn from or fashioned on historical and archival accounts. However, these sources are deliberately disguised or transformed in order to reveal the inadvertent failures of accuracy and veracity that characterize the writing of history. Like fiction, historiography is a representational form, that is, it attempts to represent a spatial or temporal absence. It does this by using systems of signification by which we make sense of the past. If the past is to serve as an object of knowledge for the present, it has to be cast in the regulative metaphors of the present. In other words, it has to be interpreted within the framework of its relevance for the present. Thus the historian often recounts the past in terms of analogies, similes, and metonymies. The past, furthermore, is only accessible as textualized remains. In other words, not only do historians engage in an act of rhetorical interpretation but they also interpret texts rather than events, thus maintaining a double distance from the actual object of investigation. The operative trope of historiography appears therefore to be Romantic irony. Irony operates in terms of the relationship historiography has to its object and the distance that separates it from that object. Like all *Darstellung,* the writing of history is infinitely approximate and appropriative representation.

The problem of representation as mediated truth is translated into poetic or prophetic truth that is in turn an affirmation of the irreducible gap between aesthetic form and logical norm. The suspension of chronological or linear flow of the narrative in these tales is one example in defiance of logical norm. Time is no longer seen as a highly codified system divided into a past, a present, and a future. It is no longer calendar time, but a framework of experience that acquires its only coherence in memory (recollection), imagination, and text.

The three tales discussed do not designate any present as their point of reference. Rather the three dimensions of time are conflated and mediated in a representational form which operates by metaphors of memory and anticipation. The past, not merely as it was but rather in its alternative configurations, remains a source of reference for the narrative present and future. Imagination and recollection as instruments of human understanding realize and anthropomorphize time in narrative.

The protagonists of the following stories are in broad terms all participants in the convention of *Bildungsreisende* (travelers on the road to education). The quest for self-knowledge, typical of the *Bildungsroman,* takes the form of encounters with the "exotic other" that appears variously as primordial nature and a glorious past in *Hyperion,* a poetic experience beyond space and time in *Heinrich*

von Ofterdingen, and the occult in *Isabella von Ägypten.* The protagonists decode this otherness by learning a new alphabet, a new
language, and a new geography. Their education constitutes an
initiation into the sacred order of poetry. The initiation takes place
in a timeless or unrepresentable time which is possessed in imagination and shared in memory.

In memory and anticipation, in suspended temporality, and
accompanied by recurrent alterity, the hero of the Romantic novel
attempts to meet the pedagogical imperative and learns to intuit the
many voices and languages of the earth, to navigate the threaten-
ing channels of ambiguity, and to waltz between necessity and freedom. The following brief encounters with Hyperion, Heinrich, and
Isabella are not conceived as full-fledged literary interpretations of
their (hi)stories. The recent history of literary criticism offers many
fine interpretive studies of German Romantic literature.[1] Rather the
following reading of three exemplary literary texts attempts to underline the metahistorical status of Romantic literature as it reflects
on its own mode of narrative operation and on concepts of temporality and alterity. It is a compact recording of these texts as voices
of a new poetic historiography. In other words, these tales are
viewed as literary historical works that purport, as Hayden White
has observed, "to be a model, or icon, of past structures and processes in the interest of *explaining what they were by representing
them*" (1973, 2). This representation of historical experience cannot
be conceived in terms of a narrowly historical documentary or
realistic notion of history but rather as a heuristic challenge to the
preconceived boundaries separating history from story.

Friedrich Hölderlin's *Hyperion*

In a review of Johann Wolfgang von Goethe's *Wilhelm Meister*
in the *Athenäum,* Friedrich Schlegel refers to the pedagogical vision
of the novel as follows: "Not this or that individual should be
educated but nature and culture themselves should be represented
[*dargestellt*] in a multiplicity of examples and summarized in simple
principles" (1958, 2: 143). This imperative coincides almost ideally
with Hyperion's pursuit. The pursuit is realized not in any action
but solely in reflection. The novel uses the epistolary form and is
restricted, with the exception of a couple of letters by Hyperion's
beloved Diotima, to a single letter writer, Hyperion. In a series of
letters to his friend Bellarmin, Hyperion reconstructs through tem-

poral voyages of memory his attempts to live as a hermit and to embrace the lesson of freedom as exemplified by nature and ancient Athens, two terms that oppose an education regulated by the dictates of modern rationalism and political absolutism. Like Schiller's letters in *Aesthetic Education*, Hyperion's letters argue that no theory of knowledge nor its attendant progress can achieve legitimacy before undergoing an aesthetic re-vision. Philosophy is not born of "mere understanding," for it is more than "the limited knowledge of what is," writes Hyperion. Nor is it born of "mere reason," for it is more than a "blind demand for a never-ending progress in combination and differentiation of some practicable matter" (1969, 1: 369). However, once the ideal of beauty illuminates reason, then reason begins to see what it is striving for. In art, which is a testament to the ideal of beauty, knowledge can ultimately exercise autonomy and become an agent of freedom.

In another text, known as "Fragment von Hyperion," Hölderlin describes the itinerary from the confining dictates of reason to the autonomy of will as the "eccentric path" (*exzentrische Bahn*; ibid., 1: 440). This path originates in the pure simplicity of nature and ends in the multiplicity of formation. This last stage is not a naïve unity with nature but an informed encounter with it. It is a conscious effort of the self to form (*bilden*) itself in a dialogue with the other. The educated approximation to nature in art and myth, in other words, in beauty, signals an infinite progression. "Oh ye who seek the highest and the best, in the depths of knowledge, in the turmoil of action, in the darkness of the past, in the labyrinth of the future, in graves or above the stars! do ye know its name? the name of the one which is one and all?" (ibid., 1: 339). Not surprisingly, this rich diversity and union of knowledge and experience is named Beauty.

In his letters Hyperion retrospectively charts the course of this progression toward the ideal of beauty. In a nonlinear order governed only by the dictates of a selective memory, Hyperion recounts childhood dreams, his trip to Athens, his encounters with the teacher figures Adamas and Alabanda, his arrival at the ideal of beauty in Diotima, his participation in the Greek war of independence, his return to Germany, and his final search for a new mythology. The time of the letters is a reconstructed time, whose anachronism orders the accounts in accordance with the perceived progress of *Bildung*. Self-representation is intimately linked to the representation of another time and place. However, neither the identity of the protagonist nor the time and space where he dwells refers to a fixed person, history, or geography. Hyperion is alternately a German and a Greek, simultaneously the narrator and the narratee. The time in which events are chronicled switches between antiquity and the eighteenth century, the setting of narrated action, between Germany, Greece, the Ottoman Empire, and the Orient at large. The status of the topoi of history or the story is, in the final analysis, equivocal. Time and space are represented both as monument and ruin and homeland and foreign land, respectively.

The locality presented is always a memorial, the locus for recollection of what has been lost, forgotten, removed, or erased through time. "Oh, it is so sweet to drink from the cup of oblivion" (ibid., 1: 336), muses Hyperion. The Greeks of the eighteenth century are subjects of the Ottoman Empire and fighting against it for independence. However, the Greece of the narrative is not the "real" Greece of the eighteenth century inhabited by a modern Slavic people but an ideal representation of what ancient Greece was. At some point, for example, Hyperion goes to Smyrna in Asia Minor. Smyrna is the ancient name of the Ottoman city of Izmir and all reference to Smyrna is to the ancient city. If the action is taking place in the eighteenth century, it is unlikely that Hyperion would visit one of the major ports of the enemy. Hyperion's father advises him to go to Smyrna to learn "the speech of cultivated peoples and their political constitutions, their views, their manners and customs" (ibid., 1: 308). Clearly, this idealized picture simply glosses over the historical fact that ancient Smyrna is now occupied by what Hyperion sees as Oriental despots. Nevertheless, there are references to actual historical events. The second letter in the first book of the second volume contains a historically accurate reference to the Cheshme naval battle with the Ottoman sultan's fleet on July 4, 1770 (ibid., 1: 405). In this way, like the vision of Romantic poetry in fragment 116 of the *Athenäum,* the narrative floats between the real and the idea(l), the historical and the fictional. John Jay Baker, in a study on Hölderlin's elegy "Brod und Wein," has observed that one approach to the elegy is "to treat its historical dimension as a rhetorical overlay," that is, to understand Hölderlin's Greece not as "the Greece of history but instead the history and product of a trope." This trope, in turn, is "the inauguration of the aesthetic character by which the West has known itself" (1986, 471).

The picture of an idealized ancient Athens in *Hyperion* can be read tropologically as an allegory of nature and freedom. This allegory is the criterion by which the phases in the process of *Bildung* of the individual and of history are judged. The memory of Athens stands in sharp contrast to Hyperion's representation of Sparta, the Orient, and, later, the Germanic North.

> More undisturbed in every way, freer from violent interference than any other people on earth, the Athenians grow into adulthood. No conqueror weakens them, no victory in war intoxicates them, no foreign religion stupefies them, no rash wisdom urges them to untimely maturity. (1969, 1: 363)

The Athenians "cannot tolerate arbitrariness, because their divine nature refuses to be upset, they cannot tolerate legality everywhere for they do not need it everywhere" (ibid., 1: 366). Hyperion draws a parallel between this picture of Athens and his happy childhood before knowledge had "ruined everything" for him. Indeed, "the child is a divine creature . . . The pressure of law and destiny does not touch it; only in the child is freedom" (ibid., 1: 298). Like Schiller, Hölderlin celebrates the inauguration of freedom in beauty. The child's freedom is one with beauty. "The first child of divine beauty is art. Thus it was among the Athenians" (ibid., 1: 365). In a sentence reminiscent of Schiller, Hyperion states that "the spiritual beauty of the Athenians produced the necessary sense for freedom" (ibid., 1: 365–366).

Sparta, in contrast, never enjoyed an unfragmented childhood situated in nature and beauty, and therefore moved into a problematic adulthood. Egyptians impassively bore "the despotism of arbitrary action" while the people of the North tolerated without resistance "the despotism of law, injustice in the form of codes of justice" (ibid., 1: 366). Here Hölderlin seems to adopt Hegel's view of the Oriental world and its submission to despotic will as a primitive stage in the history of the spirit:

> Like a supreme despot, the Eastern climate in its power and splendor casts its inhabitants to the ground. Before humans learn to walk, they must kneel, before they learn to speak, they must beg; before the heart finds equilibrium, it must bend, before the spirit is strong enough to bear flowers and fruit, fate and nature drain all its strength through scorching heat. Egyptians are devoted before they are a whole so they know nothing of wholeness, of beauty, and what they call the most

> sublime is a veiled power, an awful enigma; the dark, dumb Isis is their first and last, a hollow infinity and nothing reasonable has ever come out of it. Even the most sublime nothingness gives birth to nothingness. (ibid., 1: 367)

Nevertheless, the text maintains some trace of the Romantic notion of the Orient as a place of higher truth and learning. Alabanda, for example, leaves Hyperion to go to a mysterious unnamed place in the heart of Asia to benefit from its age-old wisdom. On the other hand, the North forces its pupils into introspection too soon. "If the spirit of the fiery Egyptian hurries forth to travel happily through the world, in the North, the spirit returns into itself even before it is ready to travel" (ibid., 1: 368). "Pure intellect, pure reason are always the kings of the North," adds the narrator.

Hyperion remains troubled by the contemporary dominance of the Nordic spirit. His imagination strives to refashion the German spirit on the image of the Hellenic ideal. But that spirit is too absorbed in the self, hence unable to divide itself to become different. The only way to freedom lies not in philosophical certainty or a belief in order but in the poetization of existence. And this starts at the point of positing and accepting difference. Hyperion observes that the great saying of Heraclitus about positing difference within oneself is an adage only a Greek could have found, "for it is the essence of beauty, and before that was found, there was no philosophy" (ibid., 1: 367). Without beauty there is no philosophy, and beauty only comes into being when the self separates from itself (posits itself) and recognizes this difference, this separation, as beauty. In art, the first child of divine beauty, divine humanity rejuvenates and renews itself. In order to present itself to its own consciousness, the self posits its beauty. "Thus human beings give themselves their gods. For in the beginning humans and their gods were one, when, unknown to itself, eternal beauty *was*" (ibid., 1: 365). This view is heavily indebted to Schelling's philosophy of art. As Schelling argues at the end of *System of Transcendental Idealism,* art is the only genuine agent and document of philosophy because it

> continues to authenticate what philosophy cannot represent in external form, namely the unconscious element in action and production and its original identity with the conscious. . . . The view of nature which the philosopher appropriates artificially [*künstlich*] is, for art [*Kunst*], the original and natural one. (1979, 272)

Thus, artistic representation coincides with a primordial, natural reality or truth. This is what Hyperion seeks. His poetic language is cast in a mythological idiom that permanently recalls Greece as a preeminent topos of divine utterance.

Hyperion charts the course of *Bildung* as a move toward a new intimacy with the divinities of a mythologized past. The present makes a mockery of an aesthetic and moral education. In his letters to Diotima Hyperion records fragmented memories of a bloody war: "It is over, Diotima! Our people have plundered, murdered indiscriminately" (1969, 1: 399). With the triumph of barbarism and the defeat of primordial Greek sensibility, language loses its emancipatory force and becomes a tool of oppression. Hyperion therefore seeks silence: "I can scarcely speak. . . . Language is a great superfluity. The best is ever for itself, and rests in its own depth like the pearl at the bottom of the sea" (ibid., 1: 400). Silence is the language of the poetic, after the poetic is disappointed by language. When Hyperion receives no word of farewell from Diotima after a long wait, he writes to her, "but you remain silent. That, too, is a language of your beautiful soul, Diotima" (ibid., 1: 402).

After his profound disappointment in modern-day Greeks—"I have nothing more to do with the Greeks" (ibid., 1: 400)—Hyperion's rendezvous with contemporary Germany proves even more devastating:

> So I arrived among the Germans. I did not demand much and was prepared to find even less. I came humbly, like the homeless, blind Oedipus to the gates of Athens. . . . Barbarians all along, they have grown more barbarous through industry and science and even religion, and are profoundly incapable of any divine emotion. . . . It is a hard saying, and yet I speak it because it is the truth: I can think of no people more torn apart than the Germans. You see artisans, but no human beings, thinkers, but no human beings, priests, but no human beings, masters and servants, but no human beings, youths and adults, but no human beings—is this not like a battlefield where hacked-off hands and arms and every other member lie pell-mell, while the life-blood drained from them vanishes in the sand? (ibid., 1: 433)

The only salvation from the memory of this bloodbath lies in re-course to the primordial unity of all beauty: "There will be but one beauty; and humanity and nature will be united in one all-embracing Divinity" (ibid., 1: 375). The locus of this transcendental recovery is poetry where a new poetic history or a new mythology is constituted in the encounter of the past with the future. This vision corroborates Schlegel's statement that only poetry serves as both model and remembrance (1958, 19: 5, no. 19). The model of Hölderlin's Greece is an allegory of the historical realization of an emancipatory and anticipatory vision. Thus, the projection of myth in Hölderlin re-calls the memory of this allegory.

The vision of a new mythology as the only feasible *Bildung* is borne out by the content of a short and incomplete text called "Das älteste Systemprogramm des deutschen Idealismus" (The earliest systematic program of German idealism) and discovered by Franz Rosenzweig among a collection of Hegel's papers and published in 1917.[2] This fragmentary document has been variously attributed to Hölderlin, Schelling, and Hegel. Lacoue-Labarthe and Nancy read the "program" as a text that introduces a disruptive break "within the philosophical, . . . a distortion and a deviation, which inaugurates the genuinely *modern* position of the philosophical (which is still our own, in more ways than one)" (1988, 29). In "Hölderlin und der deutsche Idealismus" (Hölderlin and German Idealism) Ernst Cassirer concludes that the author of the "System" is in all probability Hölderlin (1971, 132–135). Cassirer claims that, after a meeting with Hölderlin in the summer of 1795, Schelling perhaps conceived of a new duty for philosophy inspired greatly by Hölderlin's vision of the role of art. Indeed, the decisive insight of the text that "the philosophy of the spirit is an aesthetic philosophy" is the site where Idealism gives way to Romanticism. Like Schlegel's fragment 116 in the *Athenäum*, this text serves as a kind of manifesto of Romantic idealism. Its foremost item stipulates the representation of the self as absolutely free: "The first idea is, of course, the representation [*Vorstellung*] *of myself,* as an absolutely free being. With the free, self-conscious being arises simultaneously a whole *world*—from nothingness—the only true and conceivable *creation from nothingness*" (1969, 2: 647).[3] The world is created out of nothingness by the self-consciously free self. The subject's free self-presentation is the true form of the world. This reaffirms the Fichtean idea of the absolute self as self-consciousness.

The absolute freedom of consciousness is the possibility of the system: "Only that which is the object of *freedom* is called *idea*" (ibid., 2: 647). And the idea of beauty unites the ideas of consciousness, knowledge, and ethics. It is the ideal idea. It sublates all contradiction and resolves the opposition between system and freedom or, to use Kantian terms, necessity and freedom. This resolution takes place, implies the text, in the act of poetic representation. Philosophy realizes itself, becomes conscious of itself, when it represents itself in art. "I am convinced," reads the text, "that the highest act of reason, which covers all ideas, is an aesthetic act, and that *truth and goodness* are related only *in beauty*" (ibid., 2: 648). Without a sense for the aesthetic, philosophy can only be a philosophy of the letter. Hyperion sees the work of all understanding devoid of the "beauty of spirit," as a labor of mere necessity (ibid., 1: 369). If "the philosophy of the spirit is an aesthetic philosophy" (ibid., 2: 648), then poetry as *Hyperion*'s lesson shows is the teacher of humanity. Diotima assigns this pedagogical role to Hyperion who embarks on a symbolic search for the divine embodiment of beauty. In farewell Diotima says to Hyperion: "You will be the teacher of our people, you will be a great man, I hope" (ibid., 1: 375).

The "System Program" continues with a plea for a sensible religion, that is, a material form of art that engages the human senses: "We often hear that the masses need a *sensible religion*. Not only the great masses but also the philosopher needs this. Monotheism of the reason and of the heart, polytheism of the imagination and of art, that is what we need!" (ibid., 2: 648). This implies a new mythology of reason—a reconstituted mythology which stands to inherit the poetic configurations of a re-visioned idealism. And this mythology constitutes a religion of free will. "Do you know," Alabanda asks Hyperion, "why I have never given death any thought? I feel a life in me which no god created and no mortal begot. I believe that we exist through ourselves and that only through our own free desire are we so intimately bound to all." What meaning would life have if the world "were not a harmony of free beings?" (ibid., 1: 421). This freedom defines the priesthood of poetry. In Diotima's words Hyperion will be "the priest of divine nature" (ibid., 1: 429). At the height of the bankruptcy of reason, morality, and politics which informs the present age, the hope of healing lies in a new religion of the beautiful. And Hyperion heals as he writes, understands the state of affairs better as he recounts it, and understands the continuity and necessity of horror in history and the loss of Alabanda and Diotima. "We depart," he remembers Diotima saying, "only to be more intimately united, more divinely at peace with all, with ourselves. We die in order to live" (ibid., 1: 428). In this sense time flows backward and death leads to youth and birth.

The focus on a new mythology as a means of recollecting the lost lessons of history and as a moral corrective to the idolatrous worship of reason in modernity marks the path of Romantic *Bildung*. In a certain sense, this path originates in a work that was unacknowledged at the time of its publication and forgotten soon afterward but recovered and much acclaimed in recent critical history. In 1725 a distinguished Italian jurist by the name of Giambattista Vico published a book called *Scienza nuova* (The new science). The key to this new science lay in Vico's perception that the so-called primitive peoples when properly understood reveal themselves as neither naïve nor savage but instinctively poetic in their response to the world. This response issues from their inherent "poetic wisdom" (*sapienza poetica*) which governs their interaction with the world and reveals itself in forms of poetic representation such as myth and symbol. The mythical universe of the ancients is then not to be understood as a mode of ingenuous coping but as an attitude of a radically different order whose ultimate function is cognitive. The mythical accounts of creation are not supernatural visions of the primitive eye but means of encoding the world and coming to terms with its mysteries. All myths are rooted in the actual experience of the ancients and represent their attempts to impose a graspable, human shape on nature. Vico's theory of myth represents one of the earliest modern arguments to base the importance of art on the notion that abstract thought emerges from mythical imagination and iconic expression. Vico consequently reverses the rationalistic understanding of poetic tropes as forms of deviation from standard language. He regards them as both temporally and logically prior to abstract thought. In the final analysis, it is the faculty of poetic wisdom which displays a consistent ability to deploy myth and metaphor in the translation of the mysteries of nature into earthly vision. The conclusion inherent in Vico's argument is that how we articulate the world determines our way of arriving at what we call reality.

This poetic reality implicitly criticizes the idea of the Enlightenment that the world is a rationally ordered whole. Such criticism finds its forceful expression in Novalis's notion of *Romantisieren* (romanticizing) which "is nothing other than a qualitative potenti-

ation. . . . This operation is as yet quite unknown. By attibuting a
higher meaning to the ordinary, a mysterious appearance to the
commonplace, the worth of the unknown to the known, the appearance of infinity to finitude, I romanticize them" (1960, 2: 545, no.
105). In other words, knowledge is not limited to the sphere of the
rationally and quantitatively accountable and verifiable. Through
the transcendental vision of poetic wisdom, images, dreams, and
memories expand and diversify the human capacity for understanding. In *Heinrich von Ofterdingen* poetic understanding shows itself
capable of being realized both in the real world of representable
time and space and in a world that is beyond a representable reality
where time and space form a seamless continuum in memory and
anticipation.

Novalis's *Heinrich von Ofterdingen*

Of all the novel fragments and novellas of German Romanticism
Heinrich von Ofterdingen is perhaps the one that exemplifies most
consistently Schlegel's statement that a "theory of the novel would
have to be itself a novel" (1958, 2: 337). In his notebooks Novalis
lists the "unities" (*Einheiten*) of the novel as "the struggle between
poetry and non-poetry. Between the old and the new world. The
story and history of the *novel* itself" (1960, 1: 340 and 3: 639, no.
510). In fact, this novel fragment is a configuration of various literary forms which narrate the story of their own historical and formal production. The conceptual tapestry of the novel, where various reflections on the nature of understanding, interpretation, and
knowledge are interwoven, makes a ready categorization of the
work untenable. Novalis's notes of February 11, 1800, indicate that
Ofterdingen was conceived as a poetic response to Goethe's "un-
poetic" *Wilhelm Meisters Lehrjahre* (Wilhelm Meister's appren-
ticeship) (ibid., 3: 645–652). Novalis finds *Meister* "fundamentally
a fatal and stupid book—so pretentious and ornamented (artificial)" (ibid., 3: 646, no. 536). Novalis's polemic against Goethe's
work provides the former with the pretext to formulate his own
theory of the novel. For Novalis the novelist's endeavor is a hermeneutical event co-sponsored by the philosophical act of reflection
and the poetic principle of selection and combination: "The novelist
attempts to create poetry by events and dialogues, by reflection and
portrayal. . . . Everything depends on the manner and art of artistic

selection and combination" (ibid., 3: 649, no. 549). The various parts of this narrative combination are reflected, as sanctioned by fragment 116 of the *Athenäum,* in an endless series of tropological mirrors. These parts often "float" between the real and ideal, between "what is represented and what represents . . . on the wings of poetic reflection."

The notion of "qualitative potentiation" or the exponential increase in the power of the poetic integer is implemented through a frequent use of foreshadowing. In this way, dreams, songs, poems, memories, and actual happenings all recall, anticipate, and reflect on one another. This recurring shift between various representations of reality is already apparent in the first two sentences of the novel:

> Heinrich's parents were already in bed and asleep; the clock on the wall was ticking monotonously; outside the rattling windows the wind was blowing. From time to time the glimmer of the moon lit up the room. The youth lay restless on his bed and thought about the stranger and his stories. (ibid., 1: 195)

From one sentence to the next there is a shift from an everyday scene to the remembrance of things past, a reference to a mysterious stranger. The next sentence introduces the recurrent metaphor of the blue flower:

> I yearn to get a glimpse of the blue flower. It is perpetually in my mind, and I can write and think of nothing else. I have never felt like this before; it seems as if I just had a dream or as if I had been transported into another world in sleep. For in the world where I otherwise lived, who would ever bother about flowers? (ibid.)

Novalis invests the unknown with the known by assigning the stranger and the blue flower the definite article from the very beginning. The blue flower with its wide repertoire of significations is the informing allegory of the novel and points to changing concepts at different temporal levels. It is introduced as a sign of indescribable longing, then becomes a symbol of ideal love, harmony with nature, the key to the code of nature, and, in a manner of speaking, the fleur-de-lis of the future kingdom of poetry.

In spite of the many shifts between the real world of the narrative and the ideal world of poetic prophecies, memories, and dreams the first part of the story called "Die Erwartung" (Expectations) takes

place in a real time and place: medieval Germany. Furthermore, the
historical character of Heinrich is loosely based on a medieval bard
of that name. Heinrich's actual journey with his mother from
Eisenach to his grandfather's home in Augsburg constitutes the plot
in the first part of the book. During the course of what appears to
be an educational pilgrimage, Heinrich meets an unusual cast of
characters including a party of traveling merchants, a group of
crusaders, a Saracen slave girl, an old miner, a hermit in an underground library, and the poet Klingsohr and his daughter Mathilde.
Heinrich's encounters and conversations with people from exotic
worlds mark the stations of his *Bildung*. One of his early encounters
is particularly revealing in its Romantic representation of the
Orient. In his notes Novalis sketches the Saracen girl, Zulima, as
an allegory of poetry: "The Oriental woman [*die Morgenländerin*]
is also poetry" (ibid., 1: 342). Heinrich is deeply moved by Zulima's
song which tells of the woes of a stranger in a strange land. She
tells Heinrich the story of her brother who moved to Persia to apprentice with a famous poet and was never heard of again, of the
mysterious language of nature in her land, and of the poetic senti-
ments of her people:

> She lingered particularly on the praise of her country and her people.
> She described their magnanimity and their pure, great sensitiveness to
> the poetry of life and to the wonderful, mysterious charm of nature.
> She described the romantic beauties of the fruitful Arabian regions,
> which lie like happy isles amid the pathless deserts, like refuges for the
> oppressed and the tired, like colonies of paradise. (ibid., 1: 236)

In Zulima's account Arabia is a museum of natural history where
"strange, bright and many-colored figures and scenes on the old
stone slabs" have preserved the myriad signifying practices of the
past and intimate the presence of no longer presentable time and
meaning: "An obscure recollection amid the transparent present reflects the images of the world in sharp outlines, and thus one enjoys
a double world which in that way is freed of all that is crude and
violent and becomes the magical poetry and fable of our senses"
(ibid., 1: 237). In parting, Heinrich asks Zulima for her headband
adorned with unknown letters. This gesture is yet another testimony
to Heinrich's ongoing fascination with the esoteric signs of nature
and occulted history.

The tales and fables within the novel constitute, in Schlegel's definition of Romantic poetry, the endless series of mirrors that reflect the thematic concerns of the narrative. The Atlantis tale told by the traveling merchants in the third chapter of the first book introduces a compact itinerary of this novel. The song of the youth in the Atlantis tale deals with

> the origin of the earth, the appearance of heavenly bodies, plants, animals, and human beings; with the omnipotent sympathy of nature; with the primeval golden age and its sovereigns—love and poetry; with the emergence of hate and barbarism and their battles with those beneficient goddesses; and finally with the future triumph of the latter, the end of misery, the rejuvenation of nature, and the return of an eternal golden age. (ibid., 1: 225)

The theme of the song becomes part of a progression in a symbolic series. It reappears as a more elaborate narrative in Klingsohr's tale and is then summed up in the Astralis poem which introduces the second part of the novel where it shifts from a second-order—as a story within a story—to a first-order narrative. In other words, the allegorical tales that were deviations from the plot of the first book become the thematic concern of the second book. Novalis orders experience in what he calls the "geometric progression" of the novel (ibid., 2: 534, no. 34). The idea of the novel cannot be contained in a center. Unlike Kant, who discounts the possibility of a conceptual rule adequate to the "free play of cognitive powers," Novalis finds a mathematical series that coincides with open-ended signification:

> The novel is not the image or reality of a *sentence*. It is an intuitive implementation—realization of an idea. . . . An idea is *an infinite series* of sentences—an *irrational quantity*—that cannot be posited (musically)— incommensurable. . . . The law of its progression, however, can be formulated—and it is by this that a novel should be evaluated. (ibid., 2: 570, no. 212)

In spite of his wizardry with mathematical allegorizations, Novalis does not consider conceptual knowledge as an end in itself but as a means of achieving a state of informed innocence: "Knowledge [*die Erkenntnis*] is a means of arriving at *Non-knowledge* [*Nichterkenntnis*]. . . . Distant philosophy sounds like poetry—for each call into the distance becomes vocalic. . . . Everything becomes poetry—poem from afar" (ibid., 3: 302, no. 342). The Romantic

ideal of arriving at this state of conscious naïveté through *Bildung*
is realized in Heinrich's utopic experience of homecoming in the
second part of the book. Here Heinrich returns to a dimension of
theoretical innocence and poetic re-cognition. Understanding is not
always categorical, nor is it governed by a priori forms of intuition.
It can happen in the irrational world of a lost time, in hallucinations
and dreams. The unconscious assumes the force of statement just
as much as the conscious. A striking example is Heinrich's dream
of Mathilde's drowning in the sixth chapter of the first book. On
the one hand, its status in the story is one of a mere dream, for the
real Mathilde makes several appearances in person after this dream.
On the other hand, the only reference to Mathilde's actual death
is in the dream, and, therefore, its symbolic representation and its
reality become the one and the same. The force of the symbolic
spares both Mathilde and the narrator the experience of the actual
drowning or its replay at another narrative level.

Like dreams, memories are symbolic representations of knowledge. This is illustrated in a long conversation on history in the fifth
chapter of the first book. Here Heinrich and a group of his traveling
companions descend into mines in the company of a miner who has
acquired a vast knowledge of the past by decoding the language of
fossils. He was able to reconstruct a fragmented and forgotten past
by studying the material remnants and ruins of the earth. The underground journey leads to the innermost cave where Heinrich and
his companions meet Count von Hohenzollern, a hermit living in
a vast library. He greets the travelers warmly and tells them the
story of his youthful days as a soldier, of his children who were
born in the Orient and died shortly after their arrival in Europe,
and of his life with Marie, his wife who lies buried in the cave. During his conversation with Heinrich, Hohenzollern embarks on a
lengthy argument for the literary structure of history. He emphasizes the importance of the associative power of imagination in
imposing a coherent narrative form on the events of history. It is
in *Erinnerung* (as memory and recollection) that the moments of
Geschichte (as history and story) become an object of understanding and re-cognition:

> The true sense for the stories [and histories] of human beings develops
> late and rather under the quiet influence of recollection than under the
> more aggressive impressions of the present. The immediate events seem

to be only vaguely related but they *sympathize* all the more beautifully with the more remote ones, and only when one is in a position to survey a long series [of events] and to avoid not only taking everything literally but also confusing the actual order [of events] with wanton dreams, does one apprehend the secret union of the past and the future and learn to piece together history out of hope and memories.

Only those to whom all past is present may succeed in discovering the simple rule of history. We come upon only incomplete and complicated formulas and can be glad if we find, even if only for ourselves, a useful prescription which provides us with an adequate explanation of our short lives. . . . Youth reads history only out of curiosity, like an entertaining fairy tale; for those in their more mature years history is a comforting and edifying friend who through her wise conversation prepares them gently for a higher, more comprehensive career and makes them familiar with the unknown world by means of telling images. (ibid., 1: 257–258)

History is then a representation of alterity, in this case, of another time which can never be recalled in its totality. This lost time is available to present consciousness only through fragments of texts or of collective memory which, in order to be understood, need narrative coherence. In Hohenzollern's view, therefore, only poets can write history, for they can re-collect fragments of time and rearrange them as a metaphorical whole in *Darstellung*:

When I seriously reflect on all this, it seems to me that a historian must necessarily be a poet, for only poets are likely to perfect the art of skillfully configuring events. In their stories and fables I have with quiet pleasure observed their fine sense for the mysterious spirit of life. There is more truth in their fairy tales than in scholarly chronicles. Even though the characters and their fates are invented, the spirit in which they are invented is nevertheless truthful and natural. To a certain extent, as far as our enjoyment and instruction are concerned, it does not matter whether the characters in whose fates we trace out our own ever really lived or not. We want to perceive the great simple soul in the events of an age; if this wish is granted, we do not bother about the accidental existence of its external figures. (ibid., 1: 259)

In this interpretation of *Geschichte,* based on its double meaning of history and story and governed by the poetic principle of narrative coherence, the paths of history and literature as well as historiography and literary criticism converge. Consequently, history is seen, as E. L. Doctorow once observed, as "a kind of fiction in

which we live and hope to survive, and fiction is a kind of speculative history . . . by which the available data for the composition is
seen to be greater and more various in its sources than the historian
presupposes" (1983, 25). In Novalis's "speculative history," the
foregrounding of poetic operations helps identify, prior to analysis
and explanation, certain levels of experience which may pose philosophical and cognitive challenges to understanding. The rhetorical
use of language in the writing of history, the employment of tropes,
can subject phenomena represented in historical texts to a poetic
and ultimately a critical transformation.

An incident that follows the hermit Hohenzollern's discourse on
history serves as a revealing reflection that the story makes on its
own structural development. In Hohenzollern's library Heinrich
finds a book "written in a foreign language which seemed to him
to have some similarity to Latin and Italian" (1960, 1: 264).
Gripped by a strange curiosity, Heinrich turns the pages of the
book, which has no title, only to find his own image reproduced
at various stages of his past and future life. He sees himself with
his parents, present companions, and an imposing figure whom he
does not yet recognize. The pictures on the last pages of the book
get darker and blurred. When he comes to the last page Heinrich
realizes that the book has no ending. He is overcome by a strong
desire to read this occulted script: "He ardently wished he knew
the language, for the book pleased him tremendously without his
understanding a syllable of it" (ibid., 1: 264). Later Hohenzollern
tells Heinrich that the book is written in Provençal and recounts
the wondrous life of a poet. This book within the book prefigures
the structural fortunes of the novel. Like the Provençal book, which
has no title and no end, *Heinrich von Ofterdingen* remains a fragment. The actual book and the fictional book within the book, the
"real" story and the prophetic story within the story are linked
in their common structural destiny. Furthermore, this narrative
strategy is a commentary on the intertextual nature of all books.
Whether real or idea(l), books refer not to things in the world but
to other books. Many postmodern novels such as Umberto Eco's
The Name of the Rose reflect on their own intertextual heritage.
"I had thought, each book spoke of the things, human and divine,
that lie outside of books," states Eco's narrator, "now I realized
that not infrequently books speak of books: it is as if they spoke
among themselves" (1984, 342).

In the second part of the book, called "Die Erfüllung" ("The Fulfillment"), Heinrich moves from the real world of his family, his friends, his mentor Klingsohr, and beloved Mathilde to an ideal universe beyond time and space. He enters a domain of pure representation. Here the lines between different forms of narrative—story, poem, song, dream, prophecy—dissolve into a dreamlike vision. This vision is focused on reconstructing a world in a new language attuned to the pulse of nature. On this plane or planet suspended in a mythical time and space, Heinrich exists in a world of memory. He meets Sylvester, an old man intimate with the mysteries of nature. Heinrich's father had visited Sylvester's house in Rome as a young man. Sylvester is a figure from a past that would be inaccessible to Heinrich in a world of real or linear time. In the beginning of the novel Heinrich's father had recounted an earlier dream where Sylvester had appeared to him as a guide, leading him by the hand through long corridors into an open space where, like his son many years later, he is enchanted by the sight of the blue flower. A dream figure from the first part of the novel now reappears as a mediator and interpreter of fleeting and fragmentary signs of nature's languages. Sylvester instills in Heinrich an awareness of the universal signifying system that unites the disparate forms of human experience:

> Plants are the most immediate language of the earth. . . . This green mysterious carpet of love . . . is renewed every spring, and its singular script is legible only to the beloved, like the Oriental bouquet. He will read forever and yet never be satisfied, and daily he will perceive new meanings, new, more enchanting revelations of loving nature. For me this infinite satisfaction is the secret charm which inheres in traversing the surface of the earth, for each region solves different riddles for me. (1960, 1: 329)

Just as the actual world of the first part often digressed into a world of poetic imagination, the poetic universe of the second part points to actual philosophical, moral, and social concerns. When Heinrich observes that *Gewissen*, the transcendental conscience that "generates the universe and meaning," appears to him "to be like the spirit of the world poem," Sylvester replies:

> Conscience appears in every serious completion, in every cultivated truth. Every inclination and truth developed through reflection into a world picture becomes a phenomenon, a transformation of conscience.

All education [*Bildung*] leads to what one can only call freedom, regardless of the fact that what is designated by this is not a mere concept but the creative ground of all being. This freedom is mastery. The master exercises unrestricted power in a purposeful, definite, and reflective manner. The objects of his art are his and subject to his will, and they do not chain or inhibit him. And precisely this all-encompassing freedom, mastery, or sovereignty is the essence, the drive of conscience (ibid., 1: 331)

Like poetry, conscience cannot be reduced to conceptual categories, yet it insures the freedom of human life. This union of moral and aesthetic education grants human beings mastery over the world by allowing them to read phenomena poetically or intuitively. Freedom resides in *Bildung*, which opposes the forces of ignorance and bigotry, and in the human capacity for visualization and symbol making through which we order and understand experience. As a representational system that subsumes sign and symbol, language insures this freedom. "Language," observes Heinrich, "is really a little world in signs and sounds. Just as human beings rule over it, so they would also like to rule over the great world and be able to express themselves freely in it" (ibid., 1: 287).

We also approach elusive time in language. We recover it in words, in a textualized archaeology, or we internalize it in dream and memory, which, like language, are signifying systems. The noumenal world and lost time are accessible, albeit indirectly, by representational remains. "In the age we live in there is no longer any direct intercourse with heaven," states Heinrich's father, "the old stories and records are now the only source of knowledge, in so far as we need it, of the divine world" (ibid., 1: 198). The important stations in Heinrich's journey are libraries. He sees images of the past, the present, and the future in the mysterious book in Hohenzollern's library. In this library time is experienced as a continuum. Indeed, in Foucault's definition the library is the site that collapses temporal difference by rendering all historical epochs co-present.[4] Library circumscribes the field where the voyages in time, expeditions, and excavations unfold. The Romantic idea of the endless book is housed in the larger metaphor of the universal library. In "The Library of Babel" Borges employs a strikingly similar metaphor. Borges's library duplicates Hohenzollern's library by situating in its center an artifact that is an allegorical representation of the world of experience. In the latter this artifact was the Pro-

ençal book, which mirrored Heinrich's life in memory and antici-
ation. In the former it is a mirror. Talking about "the universe
which others call the Library)," the narrator notes that in its "hall-
vay there is a mirror which faithfully duplicates all appearances.
Men usually infer from this mirror that the Library is not infinite (if it really were, why this illusory duplication?); I prefer to
dream that its polished surfaces represent and promise the infinite. . . . Like all men of the library, I have traveled in my youth; I
have wandered in search of a book, perhaps the catalogue of cata-
ogues" (Borges 1964, 51). Situated between Plato's cave and
Borges's Babylon, Hohenzollern's library is a collection of the various representations of time.

The library is also a laboratory. In this case it is the site not only
of an archaeological excavation of knowledge but also of a geolog-
cal laboratory. Geology is a discipline of memory, for the study of
nature is here represented as a historical work in language and its
origins. Geology, a parent of archaeology, was one of the major
pursuits of Novalis's scientific career; during the last four years of
his life he practiced it professionally. A student of Abraham Gottlob
Werner, a preeminent geologist who blazed his own trail in the field,
Novalis was inspired by and respected his mentor's work yet was
sceptical of his emphasis on outward signs and symptoms of mineral
remains which excluded an understanding of their historical character. He criticized Werner's synchronic or atemporal, that is, merely
theoretical analysis of data which failed to elicit the significance of
their diachronic or temporal constitution (Haslinger 1981, 87).
"Both mineralogists and *organologists* seem to have taken very little
notice of the development of categories as such—of the serial degree
of increase [*Graderhöhungsreihe*] in columns" (Novalis 1960, 3:
392, no. 661). Novalis, for his part, demonstrates in metaphors of
geographical strata—mines, an underground library—that knowing
both draws on the fixed moment in the past (as tradition) and recasts it in the present. In other words, all knowledge comes into
being at the intersection of cultural and scientific heritage and theoretical and empirical evidence.

Layers of geological time constitute a form of encyclopedic
knowledge. The old miner explains his passion for mineralogy as
a passion for hidden origins. Just as Heinrich always pursues words
that could represent his dreams, so did the miner always wish as a
boy that the brilliant stones he gathered could speak so as to reveal

their mysterious origins (ibid., 1: 239–240). "You miners are al-most astrologers in reverse," says Hohenzollern, "they study the powers and effects of the constellations and you investigate the powers of rocks and mountains and the manifold effects of the strata of earth and rock. To them the sky is the book of the future, whereas to you the earth reveals monuments of the primeval world" (ibid., 1: 260). As a natural science that is also archaeological, geology, in a sense, allegorizes the study of language as a form of natural history. In a fascinating study on the discovery of geological time, which echoes Novalis's geological insights, Stephen Jay Gould, a renowned contemporary geologist and paleontologist, re-counts how two British geologists James Hutton and Charles Lyell were aided in their discoveries both by the organizing principles of time and cultural tradition and by their superior scientific knowl-edge of rocks. Gould shows how the understanding of time is com-pressed in metaphor as well as in geological layers.

> The interplay of internal and external sources—of theory informed by metaphor and observation constrained by theory—marks any major movement in science. We can grasp the discovery of deep time when we recognize the metaphors underlying several centuries of debate as a common heritage of all people who have ever struggled with such basic riddles as direction and immanence. (1987, 8)

Memory is not the ontological ground of knowing as in Hegel. In fact, memory and its discipline, history, are fragments—"the motley and living creation draws its nourishment from the ruins of past ages" (Novalis 1960, 1: 327). Memories and dreams (as the topos of knowing outside time and space) maintain the Romantic tension between epistemological certainty and metaphysical anxi-ety. Like the Provençal manuscript, which constitutes the mirror image of the larger text, *Heinrich von Ofterdingen* excludes that moment where total representation is possible, in other words, where the irreducible gap between representation and concept is closed. The moment of this closure is infinitely postponed. In "The Library of Babel" Borges writes that humanity has always lived with the desire to discover "the origin of the Library and of time." This task is an endless task of seeking the direct and immediate represen-tation of being and truth. "If the language of philosophers is not sufficient" for this end, "the multiform Library will have produced the unprecedented language required, with its vocabularies and grammars." The elusive language of truth is pursued by "official searchers, *inquisitors,*" who endlessly search all corners of the earth and "always arrive extremely tired from their journeys; they speak of a broken stairway which almost killed them; they talk with the librarian of galleries and stairs; sometimes they pick up the nearest volume and leaf through it, looking for infamous words" (1964, 55). The search is never called off. Like Scheherazade's tales in *The Arabian Nights,* the endless search for narratives in the library points to the human desire for life and survival. Human understanding and life depend on a perpetual postponement of closure. In the heart of this allegory of the cave or library lies the art of remembering the collective tales of "one thousand and one nights."

Ludwig Achim von Arnim's *Isabella von Ägypten*

When Achim von Arnim died in 1831 at the age of fifty, he was an almost forgotten figure. With the exception of his wife, Bettina, Görres, and the Grimm brothers, Jacob and Wilhelm, no one had really understood and appreciated his work. The disorienting experience of reading Arnim arises from the free and seamless association of the mimetic-representational and the fantastic. Goethe compared this work to a pitcher that overflows, because the cooper forgot to hoop it, while Wilhelm Grimm compared it to a picture framed on three sides with the fourth side open, thus allowing the picture to be painted on and on until earth and heaven are no longer distinguishable (Völker 1979, 114). In fact, the line between the real and the imaginary, the historical and the fictional, and the discursive and the occult is canceled and everything is subsumed by poetic representation. Although the unabashedly allegorical impulse of Arnim's storytelling went unappreciated during his lifetime, Heine recovers this quaint specimen of Romantic fantasy and restores it to literary memory in his *Romantic School.* Heine is vocal in his admiration of Arnim's allegorical boldness:

> Ludwig Achim von Arnim was a great poet and was one of the most original minds of the Romantic School. Fans of the fantastic would find him more engaging than any other German writer. Here [in the art of fantasy] he surpasses both Hoffmann and Novalis. He knew how to penetrate more intimately into nature than the latter and could conjure

up far more gruesome specters than Hoffmann. In fact, sometimes when I watched Hoffmann himself, it seemed to me as if Arnim had invented him. (1970–, 8: 85)

Heine's highly favorable reading of *Isabella von Ägypten* in this essay is significant, because here Heine is very critical of most Romantic literary works on the grounds that they either represent conservative ideologies or are mired in mystifying symbolism. *Isabella* instead draws unabashed praise from Heine, for in his view it is a self-consciously allegorical work that does not claim to represent a realistic view of life or history. It refigures reality in memory, imagination, and anticipation. But most important, Isabella's story presents the world of experience from a perspective of otherness, in terms of the occult and the arcane, and as an alternative to such organizing principles as reason, logic, causality, or coherence. Heine singles out *Isabella* as an exemplary text that succeeds admirably in giving life to the painful marginalization of strange or exotic constituents of society, in this case, gypsies. "Of Arnim's novellas his *Isabella of Egypt* seems to be the most precious," states Heine, "this strange fairy-tale people, with their brown faces, friendly soothsayer eyes, and sad mysteriousness come to life here. The chaotic, illusory cheerfulness veils a great mystic sorrow" (ibid., 8: 88). According to the legend, "told very charmingly in this novella," as Heine remarks, the gypsies were condemned to wander around the world for some time as punishment for the harshness with which their ancestors turned away the Virgin Mary who requested lodging for the night for herself and her child during her flight in Egypt. Because of this, people have felt justified in treating the gypsies cruelly, and they were persecuted most unjustly and brutally. It was common practice in many countries to hang them on suspicion of theft without investigation and trial.

As the novella begins, we are told that Isabella's father, gypsy king Michael, was wrongly accused and hanged, a casualty of the persecution of gypsies in Europe. In the night his people take Michael down from the gallows, wrap his royal cloak around his shoulders, place his silver crown upon his head, and lower the royally attired body into the Scheldt in the belief that the waters will carry him to Egypt. Isabella, who lives in an old, supposedly haunted house on the river at the outskirts of town, does not know of this incident. One night she hears strange murmurs coming from the water and sees the apparition of her father rising from the river in his robe. She tries to hold on to the sad ghost of her father who floats away to Egypt to be properly buried there. All alone, Isabella holds a solemn funeral feast for her father. From this moment on her destiny follows a course that goes from the margins of the Occidental society to the holy shrines of her Oriental homeland. The exotic other, excluded and misunderstood, emerges as the representation of a higher truth.

Isabella's story consists of a repertoire of familiar literary patterns, historical pre-texts, and prophetic visions which are alternately foregrounded and backgrounded. Negotiating the curves of this narrative is the adventure in Romantic reading. The effortless shift from the real to the fantastic, from the historical to the mythical, embodies Schlegel's vision of Romantic poetry gliding "on the wings of poetic reflection." One critic refers to Arnim's narrative pattern as a "hybrid" that interweaves various strands of fairy tale, history, and social criticism (Tymms 1955, 277). In "Über Goethes Meister" (On Goethe's Meister), an exemplary Romantic reception of a literary work, Schlegel observes that the characters in Goethe's *Meister* resemble a portrait in their method of representation but are nevertheless more or less general and allegorical. This allegorical nature is what makes them "the inexhaustible material and most outstanding exemplary collection for moral and social investigation" (1958, 2: 143). In a similar vein Arnim's characters in their highly variegated allegorization constitute a narrative thread of social and cultural hue.

The subtitle of the novella, *Kaiser Karl des Fünften erste Jugendliebe* (Emperor Karl the Fifth's first love), sets up the expectation that the story is a semihistorical fiction about the emperor Karl's encounter with a gypsy princess. All historical references are freely refictionalized. The anticipation of the supernatural permeates every fact of the narrative. A quality of the bizarre envelops all aspects of Isabella's life. As a woman, an Oriental, and a gypsy-witch, Isabella is the ultimate representation of the exotic other. Her otherness takes on many faces. She leads a "secret, nightly life" in a haunted house and suffers the perils of homelessness in a physical way. With her father's death she is orphaned for the second time, having already lost her mother four years earlier. Although she has the occasional companionship of Braka, an old gypsy woman, there is no one in whom she can place complete trust. She is also set apart from her own race by her noble birth, unusual beauty, and her status as the one chosen to lead her people back to their homeland. Although a stranger through and through, she is the director of choreography in this poetic dance or free play, guiding Karl and others through complicated steps of understanding an occulted nature and history. She steers the narrative from the realm of the natural and historical to that of the supernatural and the mythical. As the story opens, Isabella looks out of the window, murmuring: "Oh, look at the angel, how he laughs at me" (1981–, 1: 510). Braka shudders at the mention of an apparition. "Child," she gasps, "what do you see?" "The moon," answers Isabella matter-of-factly. Isabella moves between these two kinds of discourse, the natural and the supernatural, without effort. For her, neither reality excludes the other. Each is a form of representation, a certain language. Understanding is a form of self-reflection in the mirror of alterity. Isabella often looks into these mirrors to catch a glimpse of the extrasensory world. She is familiar with "the cycles of the moon and the stars" (ibid., 1: 524). Like Heinrich she consults dreams, esoteric texts, and signs from nature to chart the course of her destiny.

After her father's death Isabella goes through his possessions among which she finds several old manuscripts:

> Finally, in an old chest she found old writings, many decorated with exquisite seals written on beautiful paper in a foreign language, which she had not yet learned. There were also others written in Netherlandic German which she could write and read, since her mother, who had fled an old house of the counts of Hogstraaten with Michael, had instilled the love for this old language in her husband and her child. (ibid., 1: 516)

The knowledge she gleans from these texts guides her in her subsequent mission to lead her people to freedom. Her access to the occult through deciphering the secrets of language invests her with the power of invention, creation, and prophecy, all of which are domains of the poetic in the Romantic view.

Freely subscribing to the occult and steeping herself in the esoteric formulas of her newly found books, Isabella produces for starters an *Alraun,* a miniature man, from a mandrake root she pulls out from the earth. The mandrake man is to play an important role in the subsequent course of events. As the legend goes, the mandrake root sprouts at the spot where the tears of a wrongly hanged man fall on the earth. Isabella goes to the site where her father was hanged and by applying the magic formula finds herself in possession of a mandrake man who calls himself Cornelius Nepos. The narrator steps in to comment that this Nepos is not related to the famous historian of the same name. By conjuring up the *Alraun* Isabella steers the narrative into the realm of legend and myth and destabilizes the initially established historical background of her own story. The narrator compares Isabella in her act of creating the *Alraun* to a "young artist" (ibid., 1: 530). She generates life through language, creates a man by the magic of words. In the final analysis, Isabella's tale itself becomes an allegory of the construction and definition of reality in language.

After her father's death, the dilapidated house on the river becomes Isabella's refuge, since townspeople, fearing ghosts and other monsters, dare not come near it. However, one day the crown prince, Karl, having heard that the house is haunted, decides to spend the night there to prove his courage. Isabella and Braka, fearing that they might be driven away from this shelter if the prince finds out that they live there, plot to scare him away by having Isabella appear to him disguised as a ghost in the middle of the night. The plan succeeds and the crown prince flees the house in utter terror. At this point, the narrator observes that even the most daring and arrogant man harbors a deep-seated fear "of the world that cannot be named" (*der unnennbaren Welt*; ibid., 1: 521). The fast traffic between what can be named and what remains unnamed, being (*Sein*) and appearance (*Schein*), and history and story constitute both the thematic concern and the structural form of the novella. The characters are either doubled, coupled, or both. The narrative proceeds by doubling and mirroring where the difference between the actual and the double is consistently elusive, if not lost. In other words, even within the fictive frame of the novella characters are cloned, images reproduced, visions reenvisioned, and apparent narrative closures duplicated. In a sense, the fiction mimics its own fictionality and representationality. Concepts of the real and the original become faded memories amidst the bustle of ongoing duplications.

After fleeing the haunted house, Karl realizes that he has fallen in love with what he believes to be a ghost. In fact, Karl is depicted as a character who can never tell the real and its image apart. He later falls in love with Isabella's clone. The *Alraun* doubles as a caricature of the historical Cornelius Nepos and as Isabella's lover and her child. Another grotesque double is the *Bärenhäuter* (bearskin), the ghost of a slave who has sold his soul to the devil. In order to earn some extra cash, he has now risen from the dead and contracted to serve as a servant for seven years. Although he is fat and clad in bearskin, he is always cold. At one point, the whole cast of characters and their doubles travel from Buik to Ghent, the seat of the monarchy. Heine considers Arnim's rendering of this journey a spectacle that would make all the painstakingly invented recent ghost stories of the French seem to be only "the rosy morning dreams of an *opera danseuse*" (1970–, 8: 89).

In Ghent Isabella and Karl are fated to meet again. The story now takes a realistic course only to be subverted by upcoming supernatural episodes. Karl and Isabella's romance heads for the rocks as a result of the *Alraun*'s jealousy and his claim to her affections. In order to get the *Alraun* out of the picture, Karl enlists the help of a Jewish magician who creates a golem, an Isabella clone, identical in appearance with the real woman but, in fact, a soulless and shallow apparition. Karl falls for the clone and deserts the real Isabella. Abandoned and facing great difficulties, Isabella has a dream where her father, crowned and seated on an Egyptian pyramid, tells her that she is destined to bear a child who will lead her people to their homeland. Karl eventually wakes up to the truth and sees the golem for what she is. He erases the first syllable *Ae* of the word *Aemeth* inscribed on the forehead of the golem who thereupon collapses and turns into thin air. The evil spirit of the golem is exorcised by an antispell, or in this case, an antisyllable. Once more, the language of fairy tales and charms creates another dimension of reality.

Not only Isabella's dream and her subsequent vision of holding the child of the prince, in front of whom people of many lands kneel, but also a revelation the prince's minister Adrian has foreshadow the events of the story. The visions are realized in re-vision in somewhat altered form. Karl and Isabella have a son, Lrak. However, it is Isabella, not her son, who leads the gypsies back to Egypt. She dies in her homeland after a long and successful reign. After Isabella's departure Karl retires to a monastery. Both Karl and Isabella die on the same day by their own will. As Karl lies down in his coffin ready to surrender his soul, the vision of Isabella, who is also voluntarily preparing to leave this world, appears to him. Thus, Isabella's death is not related at the "realistic" level of the narrative but in Karl's vision, just as Mathilde's death in *Heinrich von Ofterdingen* was only represented in Heinrich's dream. Furthermore, the narrator invents a "historical source" for his account of Isabella's death, claiming that the detailed account of Isabella's funeral and of the burial customs of the Egyptians narrated in the novella were recorded in a two-volume travelogue written by a printer's apprentice named Zacharias Taurinius. This work, *Beschreibung einiger See- und Landreisen nach Asien, Afrika und Amerika* (Description of some sea and land travels to Asia, Africa, and America), was actually published in 1799 and 1800 in Leipzig but it contains no such record. The coeval transitions of Karl and Isabella mark the second ending of the story. Like everything else in this narrative— including the double departures from this world of Karl and Isabella—the ending is also doubled. The narrative comes to its first closure when Isabella, who has had a very ambivalent relationship with Karl, leaves him, joins her people, and heads for her homeland. Here the closure divides and continues on to the second ending. In other words, the ending is postponed only to be duplicated. The story reflects itself in several mirrors.

Isabella's story deals a decisive blow to philosophy's claims to direct or schematic representation. All conventions are installed only to have their unity divide and proliferate. A mocking reference to the idea of split subjectivity is a parody of Fichte's self and not-self dichotomy which proves to be non-sense in the *Alraun*'s words. When Braka asks him, "well, are you a ghost or a man, dear Cornelius?" he retorts, "that is a stupid question, I am I and you are not-I. . . . I don't want to hear of such damned, hair-splitting questions" (1981–, 1: 545). Of course Arnim splits every concept and convention every which way. The *Bildung,* for example, applies to not only one individual but many and its direction is not always progressive but also regressive. The *Alraun* deteriorates in every way: physically, mentally, and morally. Karl's life and deeds go the way of anti-*Bildung,* and his final and perhaps only moment of *Bildung* comes in the form of Isabella's image (*Bild*) as he dies. There is no unity of subject and narration but a multiplicity of subjectivities that institute allegorical understanding. Nature, history, and geography are no longer epistemologically reliable points of reference but players in the infinite game of the universe. Arnim dwells at the Romantic frontier and creates a poetic space that houses the disparate conventions of the objective and the mundane and the subjective and the unearthly (or uncanny).

Several elements of the story, such as the person of Karl and the persecution of gypsies (who also are an allegorical representation of the persecuted Jews), are historical. Dreams and visions are psychologically explainable. However, the materialization of the *Alraun,* golem Isabella, and the bearskin ghost resist any realistic or psychological explanation and are only possible in the realm of the fantastic. Tzvetan Todorov offers an account of the genre of the fantastic (*la fantastique*) which describes it in terms of the neighboring genres of the uncanny (*l'etrange*) and the marvellous (*le merveilleux*) (1975, 24–57). The fantastic never wanders off into these adjacent territories, no matter how strongly it may be drawn in one direction or the other nor however much it may represent the tension such a vacillation generates. Thus, the fantastic essentially manifests itself in ambiguity, in the disorientation felt by the reader who knows only natural laws and is confronted by an event which is apparently supernatural. The genre of the fantastic therefore implies not only the narration of a strange event but also a certain mode of reading, one which opts neither for a strictly allegorical reading of events nor for a poetic interpretation that would normalize and dispose of the inexplicable. The hesitation between the natural and the supernatural which the narrative generates then has to be echoed in the readers' own uncertainty about the conventionally available patterns for their individual responses. At the end, they resolve the dilemma by opting to classify the events in one or another of the neighboring areas, the uncanny or the marvellous, depending on the way they see the matter settled. Ultimately, as Todorov argues, the role of the fantastic has always been to set that which is real or capable of causal explanation against that which is imaginary or supernatural. Hence, it can only exist as a genre in a society which articulates its own experience in terms of that simple dichotomy. Todorov maintains that in challenging the certainty of these terms by posing the question of whether the events narrated are real, the genre of the fantastic may have enacted the role of the uneasy conscience of the nineteenth century.

In short, the genre of the fantastic transmits to the society the message that life is not as simple as it collectively makes out. By abolishing the concept of representational certainty in their rediscovery, reinvention, and valorization of fragmentary and mixed genres, the Romantics were instrumental in instituting the critical function of the fantastic as Todorov defines it. "In the psychological and philosophical novel," notes Schlegel, "the *absolute* fantastic and the *absolute* mimetic must be able to be juxtaposed without merging" (1957, 53–54, no. 384).[5] Thus, the ambivalence of Arnim's narrative could not be considered an obstacle to be reduced into manageable meaning. The act of reading a synthetic writer like Arnim means participating in the vicissitudes of the text. As in Goethe's *Meister,* all textual elements refer to "spectacle, representation, art, and poetry" (Schlegel 1958, 2: 131). As such, the very form of the narrative in true Romantic fashion becomes a comment on the story of its own formation or coming into being. The apparently conflicting languages of the text—natural, supernatural—become nonreferential in that they are not compelled to signify an objective reality beyond themselves and therefore need not be mutually exclusive categories.

The literary history of German Romanticism abounds with tales that testify to the lasting union of memory and imagination. History and story unfold against a background of imaginatively remembered fragments of temporality. "Like those birds that lay their eggs only in other species' nests, memory produces in a place that does not belong to it," writes de Certeau, "it receives its form and implantation from external circumstances, even if it furnishes the content (the missing detail)." The deployment of memory, he argues, inevitably involves alteration. In fact, memory draws its "interventionary" power from its "unmoored," moving position. It "is formed (and forms its 'capital') by *arising from the other* (a circumstance) and by *losing it* (it is no more than a memory)." Thus, memory alters its object and is altered by it. If memory is no longer capable of this alteration, it will fall into decay, for it "constructs itself from events that are independent of it, and it is linked to the expectation that something alien to the present will or must occur" (1984, 86–87). In this fashion the Romantic memory reinvented an exoticized history sustained by the belief in that history's power to poeticize present experience and enhance future expectation.

6. The Critical Legacy of German Romanticism

> On the whole it seems to me that "the right perception"—that is, the adequate expression of an object in the subject—is a contradictory nonentity: for between two totally different spheres such as subject and object, there is no causality, no accuracy, no expression, but at the utmost an *aesthetic* relation, I mean a suggestive transposition, a stammering translation into a radically foreign language.
>
> Friedrich Nietzsche, "On Truth and Lie in an Extra-Moral Sense"

> The sign is to be interpreted if we are to understand the idea it is to convey, and this is so because the sign is not the thing but a meaning derived from the thing by a process here called representation that is simply not generative, i.e., dependent on a univocal origin.
>
> Paul de Man, "Semiology and Rhetoric" in *Allegories of Reading*

The critical agenda of early German Romanticism generated a re-conceptualization of knowledge through an understanding of literary texts as explorations in epistemology, ethics, and aesthetics and as intertextual and interdisciplinary artifacts. The current debates in literary theory are not-so-distant echoes of the critical voices that informed Jena Romanticism. Contemporary theories of criticism express competing and conflicting views on the indeterminacy of language, the relation between grammar and rhetoric, the interaction between literary and nonliterary texts, in short, on the general problem of representing the truth or the idea. However, modern critics have not, by and large, examined the work of Jena critics in this context; instead they have indirectly drawn upon the fruits of Jena through the broader framework of German Idealistic philosophy and, most important, through Nietzsche. Nietzsche is an important figure of transition, for he is a reluctant heir to Romantic idealism yet represents in full measure the paradoxical and ironic vision of early Romanticism. He launches a massive attack on what he considers the epistemic conceit of idealistic philosophy, particularly in his early work, which I shall briefly discuss here. At the same time Nietzsche continues the task of subverting the traditional claims to critical representation which, in fact, was inaugurated in the works of Kant, Fichte, Schlegel, and Novalis. Nietzsche concludes that all claims to truth are based on a fictional configuration of metaphors, thereby confirming Romanticism's critical anxiety that all attempts to access reality may be an unending allegorical detour.

Nietzsche: The Re-vision of Romanticism's Critical Agenda

Nietzsche's earlier work constitutes the most radical complement to early German Romanticism's agenda on representation. In three early works, "Die Philosophie im tragischen Zeitalter der Griechen" (Philosophy in the tragic age of the Greeks), "Über Wahrheit und Lüge im außermoralishen Sinne" (On truth and lie in an extra-moral sense), and *Die Geburt der Tragödie* (The birth of tragedy), Nietzsche relentlessly probes the inadequacy of the sign to the concept and the irreducible difference between presence and representation. In "Nietzsche und die Frühromantische Schule" (Nietzsche and the Early Romantic School), Ernst Behler examines the relation between Nietzsche and the actors of the *Athenäum*: the Schlegel brothers, Novalis, W. H. Wackenroder, Tieck, and Schleiermacher. He notes the common search for a new mythology, the cult of the aesthetic, the scorn of philistinism, the penchant for the fragmentary, and the recovery of Hellenistic ideals of art (1978, 59–96).[1] These important thematic similarities point to broader conceptual concerns whose Romantic traces Nietzsche develops into a preamble to poststructuralist criticism.[2] These concepts include the unstable metaphorical origin of knowledge, understanding as free play, and self-representation through otherness. In "Nietzsche and Postmodern Criticism," for example, Bernd Magnus argues that "a cluster of concepts loosely associated with 'postmodern philosophy'" experienced their first renaissance in Nietzsche's work. Magnus isolates these concepts as postmodern philosophy's

> putative anti (or post) epistemological standpoint; its antiessentialism, its antirealism about meaning and reference; its antifoundationalism; its suspicion of transcendental arguments and transcendental standpoints,

its rejection of the picture of knowledge as accurate representation; its rejection of truth as correspondence to reality; its rejection of canonical descriptions and final vocabularies; and its suspicion of metanarratives. (1989, 302)

Nietzsche's "most recent rebirth" is a thorough contemplation and celebration of these concepts in postmodern criticism.[3]

Like Schlegel, for whom "the absolute" (*das Höchste*) can only be expressed allegorically because it is unutterable (1958, 2: 324), Nietzsche looks beyond the categories of time, space, and causality into the impenetrable zone of essences only intuitable as an aesthetic phenomenon. Like Schiller he sees the world of phenomena as the realm of *Schein,* a world veiled in aesthetic illusion. However, unlike Schelling, who saw art as the culmination of philosophy because art provided direct and immediate access into the absolute, Nietzsche views art as a self-conscious illusion which excites an optic desire to look beyond appearance to the abyss where comprehension faces total resistance and eventually comes to terms with the tragic vision of existence. Since art is always alerted to the nonconclusive nature of reality, it is redeemed by its self-reflexive and ironic sensibility, whereas reason and logic are trapped in what Nietzsche calls "metaphysical delusion" (*metaphysischer Wahnsinn*). The persistent irony and mobility with which Nietzsche invests art aligns his thought unmistakably with that of the early Romantics. In "Über das Studium der Griechischen Poesie," for example, Schlegel sees "the *specific character* of fine art as free play without a definite purpose" (1958, 1: 241–242). And all *Bildung* is characterized by the interaction of this free play with nature (ibid., 1: 230).

The idea of the construction of the world as free play uninhibited by moral constraints is a recurrent one in Nietzsche. In "Philosophy in the Tragic Age of Greeks," he traces the concept of the free play of being to the pre-Socratic philosophers, most notably Heraclitus and Anaxogoras. For Heraclitus, "the world is the *play* of Zeus" where "only the play of artists and children constitutes becoming [*Werden*] and passing away, building and destroying, without any moral attribution" (1956, 3: 376). The aesthetic human being (*der äesthetische Mensch*) has come to realize how "in the conflict of plurality rules and laws can nevertheless exist . . . how necessity and play, opposition and harmony, must pair to produce a work of art" (ibid., 3: 377). Heraclitus presents us with *"the theory of law in becoming and of play in necessity"* (ibid., 3: 381). Here Nietzsche revises earlier philosophical narratives to draw out the full implications of Kant's notion of the "free play of cognitive faculties" in aesthetic judgment, Schiller's idea of the effective realization of human knowledge in the play-drive, and Schlegel's belief that every play of art is a re-production (*Nachbildung*) of the endless play of the world (1958, 2: 324).

The representation of "primordial chaos," which is the raw material of all aesthetic form for Schlegel, constitutes according to Nietzsche the fundament of the Anaxagorian world view. In order to oppose a defeatist teleological view of being, Anaxagoras insists on the primacy of the "free will" of the spirit. The absolute free will can only be thought of as free of purpose (*zwecklos*) like "a child's game or an artist's play drive" (1956, 3: 413). Here Nietzsche uses Schiller's word *"Spieltrieb."* In "Truth and Lie" and *The Birth of Tragedy* the concept of free play is closely linked to the irreducible space of motion between sign and representation. As Derrida argues, Nietzsche's radical critique of metaphysics substitutes the concepts of free play, becoming, and sign without truth for being and truth:

> There are . . . two interpretations of interpretation, of structure, of sign, of freeplay. The one seeks to decipher, dreams of deciphering, a truth or an origin which is free from freeplay and from the order of the sign, and lives like an exile the necessity of interpretation. The other, which is no longer turned toward the origin, affirms freeplay and tries to pass beyond man and humanism, the name man being the name of that being who, throughout the history of metaphysics or of ontotheology—in other words, through the history of all of his history—has dreamed of full presence, the reassuring foundation, the origin and the end of the game. The second interpretation of interpretation, to which Nietzsche showed us the way, does not seek in ethnography, as Lévi-Strauss wished, the "inspiration of a new humanism." (1972, 264–265)

It is not by an accident of literary history that Nietzsche's name became the site of reference (and reverence) for modern criticism. Nietzsche's critical reflections have shown modern readers something they have always suspected: a text means more than it says, and it is irreducibly metaphorical and subverts all determinate meanings by its implicit irony, a rhetorical limit that prevents the reference of art or criticism to a univocal authorial statement. Instead of discovering or assigning meanings, Nietzsche strives to define and understand the conditions and limits of the production of meaning. The metaphor of the labyrinth Nietzsche often employs represents the intricate path of the questions he relentlessly pursues.[4] The labyrinth is a symbol of human consciousness, the metaphor of the mind coping with the undecidability of cognitive perception. This labyrinth is the site of cracks in the foundations of metaphysical knowledge that have challenged the architects of idealistic philosophy since Kant. Nietzsche uncovers the fossilized interpretive layers that cover the problem of the representational reliability of knowledge. Nietzsche's rejection of interpretive closure reaffirms a revolutionary reversal in the order of knowledge, a reversal already accredited by the early Romantics. The understanding that joins Nietzsche with his Romantic forebears is the realization that there is no minotaur of dictatorial truth at the center of the labyrinth but rather an energetic and restless inquiry consistent with the desire to face the flux of becoming.

The concepts of play, performance, dance, and music—the dynamic dimensions of experience where perception is tied neither to the a priori nor to the contingent alone—had shown a progressive movement from the margins to the center of Romantic discourse. Nietzsche for his part rejects a deduction of categories which once established define forever the form in which we can generate further knowledge. We may employ some categories and make some assumptions, yet we understand only through our own construction and configuration of phenomena. If truth is conceived as a mode of expression adequate to unconstructed facts, then there can be no truth, for there are no raw facts. Knowledge can no longer be viewed as an assemblage of representations but only as a product of creative imagination. All knowledge originates in the artistically creating subject (*künstlerisch schaffendes Subjekt*; 1956, 3: 316), a fact human beings need to forget in order not to forfeit epistemic security. In *Das allgemeine Brouillon* Novalis formulates the condition of "true knowledge" in almost identical terms: "this artistic supposition is the foundation of a true science that springs from *artistic facts*. The I has to be constructed. The philosopher prepares, creates artistic elements and goes on with the construction" (1960, 3: 253, no. 76). The formation (*Bildung*) of concepts, argues Nietzsche, emerges as a result of the horizontal layering of metaphors, so to speak. Representations of time and space, which coincide ideally with natural laws and fully account for phenomena, do so only because we ourselves attribute explanatory powers to nature:

> Everything wonderful, however, at which we marvel in the laws of nature, that requires our explanation and might seduce us into distrusting idealism, lies actually and solely in the mathematical strength and inviolability of time and space representations [*Vorstellungen*]. These, however, we produce in ourselves and project them with that necessity with which the spider spins; since we are compelled to understand all things only in these forms, then it is no longer wondrous that in all things we actually perceive only these forms; for they all must carry within themselves the laws of number, and the number is the most astonishing aspect of things. All conformity to law which so impresses us in the orbits of the stars and in chemical processes coincides, in effect, with those qualities that we ourselves attach to things, so it is we who impress ourselves. (1956, 3: 318)

Like Schlegel, who sees mythology as a "hieroglyphic expression of surrounding nature" (1958, 2: 318), Nietzsche refers to the artistic creation of Greek gods and heroes as "hieroglyphics of nature interpretation" (1956, 3: 411). The construction of concepts (*Bau der Begriffe*) is built on metaphor. Turning Kant upside down, Nietzsche states that understanding constitutes "an imitation of time, space, and number relations on the ground of metaphors" (ibid., 3: 318–319). Concepts are generated "by equating unequals" (*durch Gleichsetzen des Nichtgleichen*; ibid., 3: 313). Just as Novalis has argued that language was not the proper medium of representation for philosophy (1960, 3: 573, no. 124), Nietzsche doubts that language constitutes "the adequate expression of all realities." In fact, words are "arbitrary transpositions" (*willkürliche Übertragungen*) which have "flown way beyond the canon of certainty" (1956, 3: 311–312). In "Philosophy in the Tragic Age of the Greeks" Nietzsche argues that "words are only symbols for the relation of things to one another and to us; nowhere do they touch upon absolute truth" (ibid., 3: 390). Thus, any representation of things or concepts has no relation to their essence but constitutes a metaphor thereof. Representation is an act of "masking," "a convention of shrouding," "a stage play," or a "play on the back of things" (ibid., 3: 310). As Derrida rightly points out, philosophical thought has repeatedly belabored the arbitrariness of the sign to

throw into sharp relief the marginal status of language in relation
to thought. He notices that Nietzsche "must resort to an analogous
argument" motivated, however, by "an entirely other aim" (1982a,
178). It is only by forgetting the metaphorical and subjectively creative origin of representation and through the sedimentation of the
once fluid products of imagination that human beings can achieve
a measure of peace and security. In other words, their peace of mind
resides in the belief that objective truth is possible. Nietzsche's archaeology of words uncovers truth as:

> A mobile army of metaphors, metonymies, anthropomorphisms: in
> short, a sum of human relations, which were poetically and rhetorically
> intensified, metamorphosed, adorned and after long use appear to
> people as fixed, canonic, and binding: truths are illusions which one has
> forgotten that they *are* illusions; worn-out metaphors which have lost
> their sensory power, coins which have their obverse effaced and now
> are regarded no longer as coins but only as metal. (1956, 3: 314)

The metaphor of the coin itself is revealing, since it represents
the notion of convertibility and, in this instance, the interstice where
Nietzsche's text transforms itself from philosophical inquiry to fiction (poetic speculation, expression, or musing) and vice versa. Like
Novalis, Nietzsche's conceptual purchasing power lies in the convertibility of his metaphoric currency. In "Philosophy in the Tragic
Age of the Greeks," Nietzsche makes an important distinction between knowledge (theoretical drive) and philosophic speculation.
The first strives for certainty and proof. The second proceeds toward its goal much faster because it is accelerated by "an alien, il-
logical power—the power of fantasy" (ibid., 3: 362). Imagination
lets thought soar and, with the speed of lightning, grasps and illuminates similarities. Only later does logical reflection step in and attempt to replace "analogy with equation and synchronicity with
causality." It is interesting to note that Nietzsche divides philosophic thought into the abstract-analytic and the synthetic or the
speculative. The latter, which recalls Romanticism's cognitive metaphor of synthetic imagination, arrives at understanding in a much
less circuitous and unrestricted fashion. Thus, a workable, practical,
and liberating thought system can only be metaphorical. The figural basis of philosophical concepts offers respite from referential
constraints:

> Intellect, that master of dissimulation, is free and relieved from its usual
> service of slavery as long as it can deceive without *damaging,* and then

> it celebrates its Saturnalia. Never is it richer, prouder, more exuberant, more skilled, and daring; with creative delight it throws metaphors around and subverts the boundary points of abstractions, so that, for instance, it designates the stream as the movable way that carries man to that place where he would otherwise go. (ibid., 3: 320)

Abstractions arise as a result of an omission of differences. A leaf, for example, differs, however slightly, from every other leaf. The concept of leaf can only be formed by an omission of these differences, an omission that is entirely arbitrary (ibid., 3: 313). Concepts and abstractions suppress the multidimensional nature of phenomena and provide us with an easy shorthand and comfortable perimeters. A paradox informs the essay. On the one hand, Nietzsche reveals the totally illusory nature of concepts. On the other hand, far from wishing that conceptual world away, he envisions a freed intellect, one that, precisely because it recognizes the illusion, will be able to use it in a creative way. Intelligent survival lies in the realization that cognition is a series of re-cognitions in the free play of significations. Cognition itself is the form of appearances. Nietzsche's insight is deeply rooted in the critical sensibility of early Romanticism. "Appearance [*Schein*] is the play of representations [*Vorstellungen*]," states an entry in Schlegel's notebooks, "and play is the appearance of actions. Pleasure is the content of the impression of art; play and appearance are [its] form" (1957, 39, no. 223). *The Birth of Tragedy* provides numerous reformulations of this notebook entry.

Nietzsche's argument is firmly rooted in the affirmation of contingency. He does not criticize the Kantian notion of things in themselves beyond asserting that it is a life-sustaining and therefore necessary fiction. Without it we would be victims of a paralyzing disorientation. In fact, human beings deserve admiration for their engineering genius, since they managed to build an incredibly elaborate structure of concepts on unstable ground:

> One may here well admire human beings, who succeeded in erecting an infinitely complicated dome of concepts on a movable foundation that is at the same time on flowing water, as a powerful genius of construction. Naturally, in order to gain a foothold on such a ground it must be a construction made, as it were, from cobwebs, so fragile as to be carried away by the waves, so firm, as not to be blown apart by each wind. (1956, 3: 315)

However, Nietzsche takes the concept of atemporality inherent to scientific discourse to task. Natural laws, he argues, manifest themselves to us only in their relation to other natural laws, which in turn we know only as sums and relations (ibid., 3: 318). In a similar vein Novalis observes that "reality knows reality only through relation, form, appearance" (1960, 2: 181, no. 234). Relations and interactions can only be realized in successive time, in temporal representations. In Nietzsche's description of the long usage of metaphors rests the history of metaphor itself. Concepts freeze metaphor in time and rob it of its continuing force. Words become canonical and images lose currency. This concept of metaphor implies, in Derrida's words:

> a *continuist presupposition:* the history of a metaphor appears essentially not as a displacement with breaks as reinscriptions in a heterogeneous system, mutations, separations without origin, but rather as a progressive erosion, a regular semantic loss, an uninterrupted exhausting of the primitive meaning: an empirical abstraction without extraction from its own native soil. (1982b, 215)

What alleviates the oppression of abstraction, for Nietzsche, is the awareness that the grounds of knowledge shift to accommodate experience. An acceptance of play as an integral part of life, "the ability to continually behold a lively play" (1956, 1: 51), lends the poet his Dionysian vision. The Dionysian world represents the zone where the Apollinian world of appearances meets the limits of comprehension and crosses the border into "tragic knowledge." This knowledge is the recognition that if *Dasein* can neither provide nor sustain the unqualified truth about itself, then there is good reason to accept art as "not merely imitation of the reality of nature but rather a metaphysical supplement of the reality of nature, set beside it for its overcoming. The tragic myth, insofar as it belongs to art at all, also participates fully in this metaphysical intention of art to transfigure" (ibid., 1: 130). Nietzsche sees in tragedy the refreshing absence of representational certainty and a negation of the optimism of dialectic thought. Tragedy as an art form goes under when the epistemological conceit of Socratic philosophy advances upon the Greek stage, beginning in the work of Euripides.

The interest of Nietzsche's text for us lies in its self-consciously allegorical enactment of the problem of representation. Like Schiller's *Aesthetic Education* and Hegel's *Phenomenology, The Birth of Tragedy* unfolds to the beat of a dramatic tempo. The Apollinian, Dionysian, and the Socratic are merely convenient metaphors that imply the history of different stages (and crises) of aesthetic representation. Nietzsche states that the Apollinian and the Dionysian represent "two different worlds of art" (*zwei verschiedene Kunstwelten;* 1956, 1: 88) in the person of two dynamic and visible deities. The Apollinian world is the world of light and shine or *Schein,* a world of appearances and illusion. Here we have only the "image of appearance" substituting for reality or representations that subvert essences, whereas in the Dionysian world there is the unmediated image of the will itself. Basing his argument on Schopenhauer, Nietzsche asserts that music, the dominant form of expression in the Dionysian mode, is the universal and unmediated language of understanding. The Dionysian provides direct access into the abyss of *Dasein* and transforms the certainty of the physical world into the whirlpool of the metaphysical where no material form can be an adequate expression of the essence. The Apollinian meanwhile attempts to overcome metaphysical doubt by glorifying "the *eternity of appearance*" (ibid., 1: 93). It re-presents essences in material form, in language—as "organ and symbol of phenomena" (ibid., 1: 44)—in images, and in the plastic arts. The Dionysian desire cannot be satisfied in appearance. It has to penetrate beyond appearances to gain a glimpse into the heart of darkness that is the core of being.

Thus, both the Apollinian and the Dionysian are strategies of the subject to represent being to itself. The former does this in a mediated, controlled form. The latter plunges directly into nothingness or the abyss of being. The two modes presuppose and complement each other. To illustrate this point, Nietzsche uses the following metaphor:

> When in a forceful attempt to gaze at the sun we turn away blinded, we see dark-colored spots before our eyes, as a cure, as it were. Conversely, the bright images of the Sophoclean hero—in short, the Apollinian aspect of the mask—are necessary effects of a glance into the inside and terrors of nature; bright spots to cure eyes damaged by gruesome night, so to speak. (ibid., 1: 55)

The form of Greek tragedy itself further constitutes the Apollinian embodiment or sensible representation (*Versinnlichung*) of Dionysian knowledge (*Erkenntnisse;* ibid., 1: 53). True knowledge (*wahre*

Erkenntnis) is, as Nietzsche asserts, the insight into the terrifying
abyss of existence to which the Dionysian leads the way (ibid., 1:
48). The horror that overcomes man in this instance of knowledge
can only be made bearable in art. The *Artisten-Metaphysik* (artistic
metaphysics) that constitutes the philosophical tenor of the *Tragedy* is most clearly heard in Nietzsche's often-repeated statement
that *Dasein* can only be justified as an aesthetic phenomenon (ibid.,
1: 14, 40, 87, 131). Art, the "healing sorceress" (*heilkundige
Zauberin*), recasts the horror and absurdity of existence into representations (*Vorstellungen*) with which one can live. These representations Nietzsche names the "sublime," which is the "artistic
conquest of the horrible," and the "comic," which is the "artistic
discharge of the nausea of the absurd" (ibid., 1: 48–49).

Although the Apollinian and the Dionysian seem at first sight to
refer to diametrically opposed metaphors of lightness and darkness,
appearance and essence, physical art form and ethereal music, they
are nevertheless intimately and necessarily bound in a metaphysics
of aesthetics and of play, and play out their linked destiny in Greek
tragedy. The Socratic mode instead fully negates the vision achieved
by the joint effort of the other two. In Nietzsche's text, the Apollinian and the Dionysian faces of Greek myth are couched in
metaphors of sight and of desire for a sight beyond all seeing:

> We looked at the drama and penetrated with piercing gaze into its inner,
> animated world of motives—and yet it appeared to us as if only a par-
> able passed us by, whose most profound meaning we thought we almost
> guessed and which we wished to open like a curtain to catch a glimpse
> of the primordial picture behind it. The clearest sharpness of the picture
> did not satisfy us: for this seemed just as much to reveal as to conceal
> something, and while it urged us through its parabolic revelation to tear
> away the veil in order to uncover the mysterious background, this
> thoroughly illuminated visibility nevertheless prevented the eyes from
> penetrating deeper.
>
> Those who have never had the experience of simultaneously having
> to see and desiring to transcend all seeing will find it difficult to imagine
> how definitely and clearly these two processes coexist and are experi-
> enced in their simultaneity in the contemplation of tragic myth. (ibid.,
> 1: 129–130)

In Socratic discourse the body of the visual is reduced to the skeleton of the abstract. "To be beautiful everything must be intelligible"
is Nietzsche's summation of "*aesthetic Socraticism*" (ibid., 1: 72).

Socrates is the archetype of the "theoretical man" (ibid., 1: 99) who rests forever on the laurels of dialectic logic. Socratic philosophy accepts knowledge as the unquestionably valid representation of the idea. The greatest triumph of Kant and Schopenhauer was over the optimism embedded in the reason of logic. They were able to point to the limits of knowledge and thus raise the important question of the problem of representation. But Socrates, the arch-representative of intellectual optimism, drowns the restless spirit of the tragic in the representational conceit of the dialectic. Nietzsche's text contains frequent allusions to the tragic hero Oedipus (ibid., 1: 34, 55, 61) which underline the question of knowledge and action, the riddle of existence, and the problem of sequence and simultaneity and highlight the operative model that tragedy puts to work at all levels where it deploys itself. "Knowledge kills action" (ibid., 1: 48) and, in Oedipus's case, ends in blindness, which ironically represents that deeper insight of the Dionysian world.

The implicit presence of Oedipus in Nietzsche's text is not merely a thematic concern. In an indirect way Oedipus's famous answer to the Sphinx's question is paralleled in a radical alteration of the narrative order of *Tragedy* which collapses the distinction between sequential narration and systematic articulation. To be sure, the exchange between Oedipus and the Sphinx is not cited in Nietzsche's text. We recall that the question the Sphinx asked Oedipus was what the creature with one voice is, who has two, three, and four feet. The question presented, confused, and mixed together the three ages through which man successively travels and which he can know only sequentially: childhood when he walks on all fours, adulthood when he holds himself firmly on two legs, old age when he aids his legs with a cane. In identifying himself all at once with his young children and his old father, Oedipus, the adult with two feet, effaces the boundaries which ought to keep the father rigorously separated from the sons and the grandfather and prevent the son from replacing the father in order that each generation occupy in the course of time and in the order of the city the place assigned to it. The epistemological supremacy of the answer built on the synchronic ordering of concepts, its "excessive wisdom" (*übermäßige Weisheit*) constitutes, in effect, the tragic reversal of action and pushes Oedipus, "into a bewildering whirlpool of crime" (ibid., 1: 34). Oedipus's victory over the Sphinx makes of him not the answer which he guessed but the very question that was asked of him—a creature of confusion and chaos. The failure of Socratic understanding and the realization of the limits of logic constitute the tragic vision—which Oedipus only achieves in blindness:

> The periphery of the circle of knowledge has an infinite number of points; and while there is no way this circle could ever be fully surveyed, noble and gifted human beings nevertheless inevitably reach before the midway of their existence [*Dasein*] such boundary points on the periphery from where they stare into the impenetrable. When they see to their horror how logic coils up at these boundaries and finally bites its own tail—suddenly the new form of knowledge breaks through, *the tragic knowledge* [*die tragische Erkenntnis*] which, merely to be endured, needs art as a protection and remedy. (ibid., 1: 86–87)

The simultaneous structuring—or the form of abstraction—that lends Oedipus's answer its theoretical value can only derive from a distortion of historical sequence and the omission of difference (for example, the collapse of the distinction between child, man, and old man). In its valorization of diversity and ambiguity in face of the conceit of unity and certainty, *The Birth of Tragedy* dramatizes the questions of art and knowledge, permanence and change, and understanding and confusion as well as the riddle of the nonpresence of truth. Truth as Nietzsche sees it is a philosophical straitjacket designed by Socrates to suffocate tragic vision and kill Apollinian illusion. Nietzsche subjects any kind of discourse that exhibits an arbitrary omission of differences to a radical critique.

The story of *The Birth of Tragedy* is itself enacted in the dramatic mode. It begins, like that other dramatic narrative of Schiller, *Aesthetic Education,* upon a note of crisis, a crisis of knowledge. Through a series of flashbacks the narrative traces the crisis to its earlier manifestations. Nietzsche sets up the triad of Apollo, Dionysus, and Socrates as the structural or systematic basis for his story. The historical chronology of the appearance of these figures in Greek life is forfeited for the sake of a convenient narrative frame. In other words, time or history is not represented linearly. As Paul de Man rightly points out, "the relative weakness of the narrative becomes much less important when one realizes that the diachronic, successive structure of *The Birth of Tragedy* is in fact an illusion," for "whenever an art form is being discussed, the three modes represented by Dionysus, Apollo, and Socrates are always simultaneously present and . . . it is impossible to mention one of them without implying the others" (1979, 85). In the very performance of his own writing, Nietzsche demonstrates that representation of the past can never arrive at an epistemologically adequate form and subverts a tradition which "thinks of truth as a vertical relationship between representations and what is represented" (Rorty, 1982, 92). Nietzsche pursues the path of a horizontal truth where writing leads to more writing and interpretation to reinterpretation. This writing is not burdened with the need for an origin or a telos. As Zarasthustra's prologue states, what may be loved in man is that he is a transition (Nietzsche 1956, 2: 281).

The radical questioning of correspondences "between representations and what is represented" and between beginnings and ends as well as the questioning of the veracity of historical accounts is enacted in the rhetorical form of *Tragedy*'s self-representation. However, the text's own statements and formal self-representation should be read not only synchronically, as a self-enclosed rhetorical system, but also diachronically, as a historical response in the hermeneutic fashion to early Romanticism's unfinished agenda on the problematics of representation. After all, Nietzsche himself reads the destiny of Greek tragedy both structurally and historically. Unfortunately the deconstructionist readings of Nietzsche often detract from the philosophico-historical context in favor of a formal textual analysis. The essence of Paul de Man's reading of *Tragedy,* for example, resides in the assertion that Nietzsche's text consists of two separate statements: "metalinguistic statements about the rhetorical nature of language and . . . a rhetorical praxis that puts these statements into a question" (1979, 98). Once the second reading is subtracted from the first one, the residue of meaning can be translated into the "nonauthoritative secondary statement" which constitutes "a statement about the limitations of textual authority" (ibid., 99). In other words, if we do a rigorous reading, we discover that the text's rhetorical ploys deconstruct its own statements. De Man's reading is based on the assertion that what initially seems to be a linear, continuous narrative in Nietzsche's text depends "on discontinuous, aphoristic formulations." These formulations are not in the main text but are drawn from posthumously published notes which were written at the same time as the essay. The imaginative though arbitrary juxtaposition of these fragments with the main text leads de Man to conclude that the subversion of the continuous narrative by aphoristic fragments is "a recurrent structural principle of Nietzsche's work" (ibid., 101). That may very well be the case. However, what does the identification of a rhetorical strategy patched together from different writings and divorced from the philosophical and historical context of the text contribute to a critical understanding of Nietzsche's work?

In the beginning of his essay de Man states that in literary studies "structures of meaning" are often explained in historical rather than rhetorical terms. He finds this a "somewhat surprising," meaning naïve, "occurrence, since the historical nature of literary discourse is by no means an *a priori* established fact, whereas all literature necessarily consists of linguistic and semantic elements" (ibid., 79). It may very well be that the historical aspect of a text is not an a priori established fact, but it is just the same an inescapable fact. Literature inheres in a linguistic body, but language is not a *tabula rasa*. It is historically, politically, and ideologically not innocent. In this case the divorce of the text of the *Tragedy* from the larger problem of representation is problematic. Furthermore, the so-called main text is not necessarily linear. In these three early texts Nietzsche does not present a chronological or evolutionary reading of the history of philosophy or of Greek tragedy but rather a typological reading. The *Tragedy*'s own mode of representing itself as a dramatic diversity of voices is both an enactment of the problem it is discussing and a radical questioning of traditional intellectual history.

By virtue of what authority is methodological discourse, as opposed to literary, free from the pervasiveness of the metaphorical? How can systematic or scientific representation lay claim to accuracy and certainty? Why can epistemologies not face the ultimately metaphorical ground of their being? These are the questions Nietzsche poses in the above-mentioned texts. Although de Man does mention the significance of *Tragedy*'s historico-critical position, this insight remains somewhat marginal to the body of his argument. "Representation (mostly referred to, in this text, as *Vorstellung* or *Abbild*) functions throughout as a negative value-emphasis," writes de Man, "from a purely historical point of view, *The Birth of Tragedy* could be ordered among the preexpressionistic critical documents in which a nonrepresentational art is being prepared; this may well be the text's main function in the history of criticism" (ibid., 94–95). Indeed, Nietzsche investigates various stages of representational certainty and elusiveness in discourses ranging from Sophoclean and Aeschylean to Euripidian tragedy, from the Attic dithyramb to the Florentine opera, and from the tragic origin of music to Socratic logic. He locates the freedom of the spirit from the burdens of the representational body in the direct and immediate revelations of "the birth of tragedy from the spirit of music," as the full title goes. The essay's concern about the fragility of representation and its quest for a "nonrepresentational art" is a fitting postscript to early German Romanticism's unfinished critical agenda. The implications of this insight, however, are never fully discussed because de Man's interest remains firmly rooted in a rhetorical analysis that does not let up. De Man insists on reading this text not with an emphasis on its critical force in the context of literary history but by singling out "a simple, even mechanical inversion of the famous mistake which literature at once attracts and, rightly understood, annihilates: its suppositious power to produce integrations" (Corngold 1983, 99).

De Man's reading of the formal dimension of Nietzsche's text is micrometrically precise, and his rhetorical engagement with it is astute and tempered by irony. To be sure, the rigor of de Man's rhetorical analysis provides an invaluable insight into the complex textuality of Nietzsche's account. However, reading rhetorically need not be synonymous with reading ahistorically. Reading rhetorically is more than a confirmation that rhetoric rests on slippery ground, that it has no fixed referent. Rhetorical analysis is not an idle or self-referential exercise in pure formality. On the contrary, such analysis endeavors to understand why the use of certain tropes and topoi at certain periods empowers texts. From the ancients through the eighteenth century the object of rhetoric as the dominant form of critical analysis was the understanding of discourses designed to create certain effects and the ability to read the persuasive, dissuasive, affirmative, and negative ploys of discourse. Rhetoric understands language as discourse and is therefore engaged in its social and political context. Nietzsche's critique of representation inaugurates a form of reading that uncovers the hidden agenda of epistemological certainties in whatever guise they may appear. In "Truth and Lie" Nietzsche demonstrates how abstractions come into being as a result of the omission of differences. In order to reclaim these differences that coincide with the multiple facets of truth, the reader needs to read rhetorically, that is, with an understanding of how rhetorical protocols transform the phenomena represented in texts. In the preface, "Versuch einer Selbstkritik" (Attempt at a self-criticism), added to the *Tragedy* sixteen years after its first appearance, Nietzsche regrets having used Kant's language in his critique of knowledge, for "the problem of knowledge [*Wissenschaft*] cannot be recognized on the ground of knowledge" (1956, 1: 10). Nietzsche feels that, at the time he wrote *Tragedy,* he did not have "the courage (or immodesty?)" to allow himself to create his "individual language" (ibid., 1: 16). This then unrealized language allowed the inadequate vocabulary of nineteenth-century epistemology to govern the text. A critically informed historical context allows us to see how Nietzsche's text undertakes to correct a previous system, but in the process also creates its own impasses—often in the form of substituting one vocabulary for another.

However, in spite of the inevitable impasses any critical response encounters, Nietzsche succeeds in confronting the problems he discusses in the metalanguage of art, in the dramatic form itself. In this form the rhetoric does not constitute a second narrative level that "deconstructs" the metalinguistic, or semiotic, authority of the text, as de Man would have it. By employing the dramatic mode Nietzsche can sustain free play between the sequential and simultaneous strands of the narrative without having to abide by the principle of noncontradiction that logic demands. In scripting the problem of representation in dramatic form, Nietzsche, in the spirit of Schiller's concept of theatrical *Darstellung,* enacts a duplication of his own interpretation of rhetorical praxis. Unlike philosophical discourse, dramatic narrative can sustain more than one voice. The emancipatory force of Nietzsche's text lies not in a mere substitution of the aesthetic for the epistemic but in its insistence on constitutive differences of subjectivity and history. The multilayered rhetorical consciousness of the text and its juxtaposition of voices, metaphors, and different temporalities subverts the essentialist, undifferentiated notions of self, being, and time, and critiques the persistent re-production of these absolutes in theoretical thought.

From the Margins of Representation: Views and Reviews

Rhetorical criticism in a limited deconstructionist mode, without recourse to a critical genealogy, runs the risk of turning into its own parody. It inevitably slips away from its crucial philosophico-historical location. It allows members of the resistance (to theory) to view rhetorical analysis, often impatiently or irritably, as a simplistic acknowledgment of the slippage of language, the vicious circle of the indeterminacy of meaning, and the inevitability of misreading. When modern philosophers and historians such as Jacques Derrida, Richard Rorty, Hayden White, Michel Foucault, and Dominic LaCapra claim that all knowledge is textual, that text (like myth in Vico, Hölderlin, or Schelling) is prior to all reality, they are not interested in overthrowing established metaphysical regimes but rather suggest in a Nietzschean spirit that the equation between truth and word is neither definitive nor resolvable.

In the preceding chapters I have tried to juxtapose Romantic formulations with their modern articulations and reconceptualize the latter in the context of the former. In what follows I will briefly point to some unexpected liaisons of certain contemporary theoretical concerns with the problems already discussed. This short visit to modern critical sites is not meant to be a *tour de horizont.* Rather, my discussion is intended as a reminder that the question of representation is inscribed onto every landmark of the contemporary critical landscape. In other words, the question of the nature of truth and reality, the representation of reality, the critique of representation, and the implication of representation in our understanding of temporality and alterity inform, explicitly or implicitly, all modern forms of textual analysis. Sometimes it appears that different critical voices tend to harmonize in strange ways. However, upon closer examination, we often realize that these strange bedfellows in fact share a family history. For example, the odd rapport between pragmatism, as represented in the work of Willard Quine and later Richard Rorty, and deconstruction is based on a shared genealogy that can be traced back to the hermeneutic bias of Romantic idealism. Rorty maintains that the concept of an ideal correspondence between being and representation and the infinite search for the perfect "mirror of nature" by more and more refined methods are the burdens of traditional philosophy:

> The picture that holds traditional philosophy captive is that of the mind as a great mirror, containing various representations—some accurate, some not—and capable of being studied by pure, nonempirical methods. Without the notion of the mind as mirror, the notion of knowledge as accuracy of representation would not have suggested itself. Without this

latter notion, the strategy common to Descartes and Kant—getting more accurate representations by inspecting, repairing, and polishing the mirror, so to speak—would not have made sense. (1979, 12)

Nietzsche's critique of Kantian metaphysics has endeavored to expose the assumed certainty of a priori principles as heuristic fictions. The apparent regularity and verifiability of natural processes, he claims, are human constructs imposed by our imagination on unsuspecting nature. More recently, in a celebrated article, "Two Dogmas of Empiricism," Willard Quine takes on the myth of a priori categories embedded in metaphysical thought. Quine contests the Kantian distinction between analytic statements that attribute to their subject "no more than is already conceptually contained in the subject" and synthetic statements "grounded in fact" (1969, 399, 398). He maintains that the distinction between analytic and synthetic propositions does not hold water, for it fails to account for the constantly shifting relation between experience, knowledge, and apparent self-evidence:

> The totality of our so-called knowledge or beliefs, from the most casual matters of geography and history to the profoundest laws of atomic physics and even of pure mathematics and logic, is a man-made fabric which impinges on experience only along the edges. Or, to change the figure, total science is like a field of force whose boundary conditions are experience. A conflict with experience at the periphery occasions readjustments in the interior of the field. Truth values have to be redistributed over some of our statements. Re-evaluation of some statements entails re-evaluation of others, because of their logical interconnections—the logical laws being in turn simply certain further statements of the system, certain further elements of the field. (ibid., 413)

Quine asserts that the changes on the periphery, which constitute major shifts in experience, can always trigger complicated readjustments of truth values which make up the center and as such are considered necessary a priori truths. But if the edge of the system is to be kept squared with experience and the center with its elaborate fictions has to follow suit, then the insistence on "a boundary between synthetic statements, which hold contingently on experience, and analytic statements which hold come what may" borders on absurdity (ibid., 414). Quine states that "our talk of external things" links up for practical purposes with the objects of the outside world and our experience of the world, but the various modes of this interaction with the world cannot be confined to a priori categories: "Each man is given a scientific heritage plus a continuing barrage of sensory stimulation, and the considerations which guide him in warping his scientific heritage to fit his continuing sensory promptings are, where rational, pragmatic" (ibid., 417).

Quine's pragmatic man rewrites, in the fashion of Thomas Kuhn's paradigm shift, his "scientific heritage" to meet the demands of the changing world of experience. Quine's relentless attempt to exorcise the spirit of a covert metaphysics still haunting the domain of analytic thought leads him to a deconstructive critique of language that rejects any ultimate concept or incarnated meaning embedded in it. The modern mission to break away from the hold of logocentric thought makes strange bedfellows of critics with differing persuasions, who celebrate in their own way the return of Nietzsche's restless, questioning spirit. They appear united in their common rejection of what Richard Rorty calls "the assumption that all contributions to a given discourse are commensurable," that is, "able to be brought under a set of rules which tell us how rational agreement can be reached on what would settle the issue on every point where statements seem to conflict" (1979, 316). However, although deconstructive criticism has led Nietzsche's example to its utmost consequences and provided the impetus for a total reevaluation of interpretive theory and praxis, it has also given rise in its not so lucid moments to a bizarre totalitarian regime in the domain of textuality by forcing language to the point of implicit reversal or a confession of its own epistemological failure.

The high-handed critique of rhetorical ploys language activates raises the question whether any form of discourse, even the most methodological, is free of the ambiguity of the figural. It seems that deconstructive readings question the validity of synthetic and contingent truths and propositions, since these can be shown to be contradictory at certain points in their history. The epistemological ground of all synthetic propositions, which constitute the basis of almost every form of human utterance, can be taken to task, since such propositions are merely accounts of experience and not necessary, logical, or consistent truths. However, analytic judgments would resist deconstructive attack, since they are based on the Kantian "law of contradiction," that is, the predicate of an affirmative analytic judgment is already contained in the concept of the subject, and the truth of the predicate in relation to its subject cannot be denied without contradiction. The meaning of such analytic propositions as "Immanuel Kant is Immanuel Kant" or "either the sun is shining in Toledo or the sun is not shining in Toledo" holds true under all conditions, in the first sentence by virtue of the identity of a = a, and in the second by the tautology, "either *a* or not *a*." One question that Kant based on his prior categorization of a priori and a posteriori forms of knowledge was whether a priori synthetic propositions were possible. If so we would have to assume the existence of certain propositions that are necessarily true and also expand our knowledge of the world, that is, they would be true independent of experience but confirmed by it. Kant's distinctions between these terms have been widely accepted and applied but have also given rise to many disputes, particularly in the domain of language philosophy as Quine demonstrates. The most rigorous deconstructive readings seem to ignore the complicated lines of demarcation between different kinds of propositions and betray a predilection for a form of negative theology, that is, a desire to reduce the flesh of the text to its mere analytic bones. A case in point is de Man's reading of Nietzsche's "Truth and Lie" in the "Rhetoric of Tropes" which implicitly asserts that there is a truth that the text fails to uncover and that it hides this failure behind a series of rhetorical masks. These masks keep truth in a state of suspended indeterminacy. Moments of rhetorical insight are never synthesized for understanding. This discontinuity of cognitive moments, in other words, the rejection of the validity of synthetic moments characterizes for de Man the tropes of allegory and irony:

> The act of irony ... reveals the existence of a temporality that is definitely not organic, in that it relates to its source only in terms of distance and difference and allows for no end, no totality. Irony divides the flow of temporal experience into a past that is pure mystification and a future that remains harassed forever by a relapse within the inauthentic. It can know this inauthenticity but can never overcome it. It can only restate and repeat it on an increasingly conscious level, but it remains endlessly caught in the impossibility of making this knowledge applicable to the empirical world. It dissolves in the narrowing spiral of a linguistic sign that becomes more and more remote from its meaning, and it can find no escape from this spiral. The temporal void that it reveals is the same void we encountered when we found allegory always implying an unreachable anteriority. Allegory and irony are thus linked in their common discovery of a truly temporal predicament. ([1969] 1983, 222)

We have seen that Novalis understands the allegorical mode in terms of a synthetic operation that progressed by an open-ended dynamic of associations in time. Here the object and its representation do not coincide, but the temporality which subsumed the irreducible gap between the two became human time in narration, in language. In Romantic criticism allegory and irony are not the hapless objects of a radical scepticism but markers of infinite progressivity. Time as human time or poeticized time both constructs and deconstructs reality. I think that the strength of the Romantic notions of irony and allegory lies in their awareness and open assertion of the necessity of both analytic and synthetic procedures in the attempt to account for the flux of experience. The Romantic concept of representation subsumes the conflicting interests of synthetic production as a mode of symbol making and analytic imagination as an agent of inquiry. Like irony, reason deploys a progressive dialectic that does not rest in synthesis: "Reason is an *eternal* determination by a never-ending separation and combination" (Schlegel 1958, 18: 304, no. 1,318). Synthesis, itself, is "only a link in the chain of *analysis* (Thesis, Antithesis, Synthesis)" (ibid., 18: 354, no. 404). Irony and reason do not negate but mimic each other. Schlegel asserts that irony deploys a genuine dialectic that prevents synthesis from becoming fixed or sedimented truth. By mediating between the poles of analytic and synthetic imagination, irony dissolves the Kantian tension between necessity and freedom: "The actual *dialectic* has always been in play around necessity and freedom, the highest good, etc. Here *irony* is one and all" (ibid., 18: 393; no. 678).

The rejection of any structuring, or synthetic, consciousness characteristic of deconstructive criticism is problematic because it implies analysis without synthesis. Derrida originally defined *déconstruction* as "simply a question of (and this is a necessity of criticism in the classical sense of the word) being alert to the implications, to the historical sedimentation of the language which we use." Derrida sees the deconstructive enterprise as "the necessity of scientific work in the classical sense," and is not sympathetic toward the position that renounces "the radicality of a critical work under the pretext that it risks the sterilization of science, humanity, progress, the origin of meaning, etc." He believes that "the risk of sterility and of sterilization has always been the price of lucidity" (1972, 271).

In an essay called "Philosophical Arguments," Gilbert Ryle, like Derrida, defends the position that unpacking the lost or hidden contents of verbal assumptions and pressing them to the point where they collapse under the tension of their own unacknowledged contradictions constitutes a scientific procedure. He compares the rigor of this philosophical exercise to the performance of a structural engineer who tests the physical limits of his material for user safety:

> Engineers stretch, twist, compress and batter bits of metal until they collapse, but it is just by such tests that they determine the strains which the metal will withstand. In somewhat the same way, philosophical arguments bring out the logical powers of the ideas under investigation, by fixing the precise forms of logical mishandling under which they refuse to work. (1967, 2: 492)

Undoubtedly, scientific pursuits require analytic rigor. As long as such rigor is employed in the service of a self-reflexive critical praxis, reading can become a point of constructive intervention in social life. However, a strategy for critical reading like deconstruction that started out as a genuinely sincere attempt to create an awareness of the burden of metaphysical thought, the referential indeterminacy of language, and the metaphorical and contingent basis of methodological discourse can all too easily get caught in a web of endless and self-defeating demystification. The critical practice of German Romanticism has shown us that a critique of representation cannot be undertaken to negate or transcend representation but to understand why certain models, analogies, and heuristic fictions are valorized at certain periods while others are discredited. Romantic hermeneutics, which is the conceptual ground of modern reception theory, undertook the task of demonstrating that at any given historical moment there is a socially constructed repertoire of regulative metaphors or scientific traditions within whose range the typical reader understands and interprets texts. In its best moments, deconstructive criticism has investigated the hidden agenda of ideologically constructed differences and essentialist notions of gender, race, and class embedded in modern forms of representation. It has questioned the stubborn reproduction of these concepts and pointed to the broader ethical implications of that reproduction. At its worst, however, deconstruction has performed an ultimately futile and sterile analysis of linguistic constructs which has implicitly espoused a negative theology. In other words, it has assumed that rhetorical ploys mask the truth of the text, a truth which can be claimed by unmasking such ploys by the appropriate methodological analysis.

The critical insights of German Romanticism have shown that all truths are representational and that, furthermore, these representations are historically situated and coercive. Neither literary fiction nor scientific theory can lay claim to being an exact representation of the phenomenal world. In our century this view has been borne out by the revolutionary assertions of quantum physics and relativity theory.[5] Thomas Kuhn and Paul Feyerabend, among others, have shown that scientific truths are representations of contingent conceptualizations and not of an atemporal reality. Many fictions of science operate not on a mimetic but on a pragmatic principle. Quine, for example, cites the example of irrational numbers that have no external, "real life" referents; they are not "mirrors of nature," but simply fictions designed to "simplify our treatment of experience":

> Imagine for the sake of analogy, that we are given the rational numbers. We develop an algebraic theory for reasoning about them, but we find it inconveniently complex, because certain functions such as square root lack values for some arguments. Then it is discovered that the rules of our algebra can be much simplified by conceptually augmenting our ontology with some mythical entities, to be called irrational numbers. All we continue to be really interested in, first and last, are rational numbers; but we find that we can commonly get from one law about rational numbers to another much more quickly and simply by pretending that the irrational numbers are there too. (1969, 415)

In an insightful article on the representational dilemma of modern art and science, Valerie Greenberg recalls that Francis Bacon in his *Novum organum* (1620) had asserted that all perceptions of the mind refer not to the universe but to humans themselves and that their minds resemble "uneven mirrors" that impose their own properties on objects (1989, 49). The prevailing outlook in twentieth-century physics has been that the task of physics is not to determine ideal correspondences between so-called reality and theory but infinitely better approximations. Science, too, has established the impossibility of total or direct representation. The entities modern physics deals with cannot often be observed directly. For example, nobody has ever seen an electron; its presence can only be inferred "from various kinds of observed phenomena. Similarly one cannot see gravitational fields, or the curvature of space-time" (Morris 1987, 192). They are only understood as mathematical constructs or representational models. "Scientific theory," argues philosopher Mary Hesse, "is just one of the ways in which human beings have sought to make sense of their world by constructing schemas, models, metaphors, and myths" ("Does Ideology Stop . . .?"; 1989, 24). Heisenberg's Uncertainty Relation, furthermore, has implied that "there is no way to measure a system without interacting with it, and no way to interact with it without disturbing it. The observer and the system, or as Heisenberg has occasionally said, the subject and the object, are thus seen as an inseparable whole that cannot be subdivided without introducing the indeterminacy specified by the Uncertainty Relation" (Hayles 1984, 51). Once more we are in the world of Romantic idealism, where the object posited becomes the self-representation of the subject. Here Friedrich Schlegel's "synthetic author" creates a living reader with whom the author enters the circle of "sympoesy," in other words, establishes interactive reading. The act of reading, "whether it is reading the behavior of matter or energy in an experiment or reading a picture or a printed text, is an act of restructuring and transforming in the mind" (Greenberg 1989, 50). In brief, it is an act of the productive imagination that oversees both production and reproduction.

Representation is a productive activity. In Heidegger's words, for example, being (*Seiende*) in its totality can only be realized when posited by the "representing-producing human being" (*vorstellend-herstellenden Menschen;* 1975–, 5: 89). Walter Benjamin maintains that the labor of representation should be understood "in the sense of chemistry . . . as the production of a material by a certain process to which others are subject" (1972–, 1.1: 109). Novalis negotiates the claims of poetic synthesis and critical analysis, which constitute operative principles of the representational act, in scientific illustrations. The formation of a chemical compound, for example, is analogous to the production of metaphor. A chemist knows that "by a true mixture a *third* [element] appears which corresponds to the other two but is more than either taken individually" (1960, 2: 666–667). Novalis repeatedly points out that his philosophical praxis is predicated on the model of chemistry which "is made up of both analysis and synthesis." Facing the travails of representa-

ion, he travels "the analytic and the synthetic paths simultaneously" yet puts an extra effort in refining "the synthetic *categories*"
ibid., 2: 192, no. 272), a task both Kant and Fichte left incomplete.
For the most part Novalis locates the dialectic of understanding in
the synthetic operation. This process is considerably more difficult
than analysis: "Integration is much more difficult than differentiation. *In relation to physics* and philosophy" (ibid., 3: 127). This
is, of course, also true of chemistry, where the difficulty of producing a synthetic element under laboratory conditions far exceeds that
of a chemical analysis. Novalis applies the scientific metaphors of
synthesis and analysis to the poetic realm by implying that constructing poems is more difficult than analyzing them and that com-
petent criticism presupposes the ability to write poetry: "Whoever
cannot make poems, can only judge them negatively" (ibid., 2: 534,
no. 35). Poetic representation operates mostly by the rules of synthesis, by associating, re-membering, and compounding. The synthetic schema governs the central conceptual model in poetic and
scientific representation.[6]

In a similar vein Schlegel observes that the philosophical process
is a "chemical" one, in other words, it fulfills itself in an ongoing
act of mixing and dissolving, synthesizing and analyzing, or producing and criticizing. The trope that negotiates this dialectic is irony.
The following entry in the *Athenäum* sums up the various configurations of the process:

> Philosophy too is the result of two conflicting forces, of poetry and
> praxis. Where these two interpenetrate completely and fuse into one,
> there philosophy comes into being; and when philosophy breaks up, it
> becomes mythology or throws itself back into life. The Greek wisdom
> was constituted in poetry and law. Some assume that the highest form
> of philosophy may once again become poetry; and in fact it is a common
> experience that ordinary souls begin to philosophize in their own fash-
> ion only after they have stopped living. I believe that Schelling's original
> contribution is his enhanced representation of this chemical process of
> philosophizing, the clarification of its dynamic laws wherever possible,
> and the classification of philosophy—which must always organize and
> disorganize itself anew—into its living fundaments and the determina-
> tion of its origins. (1958, 2: 216, no. 304)

Both synthesis and analysis are thus an integral part of the representational act. Whereas the first orders the contents of repre-

Afterword

> Metaphysics founds an age by giving it the basis of its
> structure through a certain interpretation of being and
> a certain understanding of truth. This basis reigns in all
> phenomena that define the age. Conversely, in order to
> adequately reflect on these phenomena, their metaphys-
> ical basis must be apprehended in them. Reflection is the
> courage to question most rigorously the truth of our
> own assumptions and the domain of our own objectives.
>
> Heidegger, "The Age of the World Picture"

The lesson of Romanticism's critical agenda emphatically illustrates
that the equation between representation on the one hand and the
truth of being and time on the other is inherently unresolvable. Our
perceptions of the universe, of the unknown, of otherness are all
governed not by a utopic or atemporal logic of nature but by our
own sphere of understanding which is historical, that is, conditioned by a particular scientific, moral, or aesthetic heritage and
thus subject to change. At a time when the pervasive power of representation—audio, visual, journalistic, literary—asserts itself daily
in our discursive and institutional lives, an understanding of how
texts and images mediate so-called facts should be an important
item of discussion on our cultural agenda. We need to have a better
understanding of why certain tropes and topoi become fashionable
expressions of social and political reality at critical historical junc-
tions. Postmodern discourse on the whole has defined its task as a
confrontation with representation and an acknowledgment of the
demise of master narratives on knowledge and culture as canonical
truths.[1] The critical legacy of Jena Romanticism reminds us that the
conditions and limits of knowledge and ethics are governed by the
power of metaphor. The authors of the Romantic agenda have all
along known that

> it is a mistake . . . to think of linguistic usage as literalistic in its main
> body and metaphorical in its trimming. Metaphor or something like it
> governs both the growth of language and our acquisition of it. Cognitive
> discourse at its most drily literal is largely a refinement rather charac-
> teristic of the neatly worked inner stretches of science. It is an open space

in the tropical jungle, created by clearing tropes away. (Quine 1981
188–189)

It is probably correct to assume that, in a technologically advanced society, culture is created by the mass media and the images
they deploy. Today, the state-of-the-art technology is accountable
for the ubiquitous reign of linguistic and visual representation. In
"Die Zeit des Weltbildes" (The age of the world picture) Heidegger establishes the priority of representation (*Vorstellen*) as objectification of presence in the discourse of modern science and culture
providing an appropriate postscript to the Romantic project. This
essay also provides an incisive analysis of the phenomena that mark
the transition to the modern age. Heidegger lists these phenomena
as science (*Wissenschaft*), machine technology, the movement of art
into the realm of aesthetics, the view of human activity as culture,
and the loss of gods, or what he calls "*Entgötterung*." The question
he poses is what notion of truth lies at the foundation of these regulative metaphors of the modern age. In order to answer it, Heidegger singles out the issue of science and explores the modern trans-
formations in the nature of this discourse. He locates the essence
of modern science in research and investigates the conceptual stages
of scientific procedure. All processes of life when incorporated into
the body of human knowledge have to be transformed into representation (*Vorstellung*). Throughout the essay Heidegger stresses
the literal meaning of *Vorstellung* as setting before oneself and, for
this purpose, often hyphenates it as *vor-stellen*. In this way, he invests the word with a visible (or sensible) conceptuality.

The mathematical sciences demand exactitude in representation.
But the humanistic sciences (*Geisteswissenschaften*) "must necessarily be inexact precisely in order to be rigorous. A living thing
can indeed also be perceived as a spatiotemporal magnitude of motion, but then it is no longer apprehended as living" (Heidegger
1975–, 5: 79). This inexactitude, or the noncoincidence of representation and its object, is not a shortcoming but inherent in the nature
of all sciences concerned with life whose essential characteristic is
change. If the sphere of experience is to be objectified, then the
methodology used to this end has to represent "the changeable in
its changing" (*das Veränderliche in seiner Veränderung*; ibid., 5:
80). It is only in confrontation with the "incessant-otherness of
change" (*Immer-Anderen der Veränderung*) that the significance of

the particular event is understood. The interaction with otherness is also the condition of self-understanding and self-representation. The sphere of objects is brought into the sphere of representation through methodology that in turn is based on explanation. And explanation mediates between the known and the unknown. Just as Novalis has defined the task of Romantic hermeneutics as "making an object strange yet known and alluring" (1960, 3: 685, no. 668), Heidegger states that explanation "establishes an unknown by means of a known, and at the same time it verifies that known by means of that unknown" (1975–, 5: 80).

It follows that all research and methodology are intimately linked to the form of representation by which phenomena are transformed into knowledge. The objectification of being is fulfilled only in representation, and "science becomes research when and only when truth presents itself as the certainty of representation" (ibid., 5: 87). Heidegger states that he undertakes the investigation into the nature of modern science in order to understand its "metaphysical ground" (ibid., 5: 86). This metaphysical ground is the index of a particular epoch which is reflected in its "world picture" (*Weltbild*). And what is the world picture of the modern age? Heidegger suggests that posing this very question may well constitute the essence of modern consciousness. In other words, to inquire after the world picture is in itself an act of representation. The transition to modernity, argues Heidegger, did not come about merely by the replacement of a medieval world picture by a modern one but rather by the transformation of the world itself into a picture: "The fundamental event of the modern age is the conquest of the world as picture" (ibid., 5: 94). This picture, however, is no longer a copy or an imitation of the world: "The word picture [*Bild*] now means formed image [*Gebild*] produced through representing [*des vorstellenden Herstellens*]." The modern subject creates reality in representation. In other words, the world exists through the subject who produces (*herstellen*) the world by reproducing it in representation (*Vorstellen*). By a flick of the hand images of remote worlds materialize before our very eyes, worlds that are "objectified" in media representations. Access to the inaccessible, the distant, the exotic, the forgotten, or the erased is now universally possible through modern technology that can endlessly mediate, reproduce, and reconstruct images.

Heidegger's essay, which is a self-declared investigation of the

essential nature of modern science, reduplicates the insight of German Romanticism's fascination with representation and prefigures
Foucault's determination of modernity's starting point. Romantic
irony was a self-conscious reflection on the contingent nature of
"representational reality." Heidegger reminds us that all our institu-
tionally sanctioned and legitimized knowledge is representational.
Nowadays, our institutions of literary criticism see themselves as
facing yet another crisis of representation and under implicit attack
by other supposedly more rigorous disciplines for the ivory-tower
mentality of their pursuits. A genuine understanding of the role of
representation can explain how scientific research, grant alloca-
tions, conferences, and other operations of academic life engage in
practices of appropriative representation in their task of constructing histories, geographies, and cultures of otherness. A rhetorically
informed critique of representational regimes can lead to a recognition of how second-hand images and irresponsible depictions of
other cultures dictate social politics and governmental policy. "The
awareness of Near and Far Eastern literatures that characterized the
nineteenth and early twentieth centuries has been lost, at a time
when it is even more important to understand them," writes critic
Wallace Martin:

> We have for too long defined our culture through an imaginary anti-
> thesis to our "other"—those peoples who occasionally impinge on
> Western Civilization courses and whose caricatures inhabit the press.
> While social scientists and governments are amassing facts and creating
> policies to deal with our recalcitrant others, distinguished critics might
> show that literature can play a crucial role in encouraging a humility
> and humanity more appropriate to self-understanding. (Martin 1983,
> xxxvii)

In her talk at the twenty-fifth annual Nobel Conference held
at the Gustavus Adolphus College, philosopher Sandra Harding
maintained that "value-free research," that is, science free of representational prejudices of certain dominant groups, "is a delusion"
("Does Ideology Stop . . . ?" 1989, 24E). The institutional history of
academic disciplines shows how scientific discourse is conditioned
by the persuasiveness of the images we are subjected to. "We need
a visible past, a visible continuum, a visible myth of origin to reas-
sure us as to our ends," notes Jean Baudrillard (1983, 19). As Hesse
stated at the abovementioned conference, scientific theory itself "is

a particular kind of myth that answers to our practical purposes with regard to nature. It often functions, as myths do, as persuasive rhetoric for moral and political purposes" (ibid.). Today, this "persuasive rhetoric" of science lacks critical tools to reassess its self-declared status as the master discourse. It names, classifies, distances, and masters its object. On the other hand, as Roland Barthes has cogently argued, the object of criticism cannot be possessed. What the critic analyzes is language itself, not its object. Barthes maintains that the irreducible gap between criticism and object "allows criticism to develop precisely what is lacking in science . . . *irony.*" Irony puts language to test in and through language. It may be "the only serious form of discourse which remains available to criticism so long as the status of science and language is not clearly established—which seems to be still the case today" (1987, 84–90). We may here recall that Schlegel considered irony the "duty" of any philosophy whose status as either system or history was not clearly established (1958, 18: 86, no. 678). Indeed, Romantic irony articulated the possibility of the coexistence of understanding and the challenge to understanding through the ability to manipulate symbols. This, in turn, made possible the move beyond the narrowly defined rational uses of language to infinite generations of meaning.

The critical enterprise of early German Romanticism—as outlined in the *Athenäum,* university lectures, drafts of the universal encyclopedia project, and miscellaneous fragments—underlines how fiction and historiography as well as existing and future disciplines (e.g., chemistry, geology, philology, ethnology, archaeology, psychology) define and explain our experience of time and reality through narrative configurations. The unfinished agenda of Jena Romanticism reminds us that the kind of literary criticism which reflects on the constitution of reality in representational constructs need not be a merely self-referential enterprise. We can retrieve from it many valuable insights for a self-reflexive discourse and mark it as the site for intervention in social processes. A critical hermeneutics does not operate at the level of pure meaning, it participates in history and answers to its iterative crises.

Notes

Chapter 1: Introduction

1. For a detailed history of these journals, see Ernst Behler 1983.

2. A varying cast of characters became involved with the group at one point or another either by acquaintance or through correspondence. Among these were Tieck's brother-in-law, linguist Bernhardi; W. H. Wackenroder, the author of the ultimate Romantic tale, *Die Herzergießungen eines kunstliebenden Klosterbruders* (The heartfelt outpourings of an art-loving friar); poet-critic Jean Paul; philosopher Fichte; poetess Sophie Mereau; her husband Clemens Brentano; Brentano's sister Bettina, who later married Achim von Arnim; and August Ludwig Hülsen, a writer and educator much admired by Friedrich Schlegel.

3. Also in Novalis 1960, 2: 423, no. 26. This fragment was included in Novalis's collection of fragments, *Blüthenstaub* (Pollen).

4. "The proposition *A is A* (or A = A, since that is the meaning of the logical copula) is accepted by everyone without a doubt: it is admitted to be totally certain and confirmed" (Fichte 1962–, 1.2: 256).

5. "In the course of a life dedicated to letters and (at times) to metaphysical perplexity, I have glimpsed or foreseen a refutation of time, in which I myself do not believe, but which regularly visits me at night and in the weary twilight with the illusory force of an axiom" (Borges 1964, 218).

6. "All the classical poetical genres have now become ridiculous in their strict purity" (Schlegel 1958, 2: 154, no. 60).

Chapter 2: From Transcendental Philosophy to Transcendental Poetry

1. Cf. Gilles Deleuze (1984, 14): "The fundamental idea of what Kant calls his 'Copernican Revolution' is the following: substituting the principle of a *necessary* submission of object to subject for the idea of a harmony between subject and object (*final* accord). The essential discovery is that the faculty of knowledge is legislative. . . . The rational being thus discovers that he has new powers. The first thing that the Copernican Revolution teaches us is that it is we who are giving the orders."

2. In *Der Begriff der Kunstkritik in der deutschen Romantik,* Walter Benjamin argues that the theoretical basis of Fichte's system could not tolerate the notion of endlessness. Yet reflection contains two moments: immediacy and endlessness. The Romantics share Fichte's interest in the direct and immediate consciousness of knowledge. In this self-consciousness, intuition and thought, subject and object, coincide. In Fichte, however, the dialectical relationship of subject and object delimits reflection. The Romantic "cult of the endless" rejects this concept of limited reflection. For the Romantic imagination limited reflection means merely the finite form of the work of art; there is no limit to the relations between the forms of poetry (1.1: 25).

3. In this instance "the term *darstellen* quite appropriately expresses that the relationship entails sameness fully as much as otherness since anything representative of another can take its place but is different nonetheless" (Molnár 1987, 30).

4. Earlier in the discussion Novalis had stated that the self had "hieroglyphic power" (1960, 2: 107, no. 6). In other words, the self represents itself by reproducing itself in images and writing.

5. I have, of course, oversimplified Barthes's complex and very important argument to highlight its correspondences to Novalis's more straightforward scheme.

6. Barthes proposes that the third term in myth, which we call sign in language, be named the signification, that the first term (the signifier) be called the form and the second term (the signified) the concept. Thus, whereas in the first order of signification, language, the relation of the signifier to the signified generates the sign, in the second order of signification, myth, the relation of the form to the concept yields signification.

7. Here Schiller uses the Fichtean term *Wechselwirkung.*

8. See Derrida 1972, 248: "One could perhaps say that the movement of any archaeology, like that of any eschatology, is an accomplice of this reduction of the structurality of structure and always attempts to conceive of structure from the basis of a full presence which is out of play." Derrida further states that "the Nietzschean critique of metaphysics" countered "the concepts of being and truth" with those of "play, interpretation, and sign" (ibid., 250).

9. In contrast to Kant's schema the faculties in Schiller's schema have less classified and more diversified legislative functions.

Chapter 3: Representation and History

1. Similarly, Paul Ricoeur, in the three volumes of *Temps et récit* (Time and narrative; 1983–1985) demonstrates how the experience of time is shaped and configured in narrative.

2. Leopold von Ranke, one of the more influential modern historians, wrote in no uncertain terms in the prologue to his *Geschichten der romanischen und germanischen Völker*: "To history has been assigned the office of judging the past, of instructing the present for the benefit of future ages. To such high offices this work does not aspire: It wants only to show what actually happened [*wie es eigentlich gewesen*]" (Stern 1957, 57). Ranke's contemporary Johann Gustav Droysen, who taught at the University of Berlin, questioned the methodological basis of his discipline, that is, the concept of transmission of sources (*Quellenüberlieferung*) which he judged to be an extremely positivistic procedure. In his lectures Droysen (1971) stressed that the so-called objective facts, such as battles and uprisings, were only evidence of human will and activity compressed in imagination and recorded as representation.

3. Most of this work was written in 1799 but not published, except for a few extracts, until 1826. See Novalis 1960, 3: 507–524.

4. Heine's aforementioned essay, *Die romantische Schule,* is a passionate critique of what he considers to be the conservative ideology of German Romanticism embedded in the longing for an age that has outlived its historical relevance. Heine sees in the Romantic recovery of a medieval-world picture a denial to face the demands of the modern age. For a critical examination of this essay and its ties to Romanticism's own strategies of representation, see Seyhan 1989.

5. Cf. Verene 1985. Donald Phillip Verene portrays Hegel not merely as a philosopher with a metaphorical imagination but also as a master of figurative representation who provided the history of philosophy with images of the topsy-turvy world, the unhappy consciousness, the beautiful soul, and the master and the slave, among others.

6. For an extensive discussion of the distinction between symbol and allegory in German Romanticism, see Todorov 1982, 198–221.

7. "Whereas in the symbol the transfigured face of nature is fleetingly revealed in the light of redemption through the idealization of destruction, in allegory the observer is confronted with the *facies hippocratica* of history as a paralyzed, primordial landscape" (Benjamin 1972, 1.1: 343).

8. See, for example, Haslinger 1981, 153.

9. "The essence of the novel is the chaotic form—arabesque, *Märchen* [fairy tale]" (Schlegel 1957, 180, no. 1804).

10. Cf. Brown: "The arabesque is praised . . . as an allophatic remedy for the stiffness of recent writing" (1979, 95).

11. See also Novalis, "The ancients are *products of the future and of prehistory* [*Vorzeit*]" (1960, 3: 248, no. 52).

12. In this context, it is interesting that Sigmund Freud often refers to the analogy between archaeology and psychoanalysis. He interprets the excavation of memory relics archaeologically. The archaeologist reconstructs

the image of the past from unearthed material artifacts, the psychoanalyst from verbalized memories uncovered in the process of analysis. See Freud 1950, 16: 45–47.

13. In 1802 Schlegel undertook extensive research in Provençal manuscripts and Oriental studies. In 1803 he began his study of Sanskrit in Paris under Alexander Hamilton, a famed Sanskrit scholar.

14. For a brief and well-presented discussion of the Indian imagistic character see Diana L. Eck 1985.

15. See for examples Novalis 1960, 3: 278 and 3: 429.

Chapter 4: Representation and Criticism

1. See, for example, Peter Szondi, who maintains that the early Romantic notion of the self is understood as one which posits itself as an object of its own reflection. Szondi reformulates Kant's critical philosophy in terms of poetic practice: "Schlegel calls for a poetry which writes poetically about itself along with its object, which makes itself its own object, and which, through this inner division into subject and object, is doubly empowered and becomes a poetry of poetry" (1964, 11).

2. See also Schlegel 1958, 18: 265, no. 852: "Books and letters are admittedly only signs of memory, not of external perceptions but rather of all that is eternal in us."

3. See, for example, Schlegel: "A critical mimus most romanticize, in fact, almost become a novel [itself]" (1957, 77, no. 641).

4. See Fragment no. 116 in the *Athenäum* (1958, 2: 182):

Romantic poetry is a progressive, universal poetry. Its aim is not merely to unite all the separate genres of poetry and relate poetry to philosophy and rhetoric. It desires to and should mix and fuse poetry and prose, originality and criticism, the poetry of art and the poetry of nature; and make poetry lively and sociable, and life and society poetical; poeticize wit and fill and saturate art forms with every kind of solid formative material and animate them by impulses of humor. It embraces everything that is purely poetic, from the greatest systems of art which themselves contain several systems, to the sigh, the kiss that the poeticizing child whispers in artless song.

5. The vision that launched this project was Kant's conception of a universal encyclopedia. Kant saw the task of this encyclopedia as determining the position of any science in the universal framework of knowledge and expressed the necessity for a total knowledge of the world of experience so that human cognition would not merely be an aggregate of perceptions but would constitute a system.

6. Similarly, in *Die Christenheit oder Europa* Novalis attacks "philology," which as a merely methodical analysis of texts has brought about the loss of religious sense in Protestant Bible criticism.

7. First published in 1928 by Josef Körner in *Logos* 17: 1–66, they are reprinted in Schlegel 1958, 16: 33–81.

8. Schleiermacher's lectures on dialectics date from 1814 (Schleiermacher 1903).

9. See, for example, Paul de Man: "One of the most striking characteristics of literary semiology today . . . is the use of grammatical (especially syntactical) structures conjointly with rhetorical structures, without apparent awareness of a possible discrepancy between them" (1979, 6).

10. In his *Second Introduction to the Theory of Knowledge* Fichte, for example, threatens to interpret Kant "according to the spirit" of his philosophy, if interpretation according to the letter fails to bring forth results.

Chapter 5: The Site of Instruction: Literary Tales

1. Three fairly recent works in English, Alice Kuzniar's *Delayed Endings: Nonclosure in Novalis and Hölderlin* (1987), Géza von Molnár's *Romantic Vision, Ethical Context: Novalis and Artistic Autonomy* (1987), and Kristin Pfefferkorn's *Novalis: A Romantic's Theory of Language and Poetry* (1988) offer lengthy and well-focused interpretive analyses of the literary work of Hölderlin and Novalis. Another valuable work in English is Eric Blackall's *The Novels of the German Romantics* (1983). A collection of new interpretations of the literary work of German Romanticism can be found in *Romane und Erzählungen der deutschen Romantik: Neue Interpretationen* (1981) edited by Paul Michael Lützeler.

2. The manuscript, which is in Hegel's handwriting, is a copy of a text composed earlier in June or July of 1795, most probably by Schelling. Rosenzweig, who edited and extensively commented on the manuscript in the publication of the proceedings of the Heidelberger Akademic der Wissenschaften recognized the style to be Schelling's and attributed the text to him. However, Schelling seems to have written it under the direct influence of Hölderlin with whom he was in Stuttgart in 1795. The text embodies in systematic form all of Hölderlin's well-known views on the origin and task of philosophy.

3. I am quoting the "Systemprogramm" from the Insel Hölderlin critical edition used in this study. This text is, of course, also included in some Schelling and Hegel critical editions, since it is variously attributed to all three authors.

4. "Literature begins when . . . the book is no longer the space where speech adopts a form (forms of style, forms of rhetoric, forms of language),

but the site where books are all recaptured and consumed: a site that is nowhere since it gathers all the books of the past in this impossible 'volume' whose murmuring will be shelved among so many others—after all the others, before all the others" (Foucault 1977, 67).

5. Another entry in Schlegel's notebooks reads: "The parabasis in the fantastic novel must be permanent" (1957, 61, no. 461).

Chapter 6: The Critical Legacy of German Romanticism

1. For a well-documented study on the echoes of German Romanticism in Nietzsche's conception of figural language, see Lacoue-Labarthe 1971.

2. See also Behler 1988, 180: "The almost simultaneous emergence of what came to be known as *La déconstruction* and the 'new Nietzsche' in France was certainly no coincidence but the result of a profound interaction of basic trends in contemporary thought."

3. "Nietzsche's striking observation—that some persons are born posthumously—recorded in the text *The Antichrist*," writes Magnus, "was meant to be self-referring. Today I shall be concerned with his most recent rebirth—as alembic, fulcrum, and palimpsest of much recent postmodern criticism" (1989, 301).

4. "We must now refer to all the principles of art discussed so far, in order to find our way through the labyrinth, which is what we must call *the origin of Greek tragedy*" (1956, 1: 44).

5. Neither relativity theory nor quantum physics lays claim to determining phenomenal reality. Although Einstein's ideas constitute the foundation of quantum physics, there is a fundamental difference between relativity theory and quantum theory. Einstein retained a belief in the ultimate knowability of the universe and pursued a Unified Field theory to that end. He never found it nor did he construct it mathematically. Quantum theory, by contrast, is much more liberal in its acceptance of the random and indeterminate nature of reality.

6. See, for example, Link 1971, 79.

Afterword

1. See, for example, Lyotard 1984, 37–41. Lyotard maintains that postmodern knowledge can be understood as a language game that has replaced the master narratives and whose participants create new and changing social configurations through their own communicational interaction.

Bibliography

Primary Texts

Arnim, Ludwig Achim, Freiherr von. 1981–. *Die Erzählungen und Romane*. Ed. Hans-Georg Werner. Leipzig: Insel.

Benjamin, Walter. 1972–. *Gesammelte Schriften*. Ed. Rolf Tiedemann and Hermann Schweppenhäuser. Frankfurt am Main: Suhrkamp.

Bloch, Ernst. 1977. *Gesamtausgabe*. 16 vols. Frankfurt am Main: Suhrkamp.

Chladenius, Johann Martin. 1969. *Einleitung zur richtigen Auslegung vernünftiger Reden und Schriften*. Facsimile reprint of the Leipzig edition of 1742, with an introduction by Lutz Geldsetzer. Vol. 5 of the Series Hermeneutica, Instrumenta Philosophica. Düsseldorf: Stern.

Dilthey, Wilhelm. 1914–1977. *Gesammelte Schriften*. 18 vols. Stuttgart: Teubner; Göttingen: Vandenhoeck und Ruprecht.

Droysen, Johann Gustav. 1971. *Historik: Vorlesungen über Enzyklopädie und Methodologie der Geschichte*. Ed. R. Hübner. Darmstadt: Wissenschaftliche Buchgesellschaft.

Fichte, Johann Gottlieb. 1962–. *Gesamtausgabe*. Ed. Reinhard Lauth and Hans Jacob. Stuttgart: F. Frommann (G. Holzboog).

Freud, Sigmund. 1950. *Gesammelte Werke*. 18 vols. Ed. Anna Freud et al. London: Imago.

Hegel, Georg Wilhelm Friedrich. 1970. *Theorie Werkausgabe*. 20 vols. Frankfurt am Main: Suhrkamp.

———. 1980–. *Gesammelte Werke*. Ed. Rheinisch-Westfälische Akademie der Wissenschaften. Hamburg: Meiner.

Heidegger, Martin. 1975–. *Gesamtausgabe*. Ed. Friedrich-Wilhelm von Herrmann. Frankfurt am Main: Vittorio Klostermann.

Heine, Heinrich. 1970–. *Säkularausgabe*. Berlin: Akademie; Paris: Editions du CNRS.

Hölderlin, Friedrich. 1969. *Werke und Briefe*. 3 vols. Ed Friedrich Beißner and Jochen Schmidt. Frankfurt am Main: Insel.

Humboldt, Wilhelm von. 1960. *Werke*. 5 vols. Ed. Andreas Flitner and Klaus Giel. Berlin: Rütten und Loening.

Kant, Immanuel. 1983. *Werke*. 10 vols. Ed. Wilhelm Weischedel. Darmstadt: Wissenschaftliche Buchgesellschaft.

Marx, Karl, and Friedrich Engels. 1969–. *Gesamtausgabe*. Ed. Institut für
    Marxismus-Leninismus beim Zentralkomitee der Kommunistischen
    Partei der Sowjetunion und vom Institut für Marxismus-Leninismus
    beim Zentralkomitee der Sozialistischen Einheitspartei Deutschlands.
    Berlin: Dietz.
Nietzsche, Friedrich. 1956. *Werke*. 3 vols. Ed. Karl Schlechta. Munich:
    Hanser.
Novalis [Friedrich von Hardenberg]. 1960. *Schriften*. 4 vols. Ed. Paul
    Kluckhohn and Richard Samuel. Stuttgart: Kohlhammer.
Schelling, Friedrich Wilhelm Joseph. 1976–. *Werke*. Ed. Hans Michael
    Baumgartner et al. Stuttgart: F. Frommann (G. Holzboog).
———. 1979. *System des transzendentalen Idealismus*. Ed. Steffen
    Dietzsch. Stuttgart: Reclam.
Schiller, Friedrich. 1962. *Sämtliche Werke*. 5 vols. Ed. Gerhard Fricke and
    Herbert G. Göpfert. Munich: Hanser.
Schlegel, Friedrich. 1957. *Literary Notebooks: 1797–1801*. Ed Hans Eich-
    ner. Toronto: University of Toronto Press.
———. 1958–. *Kritische Ausgabe*. Ed. Ernst Behler. Paderborn:
    Schöningh.
Schleiermacher, Friedrich Daniel Ernst. 1903. *Dialektik*. Ed. I. Halpern.
    Berlin: Mayer und Müller.
———. 1977. *Hermeneutik und Kritik. Mit einem Anhang sprachphiloso-
    phischer Texte Schleiermachers*. Ed. and intro. Manfred Frank.
    Frankfurt am Main: Suhrkamp.

Selected English Translations

Benjamin, Walter. 1977. *The Origin of German Tragic Drama*. Trans.
    John Osborne. London: New Left Books.
Fichte, Johann Gottlieb. 1982. *The Science of Knowledge*. Trans. and ed.
    Peter Heath and John Lachs. Cambridge: Cambridge University Press.
———. 1984. "On the Spirit and the Letter in Philosophy." Trans.
    Elizabeth Rubenstein. In *German Aesthetic and Literary Criticism*, ed.
    David Simpson, 75–93. Cambridge: Cambridge University Press.
———. 1988. "Concerning the Concept of the *Wissenschaftslehre*." In
    J. G. Fichte, *Early Philosophical Writings*, trans. and ed. Daniel
    Breazeale, 94–135. Ithaca, N.Y.: Cornell University Press.
Harris, H. S. 1972. "Earliest System-Programme of German Idealism." In
    H. S. Harris, *Hegel's Development: Toward the Sunlight, 1770–1801*.
    Oxford: Oxford University Press. 510–512.
Heidegger, Martin. 1962. *Being and Time*. Trans. John Macquarrie and
    Edward Robinson. New York: Harper.
———. "The Age of the World Picture." In Martin Heidegger, *The Ques-*

tion Concerning Technology and Other Essays, trans. William Lovitt, 116–154. New York and London: Garland.

Heine, Heinrich. 1985. "The Romantic School." Trans. Helen Mustard. In Heinrich Heine, *The Romantic School and Other Essays,* ed. Jost Hermand and Robert C. Holub, 1–127. New York: Continuum.

Hölderlin, Friedrich. 1984. *Hyperion or the Hermit in Greece.* Trans. Willard R. Trask. New York: Ungar.

Kant, Immanuel. 1951. *Critique of Judgment.* Trans. J. H. Bernard. New York: Hafner; London: Collier MacMillan.

———. *Critique of Pure Reason.* 1965. Trans. Norman Kemp Smith. New York: St. Martin's Press.

Nietzsche, Friedrich. 1967. *The Birth of Tragedy.* Trans. Walter Kaufmann. New York: Random House, 1967.

———. 1987. *Philosophy in the Tragic Age of the Greeks.* Trans. Marianne Cowan. Washington, D.C.: Regnery Gateway.

———. 1989. "On Truth and Lying in an Extra-Moral Sense." In *Friedrich Nietzsche on Rhetoric and Language,* ed. and trans. with a critical introduction by Sander L. Gilman, Carole Blair, and David J. Parent. Oxford and New York: Oxford University Press. 246–257.

Novalis [Friedrich von Hardenberg]. 1964. *Henry of Ofterdingen, a Novel.* Trans. Palmer Hilty. New York: Ungar.

Schelling, Friedrich Wilhelm Joseph. 1978. *System of Transcendental Idealism.* Trans. Peter Heath. Charlottesville: University Press of Virginia.

Schiller, Friedrich. 1967. *On the Aesthetic Education of Man in a Series of Letters.* Trans. and ed. Elizabeth M. Wilkinson and L. A. Willoughby. Oxford: Clarendon.

Schlegel, Friedrich. 1968. *Dialogue on Poetry and Literary Aphorisms.* Trans. Ernst Behler and Roman Struc. University Park: Pennsylvania State University Press.

———. 1971. *Lucinde and the Fragments.* Trans. Peter Firchow. Minneapolis: University of Minnesota Press.

Works Cited

Aristotle. 1961. *Aristotle's Poetics.* Trans. S. H. Butcher. New York: Hill and Wang.

Baker, John Jay. 1986. "The Problem of Poetic Naming in Hölderlin's Elegy 'Brod und Wein.'" *Modern Language Notes* 101: 465–492.

Barthes, Roland. 1972. *Mythologies.* Trans. Annette Lavers. New York: Hill and Wang. Trans. of *Mythologies* (Paris: Editions du Seuil, 1957).

———. 1979. "From Work to Text." In *Textual Strategies: Perspectives in Post-Structuralist Criticism,* ed. and trans. Josué V. Harari, 73–81. Ithaca, N.Y.: Cornell University Press.

————. 1982. *Empire of Signs*. Trans. Richard Howard. New York: Hill and Wang. Trans. of *L'empire des signes* (Geneva: Editions d'Art Albert Skira, 1970).

————. 1987. *Criticism and Truth*. Trans. Katrine Pilcher Keuneman. Minneapolis: University of Minnesota Press. Trans. of *Critique et vérité* (Paris: Editions du Seuil, 1966).

Baudrillard, Jean. 1983. *Simulations*. Trans. Paul Foss, Paul Patton, and Philip Beitchman. New York: Semiotext(e).

Behler, Ernst. 1978. "Nietzsche und die Frühromantische Schule." In *Nietzsche-Studien* 7, ed. Ernst Behler et al., 59–96. Berlin: Walter de Gruyter.

————. 1982. "Friedrich Schlegels Enzyklopädie der literarischen Wissenschaften im Unterschied zu Hegels Enzyklopädie der philosophischen Wissenschaften." In *Hegel-Studien* 17, ed. Friedhelm Nicolin and Otto Pögeler, 169–202. Bonn: Bouvier.

————. 1983. *Die Zeitschriften der Brüder Schlegel*. Darmstadt: Wissenschaftliche Buchgesellschaft.

————. 1988. "Nietzsche and Deconstruction." In *Nietzsche: Literature and Values,* ed. Volker Dürr et al., 180–198. Madison: University of Wisconsin Press.

Blackall, Eric A. 1983. *The Novels of the German Romantics*. Ithaca, N.Y.: Cornell University Press.

Bolz, Norbert W. 1979. "Der Geist und die Buchstaben: Friedrich Schlegels hermeneutische Postulate." In *Texthermeneutik: Aktualität. Geschichte, Kritik,* ed. Ulrich Nassen, 79–112. Paderborn: Schöningh.

Borges, Jorge Luis. 1964. *Labyrinths: Selected Stories and Other Writings*. Ed. Donald A. Yates and James E. Irby. New York: New Directions.

Boslough, John. 1990. "The Enigma of Time." *National Geographic* 177, 3: 109–132.

Brown, Marshall. 1979. *The Shape of German Romanticism*. Ithaca, N.Y.: Cornell University Press.

Cassirer, Ernst. 1971. *Idee und Gestalt: Goethe, Schiller, Hölderlin, Kleist*. Darmstadt: Wissenschaftliche Buchgesellschaft.

Certeau, Michel de. 1984. *The Practice of Everyday Life*. Trans. Steven Rendall. Berkeley, Los Angeles, London: University of California Press.

Collingwood, R. G. (1946) 1961. *The Idea of History*. Oxford: Oxford University Press.

Corngold, Stanley. 1983. "Error in Paul de Man." In *The Yale Critics: Deconstruction in America,* ed. Jonathan Arac et al., 90–108. Minneapolis: University of Minnesota Press.

Davis, Philip J., and Reuben Hersch. 1987. *Descartes' Dream: The World According to Mathematics*. Boston: Houghton Mifflin.

Deleuze, Gilles. 1984. *Kant's Critical Philosophy: The Doctrine of the*

Faculties. Trans. Hugh Tomlinson and Barbara Habberjam. Minneapolis: University of Minnesota Press. Trans. of *La philosophie critique de Kant* (Paris: Presses universitaires de France, 1963).

Derrida, Jacques. 1972. "Structure, Sign, and Play in the Discourse of the Human Sciences." In *The Structuralist Controversy: The Languages of Criticism and the Sciences of Man,* ed. Richard Macksey and Eugenio Donato, 247–272. Baltimore: Johns Hopkins University Press.

———. 1978. "Violence and Metaphysics: An Essay on the Thought of Emmanuel Levinas." In Jacques Derrida, *Writing and Difference,* 79–153. Trans. Alan Bass. Chicago: University of Chicago Press. Trans. of *L'écriture et la différance* (Paris: Editions du Seuil, 1967).

———. 1982a. "The Supplement of Copula: Philosophy Before Linguistics." In Jacques Derrida, *Margins of Philosophy,* 177–205. Trans. Alan Bass. Chicago: University of Chicago Press. Trans. of *Marges de la philosophie* (Paris: Editions de Minuit, 1972).

———. 1982b. "White Mythology: Metaphor in the Text of Philosophy." In Jacques Derrida, *Margins of Philosophy,* 209–271.

Doctorow, E. L. 1983. *E. L. Doctorow: Essays and Conversations.* Ed. Richard Trenner. Princeton, N.J.: Ontario Review Press.

Donato, Eugenio. 1978. "The Ruins of Memory: Archeological Fragments and Textual Artifacts." *Modern Language Notes* 93: 575–596.

Eck, Diana L. 1985. *Darsan: Seeing and Divine Image in India.* 2d ed. Chambersburg, Penn.: Anima Books.

Eco, Umberto. 1984. *The Name of the Rose.* Trans. William Weaver. New York: Warner.

Fabian, Johannes. 1983. *Time and the Other: How Anthropology Makes Its Object.* New York: Columbia University Press.

Foucault, Michel. 1970. *The Order of Things: An Archaeology of the Human Sciences.* New York: Random House. Trans. of *Les mots et les choses: Une archéologie des sciences humaines* (Paris: Editions Gallimard, 1966).

———. 1974. *The Archaeology of Knowledge.* Trans. A. M. Sheridan Smith. London and New York: Tavistock. Trans. of *L'archéologie du savoir* (Paris: Editions Gallimard, 1966).

———. 1977. *Language, Counter-Memory, Practice: Selected Essays and Interviews.* Ed. and intro. Donald F. Bouchard. Trans. Donald F. Bouchard and Sherry Simon. Ithaca, N.Y.: Cornell University Press.

Frank, Manfred. 1972. *Das Problem "Zeit" in der deutschen Romantik: Zeitbewußtsein und Bewußtsein von Zeitlichkeit in der frühromantischen Philosophie und in Tiecks Dichtung.* Munich: Winkler.

Gadamer, Hans-Georg. 1960. *Wahrheit und Methode: Grundzüge einer philosophischen Hermeneutik.* Tübingen: J. C. B. Mohr (Paul Siebeck).

Gould, Stephen Jay. 1987. *Time's Arrow Time's Cycle: Myth and Meta-*

phor in the Discovery of Geological Time. Cambridge, Mass.: Harvard University Press.

Greenberg, Valerie D. 1989. "The 'Uneven Mirrors' of Art and Science: Kunert and Escher." *Mosaic* 22, 2 (Spring): 49–62.

Harding, Sandra. 1989. As quoted in "Does Ideology Stop at the Laboratory Door? A Debate on Science and the Real World." *The New York Times*, 22 October, 24E.

Harris, Errol E. 1988. *The Reality of Time*. Albany: State University of New York Press.

Haslinger, Josef. 1981. *Die Ästhetik des Novalis*. Königstein/Ts.: Hain.

Hartman, Geoffrey, H. 1980. *Criticism in the Wilderness: The Study of Literature Today*. New Haven: Yale University Press.

Hayles, Katherine N. 1984. *The Cosmic Web: Scientific Field Models and Literary Strategies in the 20th Century*. Ithaca, N.Y.: Cornell University Press.

Hesse, Mary. 1989. As quoted in "Does Ideology Stop at the Laboratory Door? A Debate on Science and the Real World." In *The New York Times*, 22 October, 24E.

Heuer, Fritz. 1970. *Darstellung der Freiheit: Schillers transzendentale Frage nach der Kunst*. Cologne and Vienna: Böhlau.

Kuzniar, Alice A. 1987. *Delayed Endings: Nonclosure in Novalis and Hölderlin*. Athens: University of Georgia Press.

Lacoue-Labarthe, Philippe. 1971. "Le Détour." *Poétique* 5: 53–76.

Lacoue-Labarthe, Philippe, and Jean-Luc Nancy. 1988. *The Literary Absolute: The Theory of Literature in German Romanticism*. Trans. Philip Barnard and Cheryl Lester. Albany: State University of New York Press. Trans. of *L'absolu littéraire: Théorie de la littérature du romanticisme allemand* (Paris: Editions du Seuil, 1978).

Link, Hannelore. 1971. *Abstraktion und Poesie im Werk des Novalis*. Stuttgart: Kohlhammer.

Lützeler, Paul Michael, ed. 1981. *Romane und Erzählungen der deutschen Romantik: Neue Interpretationen*. Stuttgart: Reclam.

Lyotard, Jean-François. 1984. *The Postmodern Condition: A Report on Knowledge*. Trans. Geoff Bennington and Brian Massumi. Minneapolis: University of Minnesota Press. Trans. of *La condition postmoderne: Rapport sur la savoir* (Paris: Editions de Minuit, 1979).

Magnus, Bernd. 1989. "Nietzsche and Postmodern Criticism." In *Nietzsche-Studien* 18, ed. Ernst Behler et al., 301–316. Berlin: Walter de Gruyter.

Man, Paul de. 1979. *Allegories of Reading: Figural Language in Rousseau, Nietzsche, Rilke, and Proust*. New Haven: Yale University Press.

———. 1983. "The Rhetoric of Temporality." In Paul de Man, *Blindness and Insight: Essays in the Rhetoric of Contemporary Criticism*, 142–228. Minneapolis: University of Minnesota Press. (First published in *In-*

terpretation: Theory and Practice, ed. Charles S. Singleton, 173–209. Baltimore: Johns Hopkins University Press, 1969.)

—. 1984. "Intentional Structure of the Romantic Image." In Paul de Man, *The Rhetoric of Romanticism,* 1–17. New York: Columbia University Press. (First published in *Romanticism and Consciousness: Essays in Criticism,* ed. Harold Bloom, 65–77. New York and London: Norton.)

Martin, Wallace. 1983. Introduction to *The Yale Critics: Deconstruction in America,* ed. Jonathan Arac et al., xv–xxxvii. Minneapolis: University of Minnesota Press.

McTaggart, J. E. 1927. *The Nature of Existence.* Cambridge: Cambridge University Press.

Merleau-Ponty, Maurice. 1962. *The Phenomenology of Perception.* Trans. C. Smith. London: Routledge and Kegan Paul. Trans. of *Phénoménologie de la perception* (Paris: Editions Gallimard, 1945).

Mitchell, W. J. T. 1990. "Representation." In *Critical Terms for Literary Study,* ed. Frank Lentricchia and Thomas McLaughlin, 11–22. Chicago: University of Chicago Press.

Molnár, Géza von. 1987. *Romantic Vision, Ethical Context: Novalis and Artistic Autonomy.* Minneapolis: University of Minnesota Press.

Morris, Richard. 1987. *The Nature of Reality: The Universe after Einstein.* New York: Farrar, Straus and Giroux.

Newton-Smith, W. H. 1986. "Space, Time and Space—Time: A Philosopher's View." In *The Nature of Time.* Ed. Raymond Flood and Michael Lockwood, 22–35. Cambridge, Mass.: Basil Blackwell.

Pfefferkorn, Kristin. 1988. *Novalis: A Romantic's Theory of Language and Poetry.* New Haven: Yale University Press.

Polheim, Karl Konrad. 1966. *Die Arabeske: Ansichten und Ideen aus Friedrich Schlegels Poetik.* Paderborn: Schöningh.

Quine, Willard V. 1969. "Two Dogmas of Empiricism." In *Problems in the Philosophy of Language,* ed. Thomas M. Olshewsky, 398–417. New York: Holt, Rinehart and Winston.

—. 1981. "Postscript on Metaphor." In Willard V. Quine, *Theories and Things,* 187–189. Cambridge: Belknap Press of Harvard University Press.

Ricoeur, Paul. 1983–1985. *Temps et récit.* 3 vols. Paris: Editions du Seuil.

Rorty, Richard. 1979. *Philosophy and the Mirror of Nature.* Princeton, N.J.: Princeton University Press.

—. 1982. *Consequences of Pragmatism: Essays (1972–1980).* Minneapolis: University of Minnesota Press.

Ryle, Gilbert. 1967. "Philosophical Arguments." In *Philosophy of Recent Times,* vol. 2, ed. James B. Hartman, 489–503. New York and London: McGraw-Hill.

Said, Edward W. 1979. *Orientalism.* New York: Vintage.

Schwab, Raymond. 1984. *The Oriental Renaissance: Europe's Rediscovery of India and the East 1680–1880.* Trans. Gene Patterson-Black and Victor Reinking. New York: Columbia University Press, 1984. Trans. of *La Renaissance orientale* (Paris: Editions Payot, 1950).

Seeba, Hinrich C. 1985. "Geschichte als Dichtung: Herders Beitrag zur Ästhetisierung der Geschichtsschreibung." *Storia della Storiographia* 8: 50–72.

Seyhan, Azade. 1989. "Cannons Against the Canon: Representations of Tradition and Modernity in Heine's Literary History." *Deutsche Vierteljahrsschrift für Literaturwissenschaft und Geistesgeschichte* 63: 494–520.

Shallis, Michael. 1986. "Time and Cosmology." In *The Nature of Time.* Ed. Raymond and Michael Lockwood, 63–79. Cambridge, Mass.: Basil Blackwell.

Stern, Fritz, ed. 1957. *The Varieties of History: From Voltaire to the Present.* New York: Meridian Books.

Szondi, Peter. 1964. "Friedrich Schlegel und die romantische Ironie." In Peter Szondi, *Satz und Gegensatz: Sechs Essays,* 5–24. Frankfurt: Insel.

Taylor, Mark C. 1984. *Erring: A Postmodern A/theology.* Chicago: University of Chicago Press.

Todorov, Tzvetan. 1975. *The Fantastic: A Structural Approach to a Literary Genre.* Trans. Richard Howard. Ithaca, N.Y.: Cornell University Press. Trans. of *Introduction á la littérature fantastique* (Paris: Editions du Seuil, 1970).

———. 1982. *Theories of the Symbol.* Trans. Catherine Porter. Ithaca, N.Y.: Cornell University Press. Trans. of *Théories du symbole* (Paris: Editions du Seuil, 1977).

Tymms, Ralph. 1955. *German Romantic Literature.* London: Methuen.

Verene, Donald Phillip. 1985. *Hegel's Recollection: A Study of Images in the* Phenomenology of Spirit. Albany: State University of New York Press.

Vico, Giambattista. 1948. *The New Science of Giambattista Vico.* Trans. Thomas Bergin and Max Harold Fisch. Trans. of the 3d ed. (1744). Ithaca, N.Y.: Cornell University Press.

Völker, Ludwig. 1979. "Naturpoesie, Phantasie und Phantastik: Über Achim von Arnims Erzählung *Isabella von Ägypten.*" In *Romantik: Ein literaturwissenschaftliches Studienbuch,* ed. Ernst Ribbat, 114–137. Königstein/Ts.: Athenäum.

White, Hayden. 1973. *Metahistory: The Historical Imagination in Nineteenth-Century Europe.* Baltimore: Johns Hopkins University Press.

Wolin, Richard. 1982. *Walter Benjamin: An Aesthetic of Redemption.* New York: Columbia University Press.

Index

Designer:	UC Press Staff
Compositor:	Prestige Typography
Text:	10/13 Sabon
Display:	Sabon
Printer:	Maple-Vail
Binder:	Maple-Vail

DATE DUE
